ON WORLD RELIGIONS

ON WORLD RELIGIONS

Diversity, Not Dissension

Edited by

Anindita N. Balslev

Indian Council for Cultural Relations
भारतीय सांस्कृतिक सम्बन्ध परिषद्

CROSS CULTURAL CONVERSATION

 www.sagepublications.com
Los Angeles • London • New Delhi • Singapore • Washington DC

First published in 2014 by

SAGE Publications India Pvt Ltd
B1/I-1 Mohan Cooperative Industrial Area
Mathura Road, New Delhi 110 044, India
www.sagepub.in

SAGE Publications Inc
2455 Teller Road
Thousand Oaks, California 91320, USA

SAGE Publications Ltd
1 Oliver's Yard, 55 City Road
London EC1Y 1SP, United Kingdom

SAGE Publications Asia-Pacific Pte Ltd
3 Church Street
#10-04 Samsung Hub
Singapore 049483

INDIAN COUNCIL FOR
CULTURAL RELATIONS
Azad Bhavan
Indraprastha Estate
New Delhi 110002, India

Published by Vivek Mehra for SAGE Publications India Pvt Ltd, Phototypeset in 10/12 pt Times New Roman by Diligent Typesetter, Delhi and printed at Saurabh Printers, New Delhi.

Library of Congress Cataloging-in-Publication Data Available

ISBN: 978-81-321-1834-3 (HB)

The SAGE Team: Supriya Das, Archita Mandal, Nand Kumar Jha, and Rajinder Kaur

This work is inspired by and dedicated to
Swami Vivekananda, the progenitor of the Interfaith
movement on the occasion of his 150th birth anniversary.

Thank you for choosing a SAGE product! If you have any comment, observation or feedback, I would like to personally hear from you. Please write to me at contactceo@sagepub.in

—Vivek Mehra, Managing Director and CEO,
SAGE Publications India Pvt Ltd, New Delhi

Bulk Sales

SAGE India offers special discounts for purchase of books in bulk. We also make available special imprints and excerpts from our books on demand.

For orders and enquiries, write to us at

Marketing Department
SAGE Publications India Pvt Ltd
B1/I-1, Mohan Cooperative Industrial Area
Mathura Road, Post Bag 7
New Delhi 110044, India
E-mail us at marketing@sagepub.in

Get to know more about SAGE, be invited to SAGE events, get on our mailing list. Write today to marketing@sagepub.in

This book is also available as an e-book.

Contents

Part I
Teachings and Traditions

Part II
Some Issues in the Context of Religious Diversity

Part III
Conversation with Eminent Personalities

Inaugural Speech by the President of India, Shri Pranab Mukherjee
(at the International Conference on the 150th Birth Anniversary of Swami Vivekananda)

I am delighted to join you in the Seminar being organized on the occasion of the 150th Birth Anniversary of Swami Vivekananda. It serves us with an opportunity to reflect on Swami Vivekananda's teachings and the values he preached, and renew our understanding of them.

A celebrated son of Mother India, Swami Vivekananda's contribution to India's cultural renaissance brought him unparalleled eminence not only in our country but throughout the world. He lived for less than 40 years but he led a life of intensity and expansiveness.

Swamiji's teachings were in consonance with the Vedanta. He brought out the divinity lying dormant in man. He said, "*I call them God whom common men call human beings by mistake.*" Being the superior creation of God, he believed that human beings and the state of their existence cannot be ignored.

He felt that religion should be a weapon for self-transformation as well as transformation of the society. His Guru, Shri Ramakrishna Paramhansa, had taught him that service to man was service to God. Swamiji made this principle the basis of his social service program.

He imbibed the message of his Guru that anything which helps to realize God in this life should be accepted as conducive to the practice of religion and realization of the Highest Truth. Swamiji never thought of his Guru in relation to his own personal life but thought of him in relation to India and the rest of the world.

Ladies and Gentlemen, Swamiji was undoubtedly a brilliant scholar and a profound thinker. He combined his wisdom with his concern for the nation and her suffering masses. He traveled extensively within the country to understand their problems.

He was deeply troubled by the abject poverty of our masses and held that the country's downfall was primarily due to suppression of the poor, who were also immersed in ignorance and superstition. He saw that what the poor people in India needed most was the basic necessities of life such as food, clothes, and shelter.

Swamiji believed that every human being is endowed with immense potentiality, but to realize it, people need self-confidence. He used to say, (quote) "*He is an atheist who does not believe in himself*" (unquote). In his speeches and teachings, he boosted the confidence of people by saying that and I quote: "*All power is within you; you can do anything and everything; believe in that, do not believe that you are weak.*"

Swamiji did not prescribe any abrupt change in society. He believed that socio-economic change can be brought about through education. He felt that people should be exposed to two kinds of education—secular education comprising knowledge about new techniques in agriculture and village industries that would help them to emancipate economically, and spiritual education to revive their sense of self-belief and worth and to give them hope for a better future.

Swamiji established the Ramakrishna Mission in 1897 to what he described as creating the "*machinery which will bring noblest ideas to the doorstep of even the poorest and the meanest.*" The Mission has since been at the service of the poor and needy, carrying out programs in the field of health care and education, women welfare, youth welfare, relief and rehabilitation, and work towards regeneration of rural and tribal areas. It has inspired other noble initiatives to come forward and contribute to social development in a meaningful way.

Ladies and Gentlemen, Swamiji attended the World Parliament of Religions at Chicago in 1893 as a true representative of his country and religion, and defined India's standing as a great ancient civilization that offers the world a beautiful opportunity to learn from its living culture and philosophy. When I visited Chicago one year back, I had the privilege of unveiling a plaque at the place where Swamiji had delivered his famous address in 1893.

Through his speeches at Chicago, and his subsequent work in America and England, Swamiji showed the universal relevance and significance of India's ancient philosophy and spiritual culture in solving many of the problems associated with modern living.

Swami Vivekananda was a bridge between the East and the West. He taught our countrymen to adapt Indian ethos to the notions of Western humanism such as individual freedom, justice, and respect for women. Netaji Subhash Chandra Bose once said and I quote: *"Swamiji harmonized the East and the West, religion and science, past and present. Our countrymen have gained unprecedented self-respect, self-reliance and self-assertion from his teachings."*

Ladies and Gentlemen, though Swamiji never gave any political message, many freedom fighters have derived inspiration and developed a sense of patriotism through his writings and speeches. I quote what Mahatma Gandhi had once said about Swamiji: *"I have gone through his works thoroughly, and after having gone through them, the love that I had for my country became a thousand-fold."*

He loved and treated all human beings as equal without any distinction of caste, religion, race, nationality, or gender. He believed in egalitarian philosophy and wanted equal opportunities for all by not bringing down the higher, but raising the lower up to the level of the higher.

Being a Universalist, Swami Vivekananda's knowledge and understanding of spiritualism went beyond Hinduism. He was deeply familiar with the messages of other religions. Swamiji laid the foundation for harmony amongst religions and also harmony between religion and science.

All through his life, Swamiji had spread his Guru's message of harmony of religions: *"Yato Mat, Tato Path"* (*As many faiths, so many paths*). Swamiji viewed religion as the "science of consciousness" and believed that religion and modern science are complementary rather than contradictory. He portrayed religion as a universal concept and liberated it from the age-old scourges of superstitions, dogma, and intolerance.

Ladies and Gentlemen, to commemorate the 150th Birth Anniversary of Swami Vivekananda, a National Committee under the Chairmanship of the Prime Minister and a National Implementation Committee, which I had chaired when I was the Finance Minister, was constituted.

It is gratifying to note that under the guidance of these committees, several activities have been undertaken to mark this event such as printing of books on the life and teachings of Swamiji in different languages, production and circulation of audio-visual material on Swamiji, propagation of his teachings through media, and conservation of monuments of different religions as a mark of respect to his views on religious harmony.

The universality of Swamiji's teachings holds great relevance in the modern world. Despite progress made by us, our society is confronted with issues challenging our ethics and morality. Swamiji's teachings should be our guiding light in our path to the future.

I hope that Swamiji's 150th Birth Anniversary would be an occasion to awaken our minds to the great contributions and sacrifices made by him towards the welfare, progress, and enlightenment of mankind. Let us rededicate ourselves to the causes for which Swamiji devoted his entire life.

Rashtrapati Bhavan
New Delhi
March 7, 2013

Foreword

In a world which, despite spectacular scientific and technological growth, is still beset with tension and turmoil, it is necessary for all those who are genuinely concerned about the future of the human race to apply their minds to the fundamental causes of the confusion and diso-rientation that are getting increasingly evident in many parts of the world. There are, of course, several factors involved in this, including economic disparity, unacceptable poverty, erratic fiscal behavior, politi-cal instability, and so on. But one important factor is the lack of harmony between the great religious traditions of humankind. Even today, many of the conflicts around the world revolve around interreligious and intra-religious tensions.

It must be admitted that religion has played a mixed role in human history. On the one hand, much that is great and noble in human civiliza-tion—architecture, art, music, spiritual texts, esoteric practices, and so on—can be traced back to one or other of the world's great religions. On the other, millions have lost their lives or been persecuted and discrimi-nated against in the name of religion. In an age when lethal weapons of mass destruction are proliferating, this situation poses a grave risk and is no longer acceptable. It is in this context that the Interfaith movement takes on a special significance.

This movement can be said to have begun in 1893 with the first Parliament of Religions held in Chicago which was attended by several thousand delegates from around the world representing various religious traditions. It was here that Swami Vivekananda, then an unknown monk from India, created a sensation and dominated the event by his remark-able speeches. Basing his presentations on the seminal words of the Rig Veda, "*Ekam sad viprah bahudha vadanti*," (Truth is one, the Wise call it by many names) and the teachings of his master, Sri Ramakrishna, Vivekananda launched a frontal attack on religious fanaticism in the fol-lowing words:

> *Sectarianism, bigotry, and its horrible descendant, fanaticism, have long possessed this beautiful earth. They have filled the earth with violence, drenched it often and often with human blood, destroyed civilisation, and sent whole nations to despair. Had it not been for these horrible demons, human society would be far more advanced than it is now. But their time is come; and I fervently*

hope that the bell that tolled this morning in honour of this con-
vention may be the death-knell of all fanaticism, of all persecu-
tions with the sword or with the pen, and of all uncharitable feelings
between persons wending their way to the same goal.

Swami Vivekananda's historic achievement was twofold. On the one
hand, he was the first to carry the noble message of Vedanta across the
legendary seven seas to the US and Europe, thereby countering the distorted and illiterate views about Hinduism that prevailed at a time. On
the other, he set up within India the Ramakrishna Math at Belur as a
seminary for the Ramakrishna Mission which today has hundreds of
branches in India and around the world. Apart from the scriptures, his
philosophy stemmed from his deep anguish at the poverty and superstition in India that he had encountered when he wandered as a barefoot
monk from Kashmir to Kanyakumari. He thundered against the ridicu-
lous taboos and superstitions that flourished in the name of Hinduism
and said that it was an insult to preach religion to someone who is starv-
ing. He stressed that the Ramakrishna Mission had a twofold goal
"Aatmano mokshartham jagat hitaya cha," work for the liberation of
your soul, but also for the welfare of society.

Swami Vivekananda lived for only 39 years, but his powerful message continues to reverberate across the globe. Born in 1863, the 150th
anniversary of his birth is being celebrated on a large scale. A National
Committee under the chairmanship of the Prime Minister has been set
up to encourage and coordinate events not only in India but in different
parts of the world. In October last year, I addressed a meeting on Swami
Vivekananda at UNESCO in Paris. Among the programs that the Indian
Council for Cultural Relations (ICCR), the premier institution for
spreading India's civilizational message of peace and harmony around
the world, is organizing, is a series of Interfaith seminars. The first of
these was held under the title "On World Religions: Diversity not
Dissension," in collaboration with the forum Cross-cultural Conversation
(CCC) whose founder Anindita Balslev was the academic coordinator of
the seminar and has edited this book.

Two unusual features of this international conference were the fact
that it was graciously inaugurated by the President of India, Shri Pranab
Mukherjee, in the Darbar Hall of Rashtrapati Bhawan, which is a rare
honor and reflects the high regard in which the President holds Swami
Vivekananda. The closing session was also unique in that it presented a
"Cross-cultural Conversation" by His Holiness the Dalai Lama

(Buddhism), Maulana Wahiduddin Khan (Islam), Reverend Mpho Tutu (Christianity), and myself (Hinduism) with Dr Anindita Balslev. All four of us answered the same four clusters of questions, and the text of that conversations is included in this book. The participants in the seminar included a number of distinguished scholars from India and abroad, all of whom presented thoughtful and thought-provoking papers on a theme of great significance to India and the world.

The collection of essays is now being presented in this volume, ably edited by Anindita Balslev. We hope that this will represent a significant contribution to the ongoing Interfaith and intercultural movements around the world which are so urgently needed if humanity is to survive its own technological ingenuity and move toward a sane and just global society.

Karan Singh

Introduction

The year 2013 marks the 150th birth anniversary of Swami Vivekananda. The Indian Council of Cultural Relations (ICCR), in association with the Forum, Cross-cultural Conversation (CCC), decided to celebrate this occasion by holding an international conference and publishing a collection of essays focusing on the theme—"On World Religions: Diversity, Not Dissension."

Swami Vivekananda had a short but a remarkable life. Born in 1863, he passed away in 1902 and yet within the brief span of these 39 years, his presence, vision, and mission ignited the moral imagination of such a large number of men and women that he is rightly said to have ushered in a new movement whose impact is felt even to this day.

On his 150th birth anniversary, it is natural to wish to recapitulate once again the most frequently recalled incidents and episodes of his personal life, highlighting the extraordinary strides and the glorious moments of his success. However, we thought that a more appropriate way of honoring his memory would be not simply by recalling past events, but by seeking to attend to the critical task of rethinking a few of his concerns and retrieving some of his bold visions while noting their relevance in our present context.

Indeed, during his lifetime, Swami Vivekananda had embarked on various forms of organizational work and had initiated many projects. Many of these have matured and have benefitted a large number of people. Some, however, remain incomplete and, as is to be expected, are still to be pursued vigorously in order to reach the desired goal.

Our aim here is to carry forward a project that was particularly close to his heart and central to his thoughts and which at the same time is of crucial importance today. This indeed is the challenging project of creating a mind-set ready to celebrate the presence of the diverse religions of the world by surmounting dissensions among them. The decisive question that comes to the forefront in this connection is how do we construe a sense of a larger identity in the context of religious diversity that does not demand homogenization in the name of "harmony" and yet can abstain from lending support to discord or from disparaging "diversity"?

While conceptualizing the event, I felt strongly that this indeed is an occasion to relive and rekindle that great aspiration which Swami Vivekananda had expressed at the First Parliament of World's Religions, held in Chicago in 1893.

Let us recall the words that he uttered at the very close of his speech—now 120 years ago—with momentous force and firm conviction:

If the Parliament of Religions has shown anything to the world it is this: It has proved to the world that holiness, purity and charity are not the exclusive possessions of any church in the world, and that every system has produced men and women of the most exalted character. In the face of this evidence, if anybody dreams of the exclusive survival of his own religion and the destruction of the others, I pity him from the bottom of my heart, and point out to him that **upon the banner of every religion will soon be written, in spite of resistance: "Help and not Fight," "Assimilation and not Destruction," "Harmony and Peace and not Dissension."**

"On World Religions: Diversity, Not Dissension" is a large and complex topic. The network of issues and concerns reflect the acute need for an open public discourse, based on critical deliberations from multiple perspectives. It is important to emphasize that when we seek to examine the religious dimension of our contemporary "interdependent" world, we need to be prepared to consider religious issues not only in terms of theology, liturgy, metaphysics, ethics, psychology, or aesthetics—important as these are for understanding the distinctness of various traditions—but be equally ready to read their implications in socioeconomic and political terms. Furthermore, it is difficult to imagine any other topic that is more befitting for honoring the memory of Swami Vivekananda. It is, indeed, no exaggeration to state that in recent history, there is hardly anyone who has emphasized more strongly the role of religion as a force that shapes human destiny, or has provided posterity with more inspiration and strength for creating harmony among the religions of the world than Swami Vivekananda. Much of his own reflections on this specifically sensitive subject are available in printed literature, comprised of his writings and speeches. However, a discernment of their profound significance and actual relevance in our contemporary context calls for continuing critical analysis, eventually with the intention of implementing these in practice, on both the personal and the collective planes of our lives.

We went ahead with the idea of celebrating his 150th birth anniversary with the view, on the one hand, of creating an event where Indians as well as members of the international community present in New

Delhi at the time of the conference could freely participate, and, on the other hand, of preparing for the publication of a volume that could reach out to a much wider public worldwide. As intended, the international conference "On World Religions: Diversity, Not Dissension" took place in New Delhi in the beginning of 2013 (March 7–9). This was an occasion that brought a number of speakers from India as well as from various parts of the globe together, and the event was attended by a considerable large number of people. Now, it is a matter of great satisfaction for me that the planned collection of essays is also ready to go to press.

The scholars and researchers who have contributed to this volume have all devoted themselves to the study of specific facets of this vast and intricate theme over many years of their respective professional careers. It is our hope that readers will find these essays to be rich in contents, having many interesting and stimulating insights. The authors of these essays are solely responsible for their own views and renditions; only minor editorial suggestions and amendments have been made. I thank all of them for their erudite and thoughtful essays. For information about the contributors, see About the Editor and Contributors section.

In these days of rapid exchange of information, it is indeed vital to know something about the principal ideas of the diverse religious traditions that are vibrant and are shaping our lives. Human experience has shown that knowledge of "real" differences among the religions of the world is not the soil from which clichés are born. Most of the time it is "imaginary" differences that cause us to project distorted images about the "otherness" of those traditions that we are not really acquainted with. Certainly, an open "cross-cultural conversation" is needed in order to explore how the intricacies of geopolitics play havoc in the global scene, be that where one nation is composed of members of diverse religious identities (including various denominations of a given religion), or where diverse nations partake of the same religious identity. We need to gradually comprehend the mechanisms by which the different facets of these identities are sustained and appealed to for various purposes, what local and global institutional infrastructures are available to resist interventions of various sorts when religious identities are actually threatened or even felt to be endangered, and how sociopolitical forces exploit these situations.

Note that among the contributors to the event and to this volume, there are spokespersons from nine religious traditions: Hinduism,

Buddhism, Jainism, Sikhism, Islam, Judaism, Christianity, Bahai, and Zoroastrianism. It is hoped that we will all find something worthwhile, something new to learn by reading these essays. Apart from the contributions from those who represented various religions that form the first of the three parts of this volume, the essays in part two contain reflections of those who work in the area of history, peace-studies, sociology, anthropology, philosophy, psychology, and literature.

Apart from the various academic sessions where individual speakers made their presentations, it is a matter of great satisfaction for me to be able to create an open conversational setting during the conversation at the India International Centre on March 9, 2013. Part three of this volume is a record of that conversation. I look at such effort as being an indispensable part of the bridge-building task among the religions of the world. If a new phase is to begin in this vital area of universal concern, the academicians—who today are the principal theory-makers—must interact with practitioners as well as with people of various walks of life to all of whom religion matters. This is essential in order to avoid repetitions of stereotypes and clichés as well as various forms of shortsightedness that have often hindered proper communication.

"Cross-cultural conversation" is not about conversing among "us" about the "otherness" of the other, nor is it only about speaking to the other but it is really about an open exchange with each other. I was truly pleased that during the conference, I was able to converse with His Holiness Dalai Lama, Maulana Wahiduddin Khan, Dr Karan Singh, and Reverend Mpho Tutu. The rich and engrossing responses by these eminent personalities to my questions were recorded and are printed here. In some cases their comments have been a bit lengthened or shortened by them for the printed version, but mostly these are just transcribed forms of the recorded version. No editorial amendments are made, not even of any linguistic inaccuracies (given that English is no one's first language) with a view to preserving the original fervor and character of their responses. The webcast of the conversation by the India International Centre is provided for the enjoyment of the viewers: http://www.iicdelhi.in/webcasts/play_webcast/on-world-religions—diversity—not-dissension/.

In a way, it is not really surprising that there is an increasing appreciation in our time with regard to why we need to attend to our multi-religious situation and be aware of the power play that seeks to capitalize on the existing plurality of religious identity. Current events, daily reported worldwide through the news channels, have made it evident that even if secular political ideologies abound, the days of committing violence in the name of religion are far from being a matter of history. It is indeed urgent to make a fresh assessment of that "force"—to put it in the words of Swami Vivekananda—"the manifestation of which we call religion" as it still is a matter of great consequence. A resolution, therefore, to do the best that we can to carry forward the "unfinished" project of Swami Vivekananda also has a pragmatic goal—it is badly needed for the sake of a peaceful collective life. Evidently, continuous commitment and repeated effort on our part, extending way beyond a birthday celebration, must be deemed to be indispensable for building an ideal multi-religious global community for which religious diversity is no longer a source for dissension.

Swami Vivekananda was fully aware of the fact how social realities intermingle with religious identities. The insightful teachings of his Guru, Sri Ramakrishna, always guided him. Sri Ramakrishna was fully supportive of religious diversity. He declared categorically— "as many views, so many paths" (*yato mata tato patha*). It is equally note-worthy that he emphasized the fact that "No one can be righteous with an empty stomach" (*khali pete dharma hoy na*). These are lessons that deeply influenced Swami Vivekananda. In fact, these two seed-ideas gradually germinated in Swamiji's heart and grew into two thriving plants located in the very centre of the Matha and Mission that he founded. These are indeed two full-fledged projects—one seeking to bring about harmony among religions and, the other, emphasizing social service to be not without religious significance, highlighting that "service to man is service to God." If nurtured by us, we like to believe, that these saplings hold the promise of turning into huge blossoming trees that can keep growing and multiplying.

Swami Vivekananda envisioned the coming of a Vedantic society—a model of a society whose principles are worth emulating anywhere in the world, as I tried to indicate in the inaugural session of the confer ence. For Swami Vivekananda, Vedanta was not merely an appellation of a theoretical discourse but it is a call to action. He coined the term "Practical Vedanta" with the view to transform human societies—socie-ties that to this day remain all over the world very largely vitiated by asymmetries and polarities of the exploiters and the exploited, the dominant and the marginalized in multiple contexts.

The great honor in which India holds his memory was amply demon-strated by the fact that the honorable President of India, Shri Pranab Mukherjee, inaugurated this conference at the Rashtrapati Bhavan itself.

His message on this occasion is printed in the very beginning of this book.

I would like to take this opportunity to thank Dr Karan Singh, President of ICCR, for his prompt appreciation of the original concept note that I had written. I felt truly honored when he suggested that I create this event on the important and auspicious occasion of the 150th birth anniversary of Swami Vivekananda.

I would also like to thank the ICCR team for their work and continuous support all along. The arrangements, beginning with the inaugural session at the Rashtrapati Bhavan, the sessions at the Azad Bhavan, and the conversation at the India International Centre, were all highly appreciated.

Undoubtedly, more discussions are needed on the multiple phases and diverse facets of the question of religion that has always been a vital part of human civilization from time immemorial. The really crucial question before us at present is how do we move on to a plane of collective existence when the presence of diversity of religious traditions will no longer to be perceived as a cause for dissension, but rather be cherished as our common resource that can enrich and empower us in ways that we cannot even imagine today.

It is hoped that this volume will be seen as a sincere attempt to understand some of the issues and concerns connected with this large and complex theme. To become increasingly aware of the importance of the religions of the world in our collective life helps us to be more determined and better equipped for removing conflicts and abolish violence that seem to repeatedly occur in the name of religion. Indeed, the more effective we become in ascertaining the guiding principles for a proper management of multi-religious societies, the greater will be the possibility for the revitalization of the sociopolitical spheres of our collective existence.

I, on behalf of all the contributors to this volume, am thankful for the opportunity to carry forward this project so powerfully envisioned by Swami Vivekananda but which has still remained unfinished to this day. May this conversation among the adherents of the religions of the world continue and help emerge a harmonious multi-religious global community, ushering in a new era of human civilization.

Anindita N. Balslev
Editor
Forum CCC

PART I

Teachings and Traditions

1

Thoughts That Transform the Religious Mindscape

A Tribute to Swami Vivekananda

Anindita N. Balslev

From the beginning to the end of his speech—so it has been conveyed by some of the eyewitnesses who were present at the first Parliament of the World's Religions in Chicago in 1893—a large gathering of people listened to Swami Vivekananda absolutely spellbound. Indeed, there are documents describing the kind of enthusiastic responses that his presence and his speech evoked from those who attended that historical event. This was the first time in his life that the young Swami, just 30 years old then, had set his foot outside of India. A journalist who reported about his early days in the US mentioned how during conversations the Swami used to refer to India as "my country," leaving the listeners deeply touched by this patriotic streak of his character.

As we are celebrating the 150th birth anniversary of Swami Vivekananda this year (2013)—120 years after that historical event—let us not merely recapitulate the incidents of his life but also carefully consider what he actually stood for that made it possible to have the kind of impact which he had on people, irrespective of which religious communities they came from. If his Vedantic message did not fall on deaf ears, what does it tell us about the religious dimension of human consciousness? To relive his thoughts and to be able to deeply appreciate his vision is indeed an important part of transforming the religious mindscape that we all partake in. A fresh assessment is vital as this can help us to take a few steps forward in the direction where lies the aspiration and mission of Swami Vivekananda. Indeed, creating harmony among the religions of the world by denouncing dissensions among them was what he expressed so eloquently at the Parliament. Can there be a better way of celebrating his 150th birth anniversary than to pursue with renewed vigor—what I am inclined to describe as—Swami Vivekananda's "unfinished project"?

With this in view, and at the same time for providing a superb example of what "cross-cultural conversation"[1] aims at and can actually achieve, I am tempted to refer to one specific response to Swamiji's famous speech in Chicago from out of the many other inspiring ones that are available in print. This episode, reported by Annie Besant and also by others, is absolutely worth dwelling upon, since it shows conspicuously how our religious mindscape can actually get transformed.

It is narrated that "one person" (in a different account referred to as "one American gentleman"), as he came out of the great hall after listening to Swamiji, exclaimed: "that man a heathen? And we send missionaries to his people! It would be more fitting that they should send missionaries to us."

To my mind, this gentleman can be said to represent any one of "us" from just about any given religious community who is brought up to think of the members of "other" religious communities in specific ways that are not always complimentary to the latter. The appellation "heathen" in his exclamation shows the kind of indoctrination that he had undoubtedly received. Obviously, the expected image of a "Hindu as a heathen" did not quite fit once he saw and heard Swami Vivekananda. This he expresses in the rhetorical question: "that man a heathen"? The process of *unlearning* a prejudice has set in, exemplifying how drastically a view about the "otherness" of the others can get modified in a situation of a real face-to-face encounter, when "cross-cultural conversation" truly takes place.

It is vital to take cognizance of the fact that we are *taught* to adopt certain attitudes toward members of "other" religious communities and that we do in fact accept many negative images about the "other" on the basis of hearsay. On the other hand, the hopeful element in such existing practices is that these can surely be corrected, since *what is learnt can also be unlearnt*. We badly need to converse with each other about a gamut of common concerns, focusing on the presence of plurality of world religions.

Evidently, the young Swami's presence had initiated a process of an authentic meeting of minds among the adherents of diverse religions. He succeeded in communicating an inspiring message that touched the

---

[1] Note that "cross-cultural conversation" is not a conversation among "us" about "others" where these "others" may or may not be present; nor is it a matter of merely addressing the "others" who are supposed to remain silent. It entails that we speak with "each other" crossing various boundaries.

religious sentiment of all, transcending the bounded space of any particular tradition. The personal aura of the Swami had such an unmistakable spiritual quality and it was evidently so transparent that this gentleman went so far as to say that he would rather have missionaries sent to the US from India, the country to which the Swami belonged. This latter remark is particularly illuminating as it poignantly demonstrates how the stance of genuinely universal religiosity can break through the specificity of any given tradition. Moreover, this gentleman—I assume—was not thereby asking for a wholesale formal conversion of his countrymen to Hinduism, but was rather expressing the wish to attain the same earnest spirit of dedication and wisdom that Swami Vivekananda embodied and disseminated in an unrestrained manner.

Indeed, as we recapitulate this episode, it is worthwhile to pause and reflect on whether our religious quests cutting across cultural boundaries essentially occupy a common space and if it was not precisely that which Swami Vivekananda's very presence actually unveiled before the attendees of the Parliament and via them to us all? Let us ask whether it is not because of our bigotry that we generally fail to acknowledge that shared space and often choose to ignore the overlaps in the recommended values in diverse religious traditions and merely reiterate their doctrinal differences? Was Swamiji seeking for a conjoint recognition of that shared space when later on he uttered the following words?

> We want to lead mankind to the place where there is neither the Vedas, nor the Bible, nor the Koran. Mankind ought to be taught that religions are but the varied expressions of The Religion, which is Oneness, so that each may choose that path that suits him best.

It is crucially important in this connection to notice that when Swami Vivekananda speaks of "universal religion," he is not wishing for the triumph of any one of the particular religions so that it becomes the religion of all by vanquishing the others. Recall his words:

> Do I wish that the Christian would become Hindu? God forbid. Do I wish that the Hindu or Buddhist would become Christian? God forbid.

The concept of "universal" is to be contrasted with that of "particular." In the philosophy of Advaita Vedanta, the underlying "non-dual" and all-pervasive reality is the "universal." This Ultimate Reality is Inexpressible; the Upanishads describe it as "where all words come to a stand-still, which is ungraspable by the mind." Thus, every attempt to express it gives rise to one "particular" view among many other possible views. The *Rig Veda Samhita* says, "Reality is one, the sages call it by many (*vahudha*) names."[2] The Upanishadic tradition has acclaimed this "*vahudha*" approach in our quest and Swami Vivekananda was fully aware of the inevitability of variations in our expressions. He, therefore, says without any hesitation:

> I do not mean one universal philosophy, or any one universal mythology, or any one universal ritual held alike by all.

It is vitally important to keep in mind that Advaita Vedanta stands for a meta-philosophical attitude, which does not seek to suppress diversity on the empirical, conventional level. On the contrary, by emphasizing the universal truth of the underlying non-dual Reality as transcendental and as ineffable, it makes room for diverse articulations which would naturally vary as these depend on the historical experience and the conceptual resource of a given community. Diversity is inexorable and no particular expression of the Inexpressible can have the prerogative of being unique, true and perfect and declare "other expressions" to be banal, false, and imperfect. The Advaitic tradition would oppose such a reading, while firmly affirming that religious pluralism is a legitimate position. This is the reason why Swami Vivekananda upholds "Advaitism" to be "the last word of religion or thought and the only position from which one can look upon all religions and sects with love."

The thrust of this statement needs to be properly understood and appreciated. It is a propagation of a philosophical reading that allows for any number of religions to prevail in an uninhibited manner just as it firmly refutes the claim of any form of exclusivism.[3] It is in tune with that understanding that Swamiji said emphatically:

> Our watchword, then, will be acceptance and not exclusion. Not only toleration—Toleration means that I think you are wrong and I am just allowing you to live...

---

[2] *Ekam Sat Viprah Vahudha Vadanti.*

[3] Thus, when he says "Advaitism is the last word," it is simply absurd to read any implication in it—even remotely—of proclaiming any supremacy of Hinduism over others.

Thus, to pay tribute to Swami Vivekananda is to think with him and follow the crucial steps of his reflections vigilantly. One can then begin to see the hitherto unexplored potency of the religions of the world and why it is so urgent to create "harmony" among these for the benefit of all. As one continues to think along this line, one learns to reimagine a world in which the criterion of religious identity no longer gets associated with any diabolical insinuation from any side and consequently the kind of transformations that can really be brought about on our collective lives. It is not indulging in a fictitious idea to claim that if we succeed in this venture that we are sure to move on to a higher level of human civilization. In such a scenario, it can be expected that the adherents of different religious traditions will learn to respect borders that distinguish "us" from "them" but they will not seek to erect hard boundaries that block communication or mutual respect. Religion is a palpable force that works imperceptibly.

Swami Vivekananda states it in an unambiguous manner that:

Of all the forces that have worked and are still working to mold the destinies of the human race, none, certainly, is more potent than that, the manifestation of which we call religion.

However, our collective behavior so far tends to demonstrate that we have been unable to perceive the "universal" that underlies the particular expressions of it and have, therefore, failed to arrive at that "point of union" in the context of religious diversity. It is because of this that the spirit of dissension has assumed a terrible form. He observes:

Sectarianism, bigotry, and its horrible descendant, fanaticism, have long possessed this beautiful Earth. They have filled the earth with violence, drenched it often and often with human blood, destroyed civilization, and sent whole nations to despair. Had it not been for these horrible demons, human society would be far more advanced than it is now.

Indeed, as one probes deeper into his vision, the task of materializing the project of creating harmony and of denouncing dissensions among religions strikes one to be a most important way of facilitating an enlightening force to manifest itself and, thereby, bring about a profound alteration in our mind-set. The possibility of success for such a project depends considerably on how far we grasp the significance of his words when he says:

> Religion is not in books, nor in theories, nor in dogmas, nor in talking, not even in reasoning. It is being and becoming…Religion is realization.

Today there are many of us who, indeed, aspire and even wish to actively work for the emergence of a truly pluralistic society, both in the national and in the global scene. Certainly some among us have begun to perceive that an advocacy of "pluralism" in the context of cultural diversity requires a strengthening of the process that would adequately inform the adherents of specific religious traditions about "other" religions.

Despite that we brag about living in an information society, the fact is that our general knowledge even about the major world-religions is very limited. This is a serious handicap. It is urgent to correct this situation and to frankly confront that negative component, which almost seems to be a part of the heritage of all religious communities over the centuries, viz. the accumulated misleading images about "others" whose religious identity differs from that of "our own community." Its consequence has been vicious. Indeed, history has shown us again and again that "No other human motive has deluged the world with blood so much as religion"—as Swami Vivekananda had also observed.

However, it is certainly possible to *unlearn* these prejudices. We need to gather the political will to participate in an open public discourse, and allow actual encounter with people and their traditions to take place.[4] It also requires active cooperation from those who are responsible for the setting up of curricula for educational institutions, for making programs, and providing material to the media meant particularly for public information in this area.

Given the fact that the largest groups of humanity derive their sense of collective identity, their norms, and values from one or another of these world religions, religious identities do play a key role in the sociopolitical spheres of our collective lives and come to exert considerable impact. This is why today when a common sharing of advanced scientific technology is connecting the world with incredible rapidity, the concern for an authentic encounter of world-religions can be expected to

---

[4] This is precisely the aim of the Forum, "Cross-Cultural Conversation."

increasingly gain importance in the contemporary conceptual as well as in societal contexts.

However, in order to fully accept diversity of religions with all its implications entails a complex conceptual process. It not only demands a simple acknowledgement of the presence of a plurality of traditions, but also a candid recognition of the differences that are there among their myths, liturgy, and doctrines that are difficult to reconcile. We, on the collective plane, have not as yet worked out where lies "the point of union" among these—to use Swami Vivekananda's own words. This is precisely why it is not enough for the members of a pluralistic society merely to let religious diversity surface, there is a strongly felt need for discerning ways and means with the view to accomplish the bridge-building task among these. Without the latter, the phenomenon of religious diversity will continue to be seen predominantly as a divisive force rather than as a common pool of resources that could enrich us all.

Undoubtedly, the question of religion has been perpetually present not only within the conceptual frames of a global History of Ideas, it has also exercised tremendous influence throughout the history of human civilization. These historical developments can be studied and explored both conceptually as well as empirically with reference to various scenarios entailing peace and reconciliation, non-violent modes of protest just as for instigating vehement forms of violent movements, leading to diverse formations of hostile social groupings.

An open-ended "cross-cultural conversation" is needed in order to explore the intricacies of the religious context of the global scene where if one nation is multi-religious in composition, there exist diverse nations sharing the same religious identity or belonging to different denominations of the same religious tradition. We do not have as yet a clear picture of how in each case the sociopolitical forces exploit these situations, or about the exact mechanisms not only for sustaining religious identity but also for instigating violence in intricate conflict situations—be that among the adherents of two different religions or of two denominations of the same religion. Moreover, it will be useful to be able to assess what local and global institutional infrastructures need to be put in place when religious identities are actually endangered or even remotely felt to be so by the members of religious communities. This is necessary in order to prevent turmoil in our multi-religious situation, nationally as well as internationally.

Records show that far too many skirmishes take place—overtly or covertly—in the name of religion. However, it is not easy to discern what exactly the teachings of the world religions have got to do with these. Speaking about the harm done by the manipulation of religion, Swami Vivekananda remarked forcefully:

> Now, in my little experience I have collected this knowledge—that for all the devilry that religion is blamed with, religion is not at all at fault. No religion ever persecuted men, no religion ever burned witches, no religion ever did any of these things. What then incited people to do these things? Politics, but never [true] religion. And if such politics takes the name of religion, whose fault is that?

It is indeed amazing that despite the current violence done in the name of religion all over the globe, we still fail to attend to this multidimensional issue of religious diversity. By and large, we generally seem to happily play the role of bystanders until and unless "we" become directly involved in a conflict situation. This lack of readiness on our part to handle the matter in time with a sense of urgency is certainly costing us dearly. Viewed on a collective plane, the contemporary "interdependent" world demands that religious issues now must be considered not only in terms of theology or metaphysics, psychology or aesthetics—important as these are for understanding the distinctness of various traditions—but that we also note all their complexities in sociopolitical terms as well.

In order to lay further emphasis on the importance of this subject let me refer to the very pertinent remark made by the catholic theologian Bryan Hehir. It is as follows:

> There is an assumption that you do not have to understand religion in order to understand the world. You need to understand politics, strategy, economics and law, but you do not need to understand religion. If you look at standard textbooks of international relations or the way we organize our foreign ministry, there's no place where a sophisticated understanding of religion is a public force in the world is dealt with.[5]

In this connection, it is equally worthwhile looking deeper into the words of Mahatma Gandhi when he observed: "Those who say that religion has nothing to do with politics do not know what religion means."

---

[5] Quoted by Madeleine Albright in her book entitled *The Mighty and the Almighty* (Harper & Collins, 2007).

Given that we have repeatedly witnessed oppositions and tensions among the adherents of various religious traditions and between that of various denominations of a given tradition, it is now time to ask whether some serious initiative on our part to open up a creative and constructive conversation could in principle raise us to a level of maturity and enable us to make sense of our differences? The key questions that inevitably come to the forefront in our contemporary context are how to proceed with the bridge-building process in order to make emerge a sense of larger identity and at the same time how to address the task of the perpetuation of religious diversity without instigating dissensions? We must now avail of the opportunities provided by the common sharing of advanced technology and obtain some basic information about those traditions from which "others" draw their sense of religious identity as we do from "ours," as without that we are simply unable to grasp the significance of the fundamental messages that are embedded in the great religions of the world.

Undeniably, we need to obtain—both on a theoretical and practical level—deeper insights into how economy, diplomacy, geopolitics entailing military power intermingle in provoking so-called religious conflicts and how religious differences, in turn, come to interfere into the former domains of human affairs.

Today when diverse worldviews and various forms of secular ideologies seek to address anew the presence of diversity in the form of multiculturalism, globalization, cosmopolitanism, etc., the really important questions that we must try not to evade are the following: Can we not really make a collective effort to reread the true import of the teachings of the religions of the world and thereby help promote the cause of coexistence, harmony, peace, and compassion—values that anyway seem to overlap irrespective of traditions? Is it really not possible to take a joint stand against treating these great traditions as divisive forces?

Evidently we need a plan of action. For this purpose, an open and constructive public discourse along with the creation of public events at regular intervals, focusing on various aspects of this complex topic, are necessary. I tend to think that knowledge of "real" differences among traditions is much less harmful than nurturing "imaginary" differences born of hearsays or based on very superficial acquaintance with the subject matter. Conversational settings where practitioners, academicians can freely interact with people of different professions and of various walks of life–for all of whom religion matters—are indispensable. This way theoreticians who weave theories will also greatly benefit by not losing sight of the ground realities and learn from that first-hand experience that conceptualizations based on "imaginary" encounters are no longer feasible.

Swami Vivekananda had himself stated in unambiguous terms that religion is the strongest of all forces that shape "human destiny." This is also precisely why he felt strongly that if we could truly succeed in creating "harmony" among the diverse religions of the world, it would unleash a colossal force that would transform the global society. He venerated the view of his Master, Sri Ramakrishna, whose watchword was "as many views, so many paths." Laying emphasis on the notion of "religion as a path" by following which one reaches the Ultimate goal, he had no reservation with regard to accepting that there are indeed many such paths. Sometimes comparing the path to a staircase needed to reach the roof, which is the goal, he says:

A man can reach the roof of a house by stone stairs or a ladder or a rope-ladder or even by a bamboo pole. But he cannot reach the roof if he sets foot now on one and now on another. He should firmly follow one path. Likewise, in order to realize God a man must follow one path with all his strength. But you must regard other views as so many paths leading to God. You should not feel that your path is the only right path and that other paths are wrong. You mustn't bear malice toward others.

This is of course an attitude that let the followers of any given path to continue their journey with veneration and confidence without coercing others to join the same. His advice was not to yield to any kind of dogmatism (which he used to call in Bengali *Matuyarbuddhi*) or to any form of exclusivism.

Swami Vivekananda, like his Master, had also expressed his surprise that anyone should refuse to grant validity to religions that others adhere to. He said in one of his lectures,

I do not understand how people declare themselves to be believers in God, and at the same time think that God has handed over to a little body of men all truth, and they are the guardians of the rest of humanity.[6]

---

[6] *The Complete Works of Swami Vivekananda*, published by Advaita Ashrama, Kolkata, IV.

It is tempting to observe that this project of creating harmony among religions seems to be hundred times more urgent in our time than when Swami Vivekananda spoke about it in late nineteenth century at the first Parliament of the World's Religions. The various construal of selfhood and the projection of "otherness" that are still lingering on based on old prejudices are not worth perpetuating any longer. "Knowing" and not merely "imagining" the "other" could truly be the antidote for all forms of religious egoism since "no one is so vain of his religion as he who knows no other," as was aptly remarked by S. Radhakrishnan.

However, an overview of the current situation shows that despite a few sporadic efforts, the project of removing discords for the sake of creating "harmony" among religions has largely remained incomplete. Are we ready today to choose to apply our energy and time in a sustained manner so that the overall benefits of such a work can tangibly influence our interpersonal relationships and bring about the needed changes to our institutions that stand in the intersections of religion, politics, and society?

Indeed,

> a civilization based on injustice cannot last long. It is a welcome sign of the times that a religion which does not make social reform and international justice as essential part of its teaching has no appeal to the modern mind. Religion is not a simple spiritual state of the individual. It is the practice of divine rule among men.[7]

We need to attend to this task, minimally speaking, for the sake of owning up to our social responsibility and shared accountability for human suffering. Hopefully, it will soon enter our collective consciousness that it is high time for us to cease to adopt the posture of bystanders in the face of violence and atrocities inflicted in the name of religious differences. Historical records show that our inability to resist the temptation of playing religious traditions against each other has had far too many tragic consequences.

In brief, it is time to allow redeeming thoughts to transform our religious mindscape. "We are what our thoughts have made us"—and for good reason Swami Vivekananda continues to say "take care about what you think...Thoughts live; they travel far."

---

[7] S. Radhakrishnan, *The Religion We Need* (BHU, 1963, second edition).

Indeed, a keen awareness with regard to the fact that we are by no means living in a post-religious era makes it obligatory on our part to aspire to live as a multi-religious global community. We cannot simply any longer underplay the demand for a philosophy of religion that can provide the rationale for why religious diversity need not be invariably a cause for dissension. In other words, the normative concept of "Religious Pluralism" cannot really inspire or even be implemented unless it is backed by a meta-philosophy that can alter our mind-set. No political slogan alone can achieve it in its fullness.

There is an array of questions waiting for answers such as what is the raison d'etre for diversity in the religious context and why must this plurality be accepted with reverence and not to be just abandoned for the sake of triumph of one single tradition? Is it possible to find a point of convergence, a unity of purpose among the diverse religious traditions, despite their doctrinal differences? There are many more issues that call for deliberations in a multi-religious setting. However, once we begin to participate in an open "cross-cultural conversation" and delve into the complexities of a long chain of concerns, we will surely learn to overcome our prejudices and take note of the overlaps that are unquestionably there in these traditions. We will also be able to unveil—in collaboration—the real sources of conflicts and how these arise under the guise of religious differences. It can be expected that our observations will become sharper in the process, raising the level of public debates and discussions.

Yes, this is one of the most challenging tasks that humanity has ever faced and it certainly requires continuous work. It is, nonetheless, worth a try, first, to seek and then to share the "wisdom" that can be derived from the religions of the world. Let me repeat that it is only through a united endeavor that we can uncover the shared context of concerns and queries, values and visions, which undoubtedly have enormous significance not only for our soteriological quests but also for our mundane existence.

It was evident to Swami Vivekananda that the Advaitic meta-philosophical stand, which has nourished the Indian cultural soil from time immemorial, made it possible for the presence of practically all the religions of the world here in India. Acknowledging one's own tradition as one among other traditions is a model of self-understanding inspired by the message of *Rig Veda Samhita*—"Reality is one, the sages call it by different names."[8] Following the insight of Advaita Vedanta, every

---

[8] *Ekam Sat Viprah Vahudha Vadanti.*

religion exemplifies a form of engagement, an endeavor to express the Inexpressible.

This is the spirit that steered the Ramakrishna–Vivekananda movement in the sociopolitical context of nineteenth century India—a critical time when the colonialists' exploitation, not only economic but also cultural, drove Indians to despair and the process of proselytization was intense.

Sri Ramakrishna's utterance, "as many views, so many paths" (*yato mat, tato path*) is not—as I have said elsewhere—just a catchphrase motivated by the same intent as the "live and let live" formula. It is not borne of political prudence, nor is it simply a slogan coined for one's own survival in the face of militant and aggressive attack. This utterance is, indeed, a flat refusal to accept one path as valid and others as false, or to organize the plurality of religions in any hierarchical order. Philosophically, the position is a reassertion of the traditional Upanishadic insight. However, the real source of power and success of the Ramakrishna–Vivekananda movement is to be traced to the kind of leadership provided by these two figures, adored as living embodiments of the spiritual message that they were tirelessly preaching.

It is indeed deplorable that some scholars read it as though this is a sort of subtle tactics for propagating a sectarian agenda. For W. Halbfass, for instance, this message stemming from Sri Ramakrishna's own living experience is no more than a "specimen" of "Neo-Hindu inclusivism." He interprets it as a position where "the Vedanta provided the encompassing context within which Christianity, like all other religions, was contained and a priori superseded."[9] He further says that "We may even suspect that the development of the idea of fulfillment among the Christian missionaries is, in part at least, a response to the Neo-Hindu inclusivism, as we find it exemplified by Ramakrishna, Keshab Chandra Sen and Vivekananda." It is obvious that such statements show little understanding of Advaita Vedanta and of the fact that it is not a contender seeking to win over others but is a meta-philosophy that makes room for religious diversity, by disclosing the utter futility of any sense of rivalry between the "self" and the "other."

Sharing his Master's insights not only with regard to treating the different views stemming from diverse religious traditions as "many paths" but also Sri Ramakrishna's insistence that "one cannot be righteous with

---

[9] cf. Wilhelm Halbfass, Chapter 3: The Missionary Approach in His India and Europe, An Essay in Understanding, SUNY, New York, 1988.

an empty stomach" (*khali pete dharma hoy na*), Swami Vivekananda envisioned the coming of a Vedantic society—a model of a society whose principles are worth emulating anywhere in the world as these highlight the theme of social justice. He tirelessly advocated that access to food, health, wealth, and education should not be confined only to the privileged but must be shared. For Swami Vivekananda, Vedanta was not merely an appellation for a theoretical discourse but a call to action. He coined the term "Practical Vedanta" so that we may eventually chart a course of action that would transform societies, societies that to this day remain all over the world very largely vitiated by asymmetries and polarities of the exploiters and the exploited, the dominant and the marginalized in multiple contexts—be that of nationality, ethnicity, gender, race, religion, or any other.

It is not easy to encapsulate in a few words what Swami Vivekananda was all about. Swami Vivekananda's call for uplifting the spirit of humanity was not confined *only* within a nationalistic agenda aimed at inspiring downtrodden people under gigantic colonialist forces of that time. He was not prompted *exclusively* by a patriotic impulse; his life's work shows him to be an internationalist at heart. In order to understand him and to capture the significance of his life's journey, one has to take note of the fact that just as he brought a powerful message to the West, his own first-hand encounter with the West also had a deep influence on him. His was an exceptionally keen and sensitive religious mind. He fought against all forms of social injustice in national as well as international contexts, yet he was not urging only for social reform pushed by humanitarian sentiment alone. His revolutionary views can well be translated into a non-violent form of a political program for pulling up all those who are marginalized, but on that ground he was not simply a political philosopher or an activist. Certainly, he did work for all those causes but yet he stood for something much more. He is a global figure, envisioning a kind of transformation that would lead humanity to a higher level of civilization, a loftier plane of existence that we cannot quite clearly preview. These are matters that must remain open for further reflection, elaboration, and interpretation.

When I look at the figure of Swami Vivekananda, I am overwhelmed by a profound sense of awe. Here I am undoubtedly in the presence of a truly rare person to whom I can say without the slightest hesitation on my part: You are indeed a consummate Advaitin, you are surely far greater than what you have demonstrably accomplished in your short but remarkable life.

2

Diversity as the Nature of Reality
A Jain-informed Approach to the
Variety of Worldviews

Jeffery D. Long

INTRODUCTION: MANY STARTING POINTS

This essay forms one portion of a larger project dedicated to the realization of Swami Vivekananda's vision of a world marked by diversity, not
dissension, among the worldviews which human beings have developed
over the course of their march toward the truth. Swami Vivekananda, in
his wisdom, taught not that everyone must adopt the same worldview,
but rather, that we all need to learn from one another: holding fast, each
of us, to our respective worldviews, while simultaneously permitting
these views to be transformed through the process of dialogue. In his
own words, "The Christian is not to become a Hindu or a Buddhist, nor
a Hindu or a Buddhist to become a Christian. But each must assimilate
the spirit of the others and yet preserve his individuality and grow
according to his own law of growth."[1] Similarly, the Christian process
theologian, John Cobb, writes that the mutual transformation of worldviews and the emergence of a global pluralistic theology need not entail
all communities adopting the same starting point. He states that

> Global theology in a pluralistic age need not cut its ties to the
> particularities of religious traditions....[T]here is no global strat-
> egy for developing global theology in a pluralistic age. The strat-
> egy is pluralistic. It will be...different for Muslims, for Hindus,
> for Sikhs, for Jains, for Buddhists, for Jews, and for Christians.[2]

[1] Swami Vivekananda, *Complete Works*, Volume 1 (Calcutta: Advaita
Ashrama, 1989), p. 24.
[2] John B. Cobb, Jr. "Metaphysical Pluralism," in Joseph Prabhu (ed.), *The
Intercultural Challenge of Raimon Panikkar* (Maryknoll, New York: Orbis
Books, 1996), p. 59.

What is needed is for each tradition to develop its own appreciative philosophical response, arising from its own distinctive worldview, to the variety of views that exist. Each such response can then contribute to the global conversation about how we might all conceive of diversity in ways that lead us beyond dissension to harmony.

A JAIN APPROACH TO THE
DIVERSITY OF WORLDVIEWS

The Jain community's response to diversity is a most fruitful one for conceiving of diversity as a consequence not of ignorance or the human capacity for self-delusion, but of the very nature of existence as itself productive of infinite variety. The Jains have developed an appreciative philosophical response to the variety of worldviews in the form of their "doctrines of relativity." These doctrines, which are three in number, are *anekantavada* (the doctrine of the complexity of reality), *nayavada* (the doctrine of perspectives), and *syadvada* (the doctrine of conditional predication).

I would now like to explore and address some issues raised by this Jain approach to truth and the diversity of worldviews. How does this approach allow us to conceive of the relationship between relativism and absolutism in a way that avoids the pitfalls of both extremes? How does it address the need for an "open system" that does not rule out possibilities for novel expressions and manifestations of truth? How does it respond to the question of whether any linguistic or conceptual system, even one as open to diversity as this one, can be adequate to the ever-unfolding reality of the diversity that one is able to perceive in the world? And to what extent does this approach allow for the possibility of a deep and thoroughgoing rejection of its own central premises? That is, is there a sense in which a Jain approach to the variety of worldviews requires one to adopt a Jain worldview, or may this approach be conceived in ways that allow it to be adopted from a variety of starting points?

One does not need to be a Jain in order to appreciate and appropriate many facets of Jain thought and practice. In fact, this relevance of Jain thought and practice beyond the Jain community is not a new thing, though the urgency of the need for Jain ideas is greater now than ever before. Jains have always been influential upon the communities and traditions that have surrounded them, having had a substantial impact, despite their small numbers, on both the Hindu and Buddhist traditions with which they have been in close conversation for millennia.

OUTLINE OF THE JAIN DOCTRINES OF RELATIVITY

The first thing that should be clarified is what, precisely, I mean when I refer to the Jain approach as involving the idea of *relativity*. This does not refer to relativism as this is commonly conceived: as the idea that there ultimately is no truth, for what we call truth is nothing but a matter of perspective. It is, rather, the idea that there is a truth, but that truth is multifaceted and can be approached in diverse, but nevertheless valid, ways.

Why do Jains teach that truth is multifaceted, and that diversity is in some sense intrinsic to the character of existence? What, precisely, are anekantavada, nayavada, and syadvada? Before showing the utility of these doctrines in arguing for a viable pluralism, it will help to give a sense of what, precisely, these three doctrines are, as well as some sense of the context from which they have emerged, that is, their immediate Jain context and their wider context in the arena of Indian intellectual history. Then we can move toward applying them to the contemporary global context.

Jainism is an ancient system of belief and practice that has exerted a tremendous influence on the better known Hindu and Buddhist traditions, with which it has emerged in conversation over the course of several millennia. Traced by modern scholars to the figure of Mahavira, a contemporary of the Buddha who lived in roughly the fifth century before the Common Era and who also hailed from the same region of northeastern India as the Buddha, Jainism is seen by its adherents as an even more ancient tradition, which Mahavira recovered and reformulated. Even if Jainism predates this period, both Jainism and Buddhism were components of a wider movement of ascetic traditions prominent in India in the first millennium BCE. This movement, known as the *sramana*—or "striver"—movement, is based on the premise that a life of asceticism and renunciation is essential to attaining freedom from the cycle of death and rebirth.[3] The presence of this

[3] For a fuller exploration of the historical issues presented in this and the following paragraph, see Jeffery D. Long, *Jainism: An Introduction* (London: IB Tauris, 2009), pp. 29–56.

movement is evident in the Hindu tradition in the thought of the Upanishads, from the same period.

According to Jain tradition, Mahavira was not, technically, the founder of the Jain tradition, though he could be called the founder of the contemporary fourfold Jain *tirtha*, or community, consisting of male and female ascetics and male and female laypersons, or householders. According to Jain teaching, Mahavira was the 24th in a series of 24 *tirthankara*s, or enlightened teachers who reestablish the Jain community in the course of a vast epoch of cosmic time. The lives of the *tirthankara*s are outlined in a variety of Jain texts, such as the *Kalpa Sutra* and the *Trisastisalakapurusacaritra*. Each *tirthankara* goes through a similar career of growing up in a context of worldly power and privilege, renouncing that power and privilege in the name of pursuing spiritual freedom, and attaining that freedom in the form of total enlightenment, or *kevalajnana*, a state of absolute bliss and omniscience resulting in freedom from the cycle of birth, death, and rebirth to which all beings are otherwise subjected. This state is the Jain equivalent of the goal of *nirvana* or *moksha* similarly pursued in the Buddhist and Hindu traditions.

Out of the 24 *tirthankara*s, most modern scholars accept the historical existence of Mahavira, as well as his immediate predecessor, Parsvanatha (the 23rd *tirthankara*), and possibly Rishabha, or Adinatha, the first *tirthankara*. All three of these figures are mentioned in non-Jain literary sources, and there are Jain scholars who have noted resemblances between iconographic depictions of Rishabha, the Hindu deity Siva, and a figure depicted in some of the artifacts of the Indus Valley Civilization.

Whatever the origins of Jainism, the tradition taught by the followers of Mahavira is characterized by several important features, some of which it shares with other Indian religious traditions, some of which it shares but with a distinctive Jain understanding, and some of which are unique to it. Like Hinduism and Buddhism, Jainism teaches that there is a cycle of birth, death, and rebirth (*samsara*) that forms the broader context of human existence: and indeed, not only human existence, but the existence of all life forms. One feature of Jainism that makes it attractive to contemporary thinkers trying to ground an ecological ethic is its non-anthropocentric insistence on the equality of all living beings.

Like the Hindu and Buddhist traditions, the Jain tradition presents itself as a path to freedom from this cycle. Like Hindus and Buddhists, Jains see this cycle as fueled by a principle of cause and effect, or *karma*.

This principle must be negated or transcended if there is to be ultimate freedom, which is called *moksha* or *nirvana* in these traditions. Unlike most Hindus and Buddhists, Jains see karma as an actual substance that pervades the universe and adheres to the soul, or *jiva*.

The mechanics of karmic adhesion to the jiva require one to cultivate a state of calm equanimity, or *samayika*, in the face of both happiness and suffering. This state of calm is deeply incompatible with any desire to cause pain, harm, or destruction to any living being. The Jain path, therefore, requires ahimsa, or nonviolence in thought, word, and deed, as an essential prerequisite to spiritual progress. Though the ideal of ahimsa is not unique to Jainism, the extent to which it is emphasized in this tradition is unsurpassed even in the Hindu and Buddhist traditions, which are well known for their commitment to the ideal of nonviolence. Jainism is the Indian tradition that is best known for its images of monks and nuns who gently sweep the ground in front of them to avoid accidentally stepping upon tiny living things, and wearing a *muhpatti*, or mouth-shield, to help avoid even accidental ingestion of such organisms in the course of breathing.

The Indian social and cultural setting in which Jainism emerged was one in which worldviews and systems of spiritual practice proliferated in great numbers and with great variety. Indeed, the majority of these worldviews and systems have come to be defined as making up Hinduism, a religion with such internal variety that some scholars will even argue that no such cohesive religion or belief system as "Hinduism" really exists. Outside of India, Buddhism, which emerged in this same setting, has spread across Asia, where it has interacted with the indigenous beliefs and practices of the areas to which it has been transmitted—including Shamanism, Daoism, Confucianism, and Shinto, as well as, in the modern period, Christianity and modern science—adding to the rich proliferation of Indian and Indian-inspired worldviews and belief systems across the globe.

In its original, highly diverse setting, the Jain community needed to develop ways of interacting with and interpreting the belief systems of those around them which would, on the one hand, uphold the integrity of Jain belief and practice, avoiding assimilation by the majority that surrounded them, and, on the other, be sufficiently accommodating to avoid excessive conflict. This desire to avoid conflict had both idealistic and pragmatic dimensions: rooted in ahimsa, but also in the Jains' minority status.

The earliest textual account of what would eventually be developed into the fully systematized doctrines of anekanta-, naya-, and syadvada can be found in the canonical literature of the Svetambara Jain community: a literature attributed to the original 11 disciples, or *ganadhara*s, of Mahavira. In response to questions posed by the *bhikkhu*, or monk, Jamali, regarding the eternality or perishability of the world and the soul—topics on which there was much contestation among competing schools of thought in India, just as there is in our world today—Mahavira responds:

> ...[T]he world is, Jamali, eternal. It did not cease to exist at any time. It was, it is and it will be. It is constant, permanent, eternal, imperishable, indestructible, always existent.

> The world is, Jamali, non-eternal. For it becomes progressive (in time-cycle) after being regressive. And it becomes regressive after becoming progressive.

> The soul is, Jamali, eternal. For it did not cease to exist at any time. The soul is, Jamali, non-eternal. For it becomes animal after being a hellish creature, becomes a man after becoming an animal, and it becomes a god after being a man.[4]

Mahavira here brings together a variety of seemingly contrary views and shows that they are not really as incompatible as they may, at first glance, appear. Is the world eternal or not? According to Mahavira, it is both, depending upon how one conceives of the term "world." Something has always existed, "is constant, permanent, eternal, imperishable, indestructible, always existent." But this thing we call a "world" does not remain in the same state perpetually. It "becomes progressive" and "regressive," which is a reference to the Jain doctrine that the world goes through an ongoing series of vast cycles of cosmic time, each segment of which is characterized by changing proportions of happiness and sorrow, order and chaos. Things change. If, by "world," one means the totality of being, then the world is eternal, for something has always existed and will always exist. But if, by "world," one means a definite state of affairs, then this is constantly changing.

---

[4] *Bhagavati Sutra* 9: 386. Translation by Matilal. Cited in Bimal Krishna Matilal, *The Central Philosophy of Jainism: Anekantavada* (Ahmedabad: L. D. Institute of Indology, 1981), p. 19.

The basic strategy for navigating diverse worldviews that anekanta-vada represents is already visible in this dialogue between Mahavira and Jamali. Various views that, at first glance, would appear to be in conflict— "The world is eternal" versus "The world is not eternal," and "The soul is eternal" versus "The soul is not eternal"—are revealed to reflect not contradictory propositions, but partial perspectives on a wider truth available to the sage with the perspicacity to perceive it. The world and the soul are each, in different senses and different respects, both eternal and non-eternal. The adherents of the worldviews that are built upon each of these respective claims need not be in conflict with one another; for each of their views is complementary to the other, and each can find its place in the wider truth perceived by Mahavira from his vantage point as an enlightened being.

It is important to note, though, that anekantavada is not only an ingenious method for negotiating the differences among worldviews. It is not merely a rhetorical strategy employed by Mahavira and his disciples to keep the peace and cultivate respect among Jains for the worldviews of others (while affirming the ultimate superiority of Jainism as the most encompassing perspective). Anekantavada, in its most fully developed form, is an entailment of fundamental Jain metaphysical commitments outlined in Jain scriptural texts and in philosophical writings such as the *Tattvartha Sutra* of Umasvati. Umasvati explains the nature of an entity as follows: "An entity is that which arises, passes away, and endures."[5]

This account of the nature of an entity is contrasted by Jain thinkers with Buddhist views of an entity as essentially a process—a flow of impermanent events that arise and then pass away—and Hindu views of an entity as an intrinsically unchanging substance. Jainism teaches that an entity is constituted by both change and continuity: by arising and passing away, but also by endurance over time. In the subsequent Jain textual tradition, Jain philosophers present their view as a middle way, integrating concepts of process and substance.

To be sure, neither the Buddhist nor Hindu traditions is completely reducible to a fundamental claim about the nature of existence, such as the *sarvam anityam* ("All is impermanence") of Buddhism, or the *sarvam khalvidam brahman* ("All this, indeed, is Brahman") of Vedanta. Both traditions are internally diverse and include many accounts which seek to reconcile the ideas of change and continuity that characterize

---

[5] *Tattvartha Sutra* 5: 29. *utpada-vyaya-dhrauvya-yuktam sat.*

experience. There is, for example, the *alayavijnana*, or "storehouse consciousness," of the Yogacara system of Mahayana Buddhism, or the Advaitic idea of *maya*, or "appearance," as well as the more realist approaches of Vedantic schools that do not accept the idea of maya. The point here is to show how the Jains sought to position their tradition as midway between these others by focusing on the fundamental conception of reality at work in each system of thought and practice.

The basic Jain metaphysical stance is the basis for the Jain "both/and" approach to diverse worldviews. The dominant Buddhist and Vedic systems of thought with which the Jains of antiquity were in dialogue staked out strong claims in the area of philosophy based on their respective adherence to a sense of reality as intrinsically impermanent and ephemeral or as intrinsically eternal and unchanging. Again, neither the Buddhist nor the Vedic intellectual traditions is completely reducible to a single metaphysical doctrine of impermanence or permanence, and each came up with its own solution to the question of how both phenomena arise as features of our common experience. The Jains, though, focus on the implications of taking each tradition's *basic* claim to its logical conclusion.

In their most radical forms, non-Jain systems of thought would cast our common human experience of the category contrary to the one that each system takes as basic as a result of illusion or false consciousness. Buddhist accounts of experience thus present the sense of continuity attaching to phenomena such as memory and self-identity as arising from a deluded craving for enduring objects of enjoyment, when the reality is a series of arising and immediately perishing moments, each of which inherits certain characteristics from the moment preceding it and passing on characteristics to the next moment. And Vedic accounts of experience—most radically that of Advaita Vedanta—similarly present the sense of constant change attaching to temporal phenomena as arising from a deluded consciousness that fails to perceive the deeper, underlying unity of being upon which the realm of phenomena is projected.

From a Jain point of view, however, both the Buddhist and Vedantic accounts of experience capture an aspect of its nature, but not its totality. According to Jainism, there is that in an entity which arises and passes away, *and* that which endures. The Buddhist account of experience correctly notes its ever-changing karmically constituted dimension. The Vedantic account, however, equally correctly notes the eternal and unchanging core of an entity—its *jiva*, or life force—as well as the general character of existence itself—or *satsamanya*—which does not change, even while particular entities undergo change with respect to their modes of existence (or *paryaya*) at given points in time. The mode of existence of an entity at a given time is in turn a function of the relationship of that entity, either positive or negative, to possibilities, or qualities (*gunas*), which it either embodies or does not embody. A pen, for example, is a positive embodiment of pen qualities, but a negative embodiment of elephant qualities—not unlike the process idea of prehensions.

The possible qualities that can occur at a given point in space and time are nearly limitless. A particular entity is an embodiment, at that point in space and time, of all of these: a positive embodiment of those that it exhibits and a negative embodiment of those that it does not. It is a nexus of positive and negative relations to all possibilities.

In this sense, an entity has a virtually infinite number of aspects which constitute it: its relations to all of these possibilities. This is what it means to say that an entity is *anekanta*, that is, possessed of manifold aspects. Anekantavada, therefore, is the doctrine of the irreducible complexity of entities. There is that in an entity which is impermanent, changing, and in a state of constant flux. There is that in an entity which is permanent, continuous, and unchanging. And the entity as a whole is a complex synthesis of all of these aspects.

From this perspective, the cardinal sin, metaphysically speaking, is to attempt to reduce all entities to one of their aspects: to claim, for example, that only that in an entity which is impermanent is real and that continuity is an illusion, or that only that which is permanent is real, and that change is an illusion. This is the error *ekantata*, or absolutism, which is understood as one-sidedness in one's metaphysical judgments.

From a Jain perspective, Buddhist and Vedantic views err inasmuch as they are *ekanta*, that is, absolutist or "one-sided," affirming only one aspect of reality as true and dismissing the other as mere appearance, or *maya*. According to *anekantavada*, a more adequate understanding of reality is one which can integrate the varied facets that reveal themselves to our experience: one which affirms both change *and* continuity, both process *and* substance, both personal *and* impersonal dimensions, and so on. That this is not a violation of the principle of non-contradiction is demonstrated when the Jains point out that they are not claiming that an entity is unchanging in the same sense in which it is changing, or personal in the same sense in which it is impersonal. Because an entity has many dimensions or aspects to its existence, one must be attentive to

which dimension or aspect one is describing when one makes an affir-
mation about an entity's nature.

So it is not that either the Buddhists or the Vedantins are entirely
incorrect in their respective claims about the nature of reality. There is a
sense in which an entity is indeed impermanent and one in which it is
indeed permanent. But each of these systems has made one part of an
entity define its whole nature.

One can clearly see a connection between the traditional Jain critique
of absolutist views of reality and contemporary views about the emergence of religiously motivated violence from the psychological process
of identity formation. It is when we one-sidedly cling, in an absolutist
way, to only one dimension of who and what we are, only one of the
multiple allegiances that make up our identity at a given time, that we
cut ourselves off from others with whom we would otherwise feel a
common bond. It is when we are unmindful of the qualities that make up
our shared humanity and identify only with our religion, nationality,
ethnicity, or some other *upadhi*, or limiting quality, that we make possible the dehumanization of the other. We then become capable, at least
within our minds, to conceive of the other as the possible object of our
violence, and thus create one of the essential conditions for actual violence in the world. And it is when we focus only on our human qualities—as I believe a good Jain would want to point out—that it becomes
possible for us to blind ourselves to the pain of non-human life forms
and to exploit them for our own purposes. Absolutism, defined as willful
unmindfulness of the complexity of reality—the elevation of one aspect
of reality at the expense of all the others—is the seed of all violence.
This is why the Jain approach to the diversity of worldviews has come
to be seen by many Jain thinkers as a form of "intellectual *ahimsa*"—the
ideal of nonviolence in thought, word, and deed translated and applied
to the realm of intellectual discourse.

The idea of anekantavada, or the complexity of reality—which is a
metaphysical or ontological claim—has its corollary in the epistemic
realm, the realm of knowledge, in the form of nayavada, the Jain doctrine of perspectives.

How does nayavada follow from anekantavada? Each of the aspects
of reality corresponds to a point of view from which it may be
approached and known. Each such approach, in turn, corresponds to a
worldview or a belief system that takes insight into this particular facet
of reality as the core or kernel of truth around which it is constructed.
Each worldview, with its corresponding practice, is a way to realize the
truth of reality through one of its many aspects.

In this way, the Jain tradition has anticipated the nineteenth century teaching of Sri Ramakrishna, *yato mat, tato path*: "As many world-views, so many paths." Buddhists approach ultimate reality through that dimension which consists of the impermanent, the changing, the inter-dependent. Advaita Vedantins approach it through its changeless and eternal nature. Scientists approach it as the observable universe. And the adherents of *bhakti yoga* and other devotional paths, such as the Abrahamic religions, approach it as a supreme person. None of these paths is false. All capture some aspect or facet of truth. At the same time, none is complete. Each path transforms human existence in powerful and measurable ways. Each adds value and richness to the world. And each can become oppressive if it is mistaken for the totality of truth and closes itself off from the others.

Finally, if we understand, through anekantavada, that reality is com-plex and has many facets to which it cannot be reduced in its totality, and if we understand, through nayavada, that each of these facets represents an entry-point through which reality can be known through a practice that takes each facet as its chosen ideal, this entails a particular mode of speech that it is best to employ when speaking of ultimate reality to those whose commitments and paths may differ from our own. This is the mode of speech taught by syadvada, the doctrine of conditional predication. *Syat* is an optative form of the Sanskrit verbal root *as*, or "be," which means, "It could be," "It may be," "It might be," or even "It should be." In Jain technical philosophical usage, however, it means, "In one sense it is the case that…" Again, the Jain doctrines of relativity do not violate the principle of non-contradiction; for they do not assert that an entity has contrary qualities in the same sense, at the same time, or in the same place. According to syadvada, if one predicates any quality of an entity and wishes to do so with proper philosophical precision, avoid-ing the kinds of one-sided claims that characterize other traditions and cause them to fall into the trap of interreligious conflict, one needs to specify the sense in which that predicate obtains. Thus, "An entity is impermanent inasmuch as it possesses particular qualities at one time but not at another."

In other words, an entity is, in one sense (*syat*) impermanent. In another sense, it is permanent. Taking into account both its impermanent and permanent aspects, it is both impermanent and permanent. Also, because an entity is infinitely complex, it possesses aspects that cannot be described in terms of impermanence and permanence.

To take another, perhaps more concrete example, is a human being an impersonal or a personal entity? In an obvious sense, a human being is a personal entity, possessing the qualities that we associate with person-hood, such as agency, volition, and memory. In another sense, however, a human being is an impersonal entity, possessing impersonal character-istics, such as occupying a certain volume of space and a certain extent in time, having mass and density, and so on.

Taking into account both personal and impersonal properties, a human being can be seen to be both personal and impersonal. And similarly, because a human being is infinitely complex, it possesses aspects that cannot be described in terms of personhood or non-person-hood.

When one encounters a religious or philosophical claim, therefore, that is contrary to one's own view, the proper attitude to take is to adhere to one's own view, but also to be open to the possibility that a kernel of truth—a genuine insight into an aspect of reality that one has not yet considered—must rest at the core of the worldview of the other. This is not relativism—throwing up one's hands in despair and asking rhetori-cally, "Who really knows the truth?" Nor is it absolutism: clinging to one's view while rejecting all others.

It is making of one's own view an open system, capable of adaptation to the truths in the views of others. This does not mean that one gives up one's own view in its entirety, but that one allows it to be transformed in ways that cannot necessarily be anticipated ahead of time, prior to encounter and dialogue with the other. The histories of the world's reli-gions and philosophies show that such mutual transformation happens all of the time. Many world religions were, in their origins, transforma-tions of the traditions from which they emerged.

Pravrajika Vrajaprana, although speaking from the point of view of the Vedanta tradition of Sri Ramakrishna, could well be summarizing the consistent application of this Jain approach to religious diversity when she writes that,

> The world's spiritual traditions are like different pieces in a giant jigsaw puzzle: each piece is different and each piece is essential to complete the whole picture. Each piece is to be honored and respected while holding firm to our own particular piece of the puzzle. We can deepen our own spirituality and learn about our own tradition by studying other faiths. Just as importantly, by studying our own tradition well, we are better able to appreciate the truth in other traditions… This is not to say that all religions are "pretty much the same." That is an affront to the distinct

beauty and individual greatness of each of the world's spiritual traditions. Saying that every religion is equally true and authentic doesn't mean that one can be substituted for the other like generic brands of aspirin.[6]

Jains, to be sure, adhere to their own view of reality, and even see it as superior to other views, precisely because it can encompass the central insights of other views, but not in an *exclusivist* fashion, regarding one's own view as simply true and others as simply false. It, rather, sees the other as participating in the same larger truth that one is also striving to articulate.

ASSESSMENT

A Jain-inspired philosophy of religious pluralism, that takes *anekantavada*, *naya-vada*, and *syadvada* as guiding principles, arguably meets three essential criteria that a pluralistic approach to the diversity of worldviews needs to meet.

First, it addresses the contradictions among the conflicting worldviews that belief systems propose. Indeed, this is the central purpose of this philosophy. It achieves this aim by affirming a metaphysics of complexity which allows the apparently contradictory claims of various worldviews to be true by assigning each of them a sphere or domain of truth: a sense in which they are, indeed, true, but not absolutely so.

A second criterion for an ideal pluralistic philosophy is that it would avoid being itself imperialistic by subordinating other views to itself, as mere facets or aspects of itself. Does this model avoid subordinating one view to another? One could argue that it does not—and that this is in fact an impossible goal; for as long as one makes any definite claim about the nature of reality, or even an aspect of reality, one is denying the truth of all claims that contradict it (such as a claim that reality is *not* complex or multi-faceted).

All philosophies of religious pluralism are, in at least this minimal sense, forms of *inclusivism*, that is, the view that there is a more comprehensive meta-view to which a variety of views may point or in which they may be said to participate. But one can also argue that inclusivist

---

[6] Pravrajika Vrajaprana, *Vedanta: A Simple Introduction* (Hollywood, CA: Vedanta Press, 1999), pp. 56–57.

models can be either more or less affirming of the distinctive truths of the various systems of thought that they seek to subsume, and more or less open to the idea that there may be truths in other systems of which the inclusivist is not yet aware, at least until further dialogue and engagement with the other. As the late Wilhelm Halbfass has argued, the Jain model of inclusivism is also minimally hierarchical, situating other systems of thought within what he calls a "horizontal" model.

> The Jains present their own system not as the transcending culmination of lower stages of truth, but as the complete and comprehensive context, the full panorama which comprises other doctrines as partial truths or limited perspectives.[7]

A shadow of what is arguably an imperialistic or paternalistic notion of the superiority of one's own view remains, but is mitigated by the removal of the kind of hierarchical ranking of other systems of thought characteristic of non-Jain doxographic literature in the pre-modern South Asian context. Again, such a sense is arguably unable to be avoided when one takes into account the logic of what it means to hold a position. If one did not think that one's own view or tradition had any epistemic advantages at all, at least for oneself at this particular point in one's spiritual journey, then one would cease to adhere to it.

This, of course, is why the Jain model is not a form of relativism in the usual, thoroughgoing sense, absent a set of definite claims about the nature of reality; for at the core of the Jain approach is the traditional Jain understanding of existence, as perceived by the *Tirthankaras* and proclaimed by their disciples, the *ganadharas*, in the Jain *agama*, or scriptural tradition.

This raises the question of the extent to which the Jain approach allows for the possibility of a deep and thoroughgoing rejection of its own central premises? That is, is there a sense in which a Jain approach to the variety of worldviews requires one to adopt a Jain worldview, or may this approach be conceived in ways that allow it to be adopted from a variety of starting points? To explore this question fully is beyond the scope of this paper; but I would suggest that the idea of Buddhist, Vedantic, Abrahamic, or secular analogues to the Jain approach is worth pursuing. As mentioned at the outset, it is not at all necessary that the

---

[7] Wilhelm Halbfass, *India and Europe: An Essay in Understanding* (Albany: State University of New York Press, 1988), p. 414.

approach of each tradition be the same. That would go against the very notion of diversity that we seek to affirm. But it may be that the attempt to see how persons beginning from various starting points might come up with similar models would be worth the effort involved. For one thing, the subtle differences in each approach may themselves be instructive for the others. A Buddhist approach, focusing on the skillful means of awakened beings, conforms well to the proposal of the Jain thinker Haribhadra, in his *Yogadrstisamuccaya*, that the variety of worldviews owes itself to the strategies of enlightened teachers in dealing with followers of differing capacities. And a Vedantic approach, such I have sought to develop in my own work, that focuses on the distinction between *nirguna* and *saguna* Brahman, and the distinctions within the realm of *saguna* Brahman, between the supreme soul (*paramatman*), the multitude of souls making up the world (the *jivas*), and the world itself (*jagat*), might draw the attention of contemporary Vedantins to an appreciative emphasis on the diverse worldviews within Vedanta—views that include realist and dualist approaches—after a long period of focus, at least among scholars and practitioners in the Western world, upon Advaita Vedanta.

Another potential point of convergence among the Jain, Buddhist, and Vedantic approaches centers around the respective responses of these traditions to the question, of how a pluralistic approach to truth responds to the question of whether any linguistic or conceptual system, even one as open to diversity as these, can be adequate to the ever-unfolding reality of the diversity that one is able to perceive in the world? An important element in the responses of all three traditions to this question is the distinctions that each makes between a realm of ultimate truth (*paramartha satya*) that ultimately goes beyond words and a realm of conventional, relative truth (*vyavahara satya* or *samvrti satya*). The Jain version of this distinction, developed by the ancient Digambara Jain philosopher and mystic, Kundakunda, is the distinction between the ultimate or final perspective of a Jina (*niscaya naya*) and the conventional perspective of those of us for whom *kevala jnana* is yet to come (*vyavahara naya*). The Jain doctrines of relativity operate on the level of the *vyavahara naya*, the conventional perspective, which is revealed to be made up of many perspectives and is not itself the ultimate truth. This is a very important point, for this is what prevents the kernel of absolutism in the Jain approach from becoming imperialistic. It is not that the Jain perspective, pluralistic and open though it may be, is simplistically equated with ultimate truth. The Jain perspective is instead a wider vision of the relative truth. Ultimate truth can never be expressed in its fullness through words or concepts alone, but must be experienced directly. The realization of the Jina, the direct experience of truth, is what is absolute, rather than any particular verbal formulation of it.

CONCLUSION

Finally, a Jain-inspired model not only allows, it encourages—and arguably creates a mandate for—further dialogue and exploration of the many facets of reality. If the truth that discloses itself to all of us who for whom the goal of *kevala-jnana*, the omniscience of the enlightened Jina, remains in the future is one of virtually infinite multiplicity, then it seems that there is no limit to the truths that may yet disclose themselves through the process of dialogue among worldviews.

This can be seen as the distinctively Jain contribution to the vision expressed by Swami Vivekananda over a century ago.

> Each religion, as it were, takes up one part of the great universal truth, and spends its whole force in embodying and typifying that part of the great truth. It is, therefore, addition, not exclusion. That is the idea. System after system arises, each one embodying a great idea, and ideals must be added to ideals. And this is the march of humanity.[8]

---

[8] Vivekananda, Volume 2, pp. 365–366.

3

Sikhism: Transcendental and Interfaith Message

Mohinder Singh

I am thankful to the organizers of this Interfaith conference for inviting me to present the Sikh perspective on the above theme. Being a student of history, I am reminded of a similar situation which prevailed in the medieval times. Political turmoil created by conflict between the ruling elite and the majority population led to a debate as to which religion was superior. Rather than entering into polemics Guru Nanak and other saints and *Bhakta*s of his time brought about emotional integration of India through preaching loving devotion to God. The major emphasis of the teachings of the medieval *Bhakta*s and the Sufi saints was transcending religious boundaries. They emphasized that different religions were the means to reach the similar goal. In modern times, similar message was given by great Indian sage Ramakrishna Paramhans who emphasized that the aim of each religion was comparable to climbing the stairs of one's house. Once you reach the roof, you see the same sky, stars, planets, and the heavens. At a time when the Indian society is facing conflicts on various fronts it would be a befitting tribute to Swami Vivekananda to preach transcendental vision of the Ultimate which is the core of religious scriptures of different faiths. Let me share with the audience transcendental vision and Interfaith dialogue and message of universal love taught by Guru Nanak and other saints and sages whose hymns are enshrined in *Guru Granth Sahib*, the Sikh scripture.

DEFINING SIKHISM

The word Sikh is derived from Sanskrit *Shishya* or Pali *Sekha* both meaning disciple or learner. Thus those who followed the path shown by Guru Nanak (1469–1539), the founder of the new faith, came to be known as the Sikhs. They were also known as *Nanakpanthi*s, meaning those who constituted the *panth* (order) founded by Nanak. However, it

33

was not till 1925 that a legal definition of a Sikh was provided by the Sikh Gurdwaras and Shrines Bill passed in the Legislative Council of the undivided Punjab. According to the Act, "Sikh means a person who professes the Sikh religion." The Act further clarifies that in case of doubt a person shall be deemed to be a Sikh if he/she subscribes to the following declaration, "I solemnly affirm that I am a Sikh, that I believe in the *Guru Granth Sahib*, that I believe in the ten Gurus and that I have no other religion." An Act passed by the Indian Parliament in 1971 to regulate the management of Sikh *Gurudwara*s in National Capital of Delhi, a Sikh is defined as "a person who professes the Sikh religion, believes and follows the teachings of Sri Guru Granth Sahib and the ten Gurus only and keeps unshorn hair."

Unfortunately, both the legal definitions are far away from the spiritual definition of a Sikh given in *Guru Granth Sahib* which mentions:

He, who calls himself a disciple of the True Guru,

Let him rise early in the morn and contemplate the Lord's Name.

Let him attune himself to the Lord and Bathe in the Pool of Nectar at this early hour.

Let him dwell upon the Lord through the Guru's Word that all his Sins are washed off.[1]

How many of us meet the legal and spiritual requirements of being a Sikh remains a debatable issue.

THE FOUNDER AND THE MESSAGE

Born in 1469 in Talwandi, later renamed Nankana, now in Pakistan, Nanak was a precocious child with a deeply meditative cast of mind. His father soon despaired as all attempts to engage him in worldly pursuits failed. Sent to the fields to mind the cattle, he would enjoy sitting under a tree lost in his own thoughts. Complaints of the cattle trespassing provoked the wrath of his father. In school, he was good at figures and quick to learn though he liked best to wander and be alone and sing the glory of the Lord. A story is told that his father gave him some money and sent

---

[1] *Guru Granth Sahib*, p. 306, English translation by Dr Gopal Singh, pp. 297–298.

him to a neighboring town to do some profitable business. On the way Nanak met some *sadhus* who had not eaten for many days. He purchased food with the money his father had given him and fed the hungry *sadhus*, forgetting all about the business plan. He returned home empty-handed. When father asked him what he had done with the money, he replied that he had made a "profitable bargain" described in the Sikh parlance as *Sacha Sauda*.

His marriage was arranged in the hope that he would settle down with his new responsibilities but it made no difference. Through the good offices of his sister Nanaki's husband Jairam, Nanak was employed by Daulat Khan Lodhi, the Muslim Governor of Sultanpur in Kapurthala District of Punjab, to look after his stores. Though Nanak discharged his duties honestly and diligently but his heart wasn't in it. Mardana, the Muslim rebeck player, his friend from his birthplace, Talwandi, also joined him and became his constant companion. When the spirit moved him Nanak would indicate to Mardana to play the rebeck and he would sing, which was later reduced to writing and is popularly known as Nanak Bani.

GURU NANAK'S ENLIGHTENMENT

It was during his stay in Sultanpur that Nanak attained Enlightenment, at the age of 36. Gripped by an increasing restlessness, he wondered what he was doing with his life after he had worked for about two years for the *Nawab*. According to popular accounts, when he went for the customary dip in the river Bein flowing nearby, absorbed in thoughts of God, Nanak mysteriously disappeared. According to popular Sikh tradition, Nanak was ushered into the Divine Presence offered a cup full of nectar and blessed by the Almighty and told to go forth and preach the holy Word. The first words that Nanak, the Guru, uttered after his enlightenment were: "There is no Hindu, there is no Musalman."

At a time when Hindus and Muslims were engaged in sectarian conflicts these words formed a major plank in Guru Nanak's creed. This statement of Guru Nanak is generally interpreted as a mission of reconciliation between the conflicting Hindu and Muslim traditions. But Nanak's new mission seems to have a deeper meaning that the differences among various religious groups had overshadowed the underlying spirit of religion that the Supreme Power is One, all else its manifestation.

Accompanied by Mardana, Nanak, the Guru, set out on long spiritual journeys to preach his message of love. He traveled to different parts of India and neighboring countries and visited the religious centers of the Hindus and the Muslims. Realizing the religious diversity of India the Guru emphasized the essential unity of faiths through the medium of dialogue. "So long as one lives in the world one should first listen to others before uttering one's sermon," said Nanak. His travels in India took him to Banaras, the holy city of the Hindus, and further east of Assam. He traveled to the north as far as Tibet where Buddhism was practiced. According to popular stories, Buddhist monks were so impressed by the teachings of Nanak that they reverently called him Nanak Lama.

MESSAGE OF GURU NANAK

Guru Nanak preached strict monotheism and described the Creator as *Ikk*, the One without a second. Guru Nanak's philosophy of God is best described in the *Japji*, the primal creed of the Sikh faith. In his teachings there is no room for worship of any deity or human teacher other than the Formless One. Contrary to the medieval Indian practice of renouncing the world for spiritual elevation, Guru Nanak believed that "This world is the abode of God and the True One lives therein."

Guru Nanak believed that it was possible to live pure among the impurities of life.

As the lotus liveth detached in waters, as the duck floats carefree on the stream, so does one cross the Sea of Material Existence, his mind attuned to the Word. One lives Detached, Enshrining the One Lord in the Mind, shorn of hope, living in the midst of hope.[2]

Two stories illustrating the way Guru Nanak made a point can bear repetition. In Haridwar, he found devotees offering water in the direction of the rising sun which was intended to reach the spirits of their deceased ancestors. He joined the group but, scooping the water in his hands, threw it vigorously in the opposite direction. When questioned, he replied that surely by the same logic it should reach his fields in the Punjab which lay west. And in Mecca, he was berated for being disrespectful

[2] *Guru Granth Sahib*, p. 938, English translation by Gopal Singh.

because his feet pointed in the direction of the Ka'aba, where the Faithful believe God resides. He apologized, and asked that his feet be turned away to whichever direction where God was not present. It is important to emphasize that Guru Nanak was clearly emphasizing on diversity in religious traditions of India without expressing any disrespect or dissention.

The New Society Established by Guru Nanak

Towards the last phase of his life, Guru Nanak settled on the banks of the river Ravi (now in Pakistan) on the piece of land donated by a disciple. A small village came up there and he called it Kartarpur, the Abode of God. He worked tilling the fields, leading a band of disciples in prayer and devotion, and sharing all that the land produced. His family consisted of his wife, two sons, and a handful of disciples both Hindu and Muslim including Lehna, a rope-maker, who proved himself to be the most devoted among the disciples close to Nanak, was renamed Angad, meaning a limb of his body, and was appointed his successor.

The community of disciples at Kartarpur was not by any means a monastic order but a fellowship of ordinary men and women from different religious traditions engaged in the normal occupations of life, earning their livelihood through honest means and sharing the fruit of their labor with others. Guru Nanak's life for the period of 20 years at Kartarpur was an example of community living, a model, which became the basis for the development of Sikh society and Sikh value system over the years.

The Guru and his followers got up before dawn and after their ablutions said their prayers as has been the custom among travelers on the spiritual path since times immemorial. The next step, however, was revolutionary. The Guru and his followers then partook of the sacred food from the community kitchen all sitting in one line before they attended to the day's work. In the evening they again assembled at a common place and collectively recited their evening prayer and shared the evening meal. Before going to bed, they all recited the *Kirtan Sohila*, songs of Acclaim. Thus the devotees went to bed with God's name in their mind and heart and repeated the same next morning after ablutions. Teachings of the Gurus and *Bhakta*s emphasize that the purpose of meditation was to transform an individual from *Manmukh* (self-centered) to *Gurmukh* (God-centered). In his composition *Japji*, Guru Nanak describes these stages of spiritual evolution as

Dharamkhand (realm of duty), *Giankhand* (realm of knowledge), *Saramkhand* (realm of aesthetics), *Karamkhand* (realm of action), and *Sachkhand* (realm of truth)—the stage of the Ultimate Vision. After transformation of an individual from *Manmukh* to *Gurumukh* the seeker becomes one with the Creator. Zenith of spiritual glory is achieved when it is not the seeker who is seeking God but the other way round. Bhagat Kabir beautifully describes this transformation in the following hymn:

> Kabir like the waters of Ganga
> Pure is now my mind.
> And, lo, the Lord now follows me,
> Saying "Thou art mine, Thou art mine."[3]

The twin institutions of *Sangat* and *Pangat* derive from this routine. All are expected to assemble in a congregation (*sangat*) and partake food from the community kitchen (*langar*), sitting in one line (*pangat*), ensuring that there was no distinction between high and low, nor between rich and poor. There was only the fraternity, the brotherhood of man, and in the eyes of God all were equal. This tradition is followed by the devout at home and abroad even today.

Because the emphasis of Guru Nanak's teachings was on good actions and transcended the boundaries of color, caste, or creed he attracted a following from among both the Hindus and Muslims of his time. A story is told that when the Guru's end was near there was a dispute among the followers whether he should be cremated according to the Hindu practice or buried according to the Muslim tradition. The Guru advised them, "You place flowers on either side, Hindus on my right, Muslims on my left. Those whose flowers remain fresh tomorrow will have their way." So saying, he asked them to pray. When the prayer was over, Nanak pulled the sheet over him and went to his eternal sleep. The next morning, when they raised the sheet, they found the body had disappeared. The flowers of both communities were fresh. The moral of the story given in the *Janamsakhi* is clear. Guru Nanak is still fondly remembered as:

> Baba Nanak Shah Fakir
> Hindu ka Guru, Musalman ka Pir.

[3] *Guru Granth Sahib*, p. 1367, English translation by Dr Gopal Singh.

THE SIKH SCRIPTURE

The catholicity of the Sikh faith and its ecumenical spirit are best demonstrated in the *Guru Granth Sahib*, the Sikh scripture. While the hymns of Guru Nanak, and of his successors Angad Dev, Amar Das, and Ram Das, were already in circulation in some form or the other, Guru Arjan Dev, the fifth Guru, thought it proper to prepare an anthology of the hymns. It was intended that they themselves could become the focal point for the emerging community of followers. For this purpose Guru Arjan Dev acquired the *pothi*s containing the hymns of the Gurus from Baba Mohan, son of the third Guru, Guru Amar Das, and also invited compositions from various other Hindu *Bhakta*s and Muslim saints who were at the same spiritual wavelength. After having collected the required material, Guru Arjan Dev began to dictate the hymns to Bhai Gurdas at Ramsar in the holy city of Amritsar. The volume was completed in 1604 and the Guru formally installed it as the *Granth* in the sanctum sanctorum, Hari Mandir Sahib, at Amritsar. Another devout Sikh, Baba Buddha, was appointed the first *Granthi*.

The hymns of the *Guru Granth Sahib* are not arranged author-wise but are divided into musical modes indicating how they should be sung. The scripture has now been standardized to a format of 1,438 pages. It contains nearly 6,000 hymns, the largest number being those of the fifth Guru, Arjan Dev at 2,218, followed by those of Guru Nanak (974), Guru Amar Das (907), Guru Ram Das (679), Guru Tegh Bahadur (115), and Guru Angad Dev (62). Besides hymns of the Gurus and those of the Hindu *Bhakta*s and Muslim saints belonging to different regions—Jaidev of Bengal, Namdev, Trilochan, and Parmanand of Maharashtra, Sadhna of Sindh, Bene, Rama Nand, Kabir, and Ravidas from Uttar Pradesh, and the famous Sufi saint Sheikh Farid from Pak Pattan (now in Pakistan)—hymns of the Bhatts (bards) are also included in the *Guru Granth Sahib*.

It is important to mention that the Sikhs do not worship any idol or human teacher. Since the *Guru Granth* itself is the eternal Guru, it occupies a central place in a Sikh Gurudwara. It is installed on a platform with a canopy covering it as a mark of respect while an attendant generally fans it with a whisk, standing behind the *Granthi*. On entering the Gurudwara, the followers bow before the Book and make a ceremonial offering as a mark of respect. Then they sit, with heads covered, in a silent posture to listen either to the hymns being recited by the *granthi* (reader of the scripture) or to the *kirtan* (singing of hymns) rendered by the musicians known as *Ragi*s.

The *Guru Granth Sahib* opens with *Japji*, the primal creed of Sikh faith, and ends with the *sloka*s of the ninth Guru, Guru Tegh Bahadur, thus spanning a period of about 200 years.

JAPJI: THE PRIMAL CREED

Japji is the composition which most followers of the Sikh faith recite early morning generally described as *amrit vela*, the ambrosial hour. It consists of 38 *Pauri*s (stanzas) beginning with the *Mool Mantra* and ending with a *sloka*, often written as Salok following the Punjabi pronunciation.

Written in the traditional Punjabi or northern *Sant Bhakha*, the *Japji* deals with a deeply spiritual theme in a most logical and analytical manner. The *Mool Mantra* defines God through various attributes while categorically stating that the Creator is One. The translation reads: "There is but one God; *Sati* (Truth) by name; the Creator all-pervading, without fear, without enmity, whose existence is unaffected by time, who does not take birth, (is) self-existent; (to be realised) through the grace of the Guru."

The *Mool Mantra* begins with the numeral one. Words may change their meanings in the course of time, but the connotation of a numeral always remains the same. Unity of God is thus emphasized at the very outset to wean away the disciples from the worship of the innumerable gods and goddesses of the Hindu pantheon. In several hymns the Guru has portrayed this unity in moving terms:

The mighty Sing of Thy Might
And the Blessed of Thy Light
His Goodness, Greatness, Beauty:
Of Knowledge hard to classify.[4]

SIKHISM AND OTHER RELIGIONS

Guru Nanak, the founder of the Sikh faith, had cordial relations with both the Hindus and the Muslims. He was born at a time when there was

[4] *Guru Granth Sahib*, p. 1, English translation by Dr Gopal Singh.

a conflict between the two major religious traditions in India—Hinduism and Islam. Guru Nanak seems to have played the role of reconciler by giving the message to transcend narrow religious boundaries and talked of higher values in which religiosity had no place.

During his long spiritual journeys Guru Nanak's constant companions were Bala, a Hindu, and Mardana, a Muslim. In the popular calendar art we see a picture of Guru Nanak flanked by these two companions thereby conveying a message that the Guru acted as a bridge between the two major religious communities of his time. Guru Nanak's affinity with the two traditions has led some historians to believe that his was a syncretic religion with some ideas borrowed from Hinduism and others from Islam. Guru Nanak's belief in one God—Ek Onkar—was seen as Islamic and his emphasis on loving devotion to God as Bhakti or Hindu influence. However, a careful study of the teachings of Guru Nanak reveals that he had an independent message of his own. According to Sikh tradition, Guru Nanak during his meditation on the Kali Bein was called to the Court of God where he was made to drink the cup of divine Name and asked to preach the new religion revealed to him which was of transcendental nature. Besides the belief in One God, Guru Nanak taught that God had no form or garb by which one could call Him to be a Hindu God or the Muslim God. "My Master is one, the One alone exists."

SIKHISM AND INTERFAITH DIALOGUE AND ACTION

Sikh Gurus were pioneers in Interfaith dialogue and action. Guru Nanak, the founder, was a great traveler who went on long spiritual journeys popularly called *Udasis*. During his travels over two decades, Guru Nanak met a number of leaders of other religious and spiritual traditions and had long encounters with them. It is believed that he traveled over 48,000 miles mostly on foot in search of individuals whose mind and soul was imbued with Divine Revelation. During these travels and Interfaith dialogues Guru Nanak and his successive Gurus created emotional unity of India. Guru Nanak emphasized that it was the genuine quest, which was most important than debate for the sake of debate. Guru Nanak's journeys began from Punjab and progressed towards east, south, north, and west. During his journey towards the east, the Guru passed through Delhi, Uttar Pradesh, Bihar, Bengal, Assam, Manipur, and Tripura and returned through Odisha and Madhya Pradesh. During his second journey towards the south the Guru is said to have covered large territory of Rajasthan, Gujarat, Maharashtra, and Karnataka. In his northbound journey through the mountainous regions of Kashmir, Himachal, Nepal, Tibet, Sikkim, and Bhutan, the Guru is also believed to have entered the borders of China. In his final journey, he visited most of the middle-eastern countries and a Gurudwara was built in his memory in Baghdad. It is obvious that during these long journeys the Guru met various religious and spiritual masters from other traditions with whom he exchanged his ideas. From the *janamsakhi*, popular hagiographic account of Guru's life, we learn that on the festival of Shivratri Guru Nanak had an encounter with the *Siddhas* of Achal Batala. A little away from *Siddhas'* pavilion the Guru sat under a tree and began singing praises of God. While there were serious differences of opinion about approach to life, it is interesting that the dialogue remained polite throughout and did not lead to any dissention. While *Siddhas* believed in denouncing the world, the Guru emphasized the world was worth living and there was no need to give up the world for attaining salvation. Later, during his visit to Mecca the local divines asked the Guru, "Pray, open your book and tell us who is better Hindu or Muslim?" The Guru politely replied, "Bereft of good actions both are of no consequence."[5]

The spirit of Interfaith dialogue and cooperation is at its best in the *Guru Granth Sahib* wherein the fifth Guru created emotional unity of India by including hymns from Guru Nanak and his successors as also those of the Hindu *Bhakta*s including some of the so-called low castes and the Muslim saints. In a Gurudwara when a devotee bows before the Holy Book, he bows before the corporate body of the *Guru Granth Sahib* and not before the hymns of any particular Guru, *Bhakta*, or saint. *Ardas*, the Sikh prayer, ends on this altruistic note:

Nanak nam charddi Kala tere bhane sarbatt ka bhala.

[Thy Name, Thy Glory, be forever triumphant, Nanak, and, in Thy Will, may peace and prosperity come to one and all.]

---

[5] *Varan Bhai Gurdas, Var* 1–13.

4

Ramakrishna Movement's Approach to Religious Diversity

Swami Bhajanananda

The Ramakrishna Movement is centered around the life and teachings of Sri Ramakrishna as interpreted and put into practice by his foremost disciple Swami Vivekananda. Sri Ramakrishna was born in 1836 in a remote village of Bengal in a poor, priestly family, and had only the rudiments of formal schooling. It may appear to be strange that such an unlikely person came to be hailed later on as the Prophet of harmony of religions. In mid-nineteenth century, when the conservative Hindu society was bound by rigid caste rules, it needed extraordinary courage for a person born in an orthodox Brahmin family to go to a nearby mosque and offer namaz there, to meditate on Jesus Christ as God Incarnate, and to declare *Yato mat, tato path*, "As many faiths, so many paths."

What made Sri Ramakrishna follow different spiritual paths? It was not the desire for name and fame or social compulsions, which made Sri Ramakrishna an advocate of harmony of religions. The primary reason was that, being a great lover of God, Ramakrishna wanted to enjoy the bliss of communion with God obtainable through diverse spiritual paths. It was his personal discovery that diverse spiritual paths led to the transcendental experience of different aspects of the same Ultimate Reality or supreme Godhead that made him propound the doctrine of *dharma-samanvaya* or harmony of religion. Sri Ramakrishna's verification of the truth that different religious paths can lead to transcendental experiences of different aspects of the same ultimate Reality is what gives authenticity to the modern interreligious attitude known as Pluralism. It is the idea that harmony of religions is an experiential truth, and not merely a philosophical concept or a sociological expedient which is the distinctive hallmark of the ideal of harmony of religions followed in the Ramakrishna Movement.

But before discussing that, it is necessary to have a brief survey of different approaches to the problem of religious diversity and different interreligious attitudes.

APPROACHES TO DIVERSITY

There are several approaches to the problem of religious diversity or plurality, such as political approach, scriptural approach, philosophical approach, sociological approach, and mystical approach.

Political Approach

By political approach is meant the policy adopted by the government toward religion. In modern times, this approach has assumed paramount importance because, without it, the other approaches become ineffective. In modern times, even theocratic countries have the presence of large multireligious communities in the workforce, and so the governments in those countries have to follow a policy of religious toleration. In democratic countries, such as the US and India, the political approach followed is to declare the State to be secular. Secularism has been much criticized, and is often challenged in India also. Nevertheless, it does at least one thing: it denies legitimacy to fundamentalism and social injustice in the name of religion.

Scriptural Approach

One of the difficult problems in dealing with world religions is that they are based on scriptures, which differ widely from one another in their contents and aims. All religious scriptures, however, stress certain universal virtues such as truthfulness, love, compassion, selflessness, service, etc. The correct approach to world scriptures should be to highlight these common virtues and interpret those passages with a view to fostering universal love, brotherhood, and cooperation. However, scriptures also imply several theological or philosophical issues. These issues have to be reconciled or harmonized. This calls for a universal hermeneutics. From the Protestant theologians Schleirmacher and Dilthey to the present-day postmodernists several attempts have been made to develop a universal hermeneutics. Swami Vivekananda has also made significant contributions to this endeavor.

Philosophical Approach

Unlike the theological approach that deals with individual religions and is centered on scriptural studies, the philosophical approach takes religious phenomenon as a whole and studies the ontological, episte-mological, and axiological principles involved in that phenomenon. However, standard textbooks on philosophy of religion by Galloway, John Hick, and others deal only with the so-called Abrahamic reli-gions: Judaism, Christianity, and Islam. In recent years an attempt is made to study philosophy of religion from the postmodernist stand-point. A comprehensive philosophy of religion that covers religions of Indian origin and other religions can help much in fostering inter-religious understanding.

Sociological Approach

Sociological study of religion, which has now become an independent discipline, has helped a great deal in understanding religion as a univer-sal phenomenon. Sociology of religion shows how all religions, irre-spective of their differences, help people to orientate themselves to the Ultimate Reality, find meaning and solve the existential problems of life, sacralize secular activities, face the sufferings and difficulties of life with courage, and so on. The work of social anthropologists such as E. B. Tylor, Bronislaw Malinowsky, Radcliff Brown, and Ruth Benedict has shown that religious consciousness is an inherent faculty of the human mind.

Religious Studies as an Independent Approach

The approaches to the phenomenon of religious diversity or plurality we have discussed thus far are parts of other disciplines such as history, theology, philosophy, and sociology. Apart from these, the study of world religions itself has now become an independent discipline. Several universities have opened departments of religious studies or conduct courses on world religions.

There are two methods of studying religion. One is the usual sci-entific method based on correct observation, collection of all data, and making impartial judgment. The second method of studying reli-gion is the phenomenological method. In this method, one observes other religions without prejudice, without projecting one's precon-ceived notions upon other religions, and, at the same time, try to share the religious experiences, feelings, and sentiments of the fol-lowers of those religions. In other words, the phenomenological method is a way of seeing each religion through the eyes of its sincere followers.

A more recent method is to study religion from the postmodernist standpoint.

Mystical Approach

Lastly, we come to the mystical approach. This approach is based on the view that the essence and aim of religion is to gain direct, transcendental experience of the Ultimate Reality or God, and that faith, acceptance of a creed, external observances, and customs have only a supportive role to play in religion. Every religion is based on the direct experience of the Ultimate Reality gained by its prophets or sages. Majority of the people remain satisfied with their faith in the founders. But there are spiritual seekers, who feel the urge in the depths of their souls to have the direct experience of their true inner nature and the true nature of God; they are the mystics or spiritual seekers. All the major religions have highly developed mystical traditions, and have produced many great mystics who are venerated as saints or sages.

Sri Ramakrishna and Swami Vivekananda were mystics of the highest order. As already stated earlier, it was the mystical approach that Ramakrishna followed in understanding the diversity of religions and in establishing harmony of religions. Swami Vivekananda expounded the universal significance of Sri Ramakrishna's experiences and made the mystical approach the true basis of harmony of religions.

It may be noted here that the six approaches discussed above are not alternatives but complementary to one another. For the establishment of religious harmony in the present-day world situation, all the approaches need to be pressed into service.

SEVEN INTER-RELIGIOUS ATTITUDES

The six approaches that have been outlined above are six ways of dealing with religious diversity. But in practical life it is the attitude of people toward religions other than their own that determines their behavior in a multireligious society. Scholars have identified seven interreligious attitudes in the modern world. They are: Indifferentism, Relativism, Syncretism, Exclusivism, Inclusivism, Pluralism, and Universalism. These are briefly explained in the following paragraphs.

Indifferentism

This is the view that there is no essential difference among religions and they are basically the same. Such a belief seems to have been deeply ingrained in the Indian psyche from ancient times. It enables common people belonging to different religious traditions to live in harmony with one another. But this simplistic idea is based on ignorance of other religions, and ignorance cannot be a sound basis for harmony.

Relativism

At the other extreme is the attitude known as relativism. It is the view that all religious truths are relative, there is no absolute or ultimate Truth, and religions of the world are different pathways to different goals.

Syncretism

Syncretism is the view that harmony of religions means to combine good points from different religions to create a new synthetic religion. In modern times, the print and electronic media make available the spiritual truths of different religions to people all over the world, and many people now follow a syncretic attitude.

Exclusivism

Exclusivism is the view that one's own religion alone is true and all the other religions are false. According to this view, there can be only one true revelation and one true way to salvation. Such a view opposes the very idea of harmony of religions.

Exclusivism was the view that prevailed in the West until modern times. It still prevails in many parts of the world.

When exclusivism finds aggressive expression, it becomes fundamentalism, which is a major threat to peaceful life even in the same religious community.

Inclusivism

Inclusivism is the view that one's own religion alone is true, but the other religions are not false as they are *included* in one's own religion.

It also holds that although revelation can take place in other religions also, revelation in one's own religion alone is full and true, whereas revelations in other religions are partial or imperfect.

Some form of inclusivism is found in all religions. In recent years it was formulated as a distinct interreligious attitude by the German Catholic theologian Karl Rahner. After the second Vatican Council, many Catholic and Protestant theologians have tended to hold this view.

Inclusivism raises the status of one's own religion by lowering the status of other religions. Such a view cannot be acceptable to all.

Pluralism

Religious Pluralism can mean that (1) the major religions of the world are true in so far as they represent different pathways to salvation; or that (2) the ultimate Truth has revealed itself in several ways in different places. In the words of its most prominent exponent Professor John Hick, Pluralism means that "the great religious traditions are to be regarded as alternative soteriological spaces within which, or ways along which, men and women find salvation/liberation/fulfilment."[1]

Pluralism does not ignore the differences among religions or the uniqueness of each religion. States Professor James Michael Lee:

Genuine religious pluralism is not a melting pot in which all diverse religions are liquefied into sameness. On the contrary, genuine religious pluralism is a mosaic in which all religions occupy privileged, autonomous and interactive positions, which reveals the full reality of God less inadequately than any single religion is able to do by itself.[2]

In the practical field Pluralism asserts the right of every religion to exist independently, and the right of every person to follow any religion.

It may be noted in this context that pluralism is no longer a matter to be decided by theologians or Church authorities. It has become the

[1] John Hick, quoted in Grant Shockley, "Religious Pluralism and Religious Education," in Norma H. Thompson (ed.), *Religious Pluralism and Religious Education* (Birmingham, Alabama: Religious Education Press, 1988), p. 141.

[2] James M. Lee, "The Blessings of Religious Pluralism," in Norma H. Thompson (ed.), *Religious Pluralism and Religious Education* (Birmingham, Alabama: Religious Education Press, 1988).

concern of the common man. The social revolution that swept through America and Europe in the 1960s, the influx of oriental spiritual leaders and ideas into the West, secularization of moral authority, and other factors have weakened the hold of institutional religions on the minds of Western people. On the other hand, the large presence of immigrants professing different religions and the easy availability of the spiritual truths of different religions through books and especially through the Internet, have made multireligious awareness a compelling reality in Western society. As a result of all this, the pluralistic attitude is gradually gaining ground in the Western society.

More importantly, Sri Ramakrishna's life and message form the ultimate source and authentication for the doctrine of Pluralism, discussed below.

Universalism

We have briefly discussed six types of interreligious attitudes; we now come to the seventh and last one, *universalism.*

Universalism is the view that there are universally valid spiritual truths common to all religions. Whereas Pluralism emphasizes the differences among religions, Universalism emphasizes the common ground among religions.

Sri Ramakrishna laid the foundations of Pluralism. Swami Vivekananda took his Master's doctrine one step further by showing that Pluralism must culminate in Universalism. Swamiji's idea of universalism is quite different from the ideas of universalism known till now. It will be dealt with later.

Our discussion so far has been intended to serve as a sort of introduction or background to understanding Sri Ramakrishna and Swami Vivekananda's approach to the phenomenon of diversity or plurality of religions.

SRI RAMAKRISHNA'S DOCTRINE OF
HARMONY OF RELIGIONS

Sri Ramakrishna's doctrine of *dharma-samanvaya* or "harmony of religions" is the Indian version of religious pluralism. A pluralistic outlook was the common and distinctive religious attitude of the people of India during the ancient period. This ancient pluralistic outlook was based on the realization of the principle of "unity in diversity" by ancient sages. The *Rishi*s or sages discovered that behind the infinite variety of ever-changing objects in the universe there is the one infinite, ultimate, eternal, unchanging Absolute Reality known as Brahman, which is of the nature of infinite consciousness, *sat-cit-ananda*, "Absolute Existence-Awareness-Bliss." The sages of the Upanishads spoke of this ultimate Reality, Brahman, as something to be directly experienced by transcending ordinary sense awareness.

Attempts were made by philosophers to define this ultimate Reality and its relation to the world in the form of philosophic concepts. This gave rise to different schools of philosophy and religious sects. As a result, the original vision of "unity in diversity" got eclipsed and the pluralistic approach was to some extent lost. In modern times, Sri Ramakrishna and Swami Vivekananda revived and reestablished the ancient pluralistic outlook of the Indian people.

Sri Ramakrishna's doctrine of "harmony of religions," *dharma-samanvaya*, is based on certain principles of praxis which he followed in his life. The first one is the principle of *direct experience*. As stated earlier, Sri Ramakrishna's doctrine of harmony was not derived from books or intellectual reasoning, but from his own direct transcendental experience. For him religion meant direct experience, and not dogmas or rituals.

The second principle Sri Ramakrishna followed in his life was to understand each religion through the eyes of its followers. In fact, he even followed the ways of life of the followers of other religions at different times. For instance, when he was practicing the Islamic spiritual discipline, he dressed like a Muslim and performed namaz, and did not visit the temple during that period. As stated earlier, this is similar to what is known as the phenomenological method. The only difference is, modern phenomenologists only talked, whereas Sri Ramakrishna actually practiced the principle.

The third principle which Sri Ramakrishna observed all through his life was, not to criticize any religion or sect. Nor did he allow anybody to criticize any religion or religious leader in his presence. He showed great reverence toward the great founders of all religions and sects. This reverential attitude toward all religions and their founders is a living tradition in the Ramakrishna Movement.

The main tenets of Sri Ramakrishna's doctrine of harmony of religions, *dharma-samanvaya*, are briefly stated here:

1.   The Ultimate Reality or God is only one but is known by different names in different religions; it is Personal as well as Impersonal.
2.   Realization of the Ultimate Reality is the true goal and purpose of human life. It is also the main purpose of all religions. It is this direct transcendental experience, and not books, that gives validity to religions.
3.   There are several paths to the realization of the ultimate Reality. Each religion is such a path. *Yato mat, tato path*, "As many faiths, so many paths." As paths to the same ultimate goal, all the world religions are valid and true.
4.   Each person may, however, remain steadfast in his own path in a spirit of *ishtanishtha*, without thinking that his path alone is true and perfect.
5.   Furthermore, one should respect the founders of all religions as special manifestations of God and, knowing that God dwells in all people, one should serve all without any distinctions of caste, creed, or race.

These five tenets constitute the essence of Sri Ramakrishna's doctrine of *dharma-samanvaya* or "harmony of religions," which is Sri Ramakrishna's version of Pluralism. Unlike the Western concept of Pluralism, which is vague and evasive, Sri Ramakrishna's concept of Pluralism is clear and definitive and at the same time, all-inclusive.

SWAMI VIVEKANANDA'S DOCTRINE
OF UNIVERSAL RELIGION

Swami Vivekananda's approach to the phenomenon of religious diversity is characterized by two important ideas which are not so well known or understood. The first point is Swamiji looked upon religious diversity not at all as a problem but as a blessing, as an existential necessity for an individual's spiritual development. Every person's personality is structured according to a certain basic pattern and every person is endowed with many tendencies, capacities, and talents, all of which constitute what is known as his *svabhava* or "law of being." A person can grow and develop only according to his law of being. Therefore, every person needs a religion which is in tune with his svabhava or law of being. To quote Swamiji's words: "I do not deprecate the existence of sects in the world. Would to God there were twenty millions more, for the more there are, there will be a greater field for selection."[3] In another place Swamiji states: "No one form of religion will do for all. Each is a pearl in a string.... No man is born into any religion; he has a religion in his own soul. Any system which seeks to destroy individuality is in the long run disastrous."[4]

Since there are varieties of temperaments, people should choose and follow the paths of religion which suit them most. At the same time, it is necessary to have harmony, unity in diversity. This is necessary for the well-being of the society as a whole. How can we attain harmony with all, especially in the religious field, without harming our individual temperament, without ignoring the law of our inner being? Referring to this problem Swami Vivekananda states:

> Many have admitted that all the religions of the world are right; but they show no practical way of bringing them together, so as to enable each of them to maintain its own individuality in the conflux. That plan alone is practical which does not destroy the individuality of any man in religion and at the same time shows him a point of union with all others.[5]

What is that plan?

Swamiji found the answer to the above question in a new concept of Universal Religion. By universal religion Swamiji meant a view of religion which transcends ordinary conceptual differences of religions and sects. This is a new understanding of the term "universal religion." Before Swamiji came, the term "universal religion" meant any religion which is not limited to a particular area or race or culture but is open to all people all over the world. George Galloway in his well-known book *Philosophy of Religion* classifies world religions into two groups: *ethnic* religions which include Hinduism, Judaism, and Zoroastrianism and *universal* religions which include Christianity, Islam, and Buddhism. This was not what Swamiji meant by Universal Religion. He has given three concepts of Universal Religion as follows:

1. The *first concept* is that there is one eternal boundless religion which manifests itself as world religions. In the words of Swamiji,

---

[3] *The Complete Works of Swami Vivekananda*, Volume 1 (Kolkata: Advaita Ashram, 1992), p. 325.

[4] *The Complete Works*, Volume 6, p. 82.

[5] *The Complete Works*, Volume 2, p. 384.

"One infinite Religion existed all through eternity and will exist, and this Religion is expressing itself in various countries in various ways."[6] The great scholar and thinker A. N. Whitehead has expressed a similar idea: "The great rational religions are the outcome of the emergence of a religious consciousness which is universal, as distinguished from tribal or even social."[7]

2. Swamiji's *second concept* is that Universal Religion is the sum total of all the existing world religions. Regarding this Swamiji stated:

> I believe that they [the world religions] are not contradictory; they are supplementary. Each religion as it were takes up one part of the great universal truth... It is therefore addition not exclusion. My idea, therefore, is that all these religions are different forces in the economy of God working for the good of mankind...[8]

3. *Third concept*: The first two concepts refer to the existing world religions. The third concept goes beyond traditional religions and refers to humanity's eternal quest for supreme peace, supreme knowledge, supreme love, and supreme joy. It represents Swamiji's vision of an "Ideal Religion." It is meant for all without any distinctions of caste, religion, or race. It is based on the manifestation of the Divinity potentially present in man, and aims at the total development of human personality and the equal development of the capacities of reasoning, emotion, willing, and action. It harmonizes the sacred and the secular, religion and science, the ancient and the modern. It is beyond all scriptures but incorporates the good aspects of all religions. Swamiji said: "We want to lead mankind to the place where there is neither the Vedas, nor the Bible, nor the Koran; yet this has to be done by harmonizing the Vedas, the Bible, and the Koran."[9]

For Swami Vivekananda religion is not mere belief in God, allegiance to a creed, or following certain rituals or customs. For him religion is nothing short of the transformation of human life into Divine Life. It involves one's whole life. It is the conversion of every thought,

---

[6] *The Complete Works*, Volume 4, p. 180.
[7] A. N. Whitehead, *Religion in the Making* (Cambridge: Cambridge University Press, 1926) p. 37.
[8] *The Complete Works*, Volume 2, p. 365.
[9] *The Complete Works*, Volume 6, p. 416.

feeling, and action into a spiritual discipline. It is the divinization of individual and collective life.

DAWN OF A NEW AGE

In the second decade of the twenty-first century, humanity is now witnessing the dawn of a new age. In this age, the ideas of Sri Ramakrishna and Swami Vivekananda, particularly their concepts of harmony of religions and universal religion, assume great significance. To understand the true significance of these concepts we have to look at the world around us. At first what strikes our eyes may be the enormous increase in crime, violence, immorality, broken homes, attack on women and children, corruption, political instability, economic recession, and, above all, the spreading menace of global terrorism and wanton destruction of human life. But if we look beyond the shadows of these negative forces, we can see the dawn of a new age breaking upon the horizon of human culture. This new age is characterized by several mega-trends.

The first mega-trend is the "knowledge revolution," caused by advancements in information and communication technology, which is bringing into existence the "knowledge society." In the knowledge society, knowledge itself is power, and not brute force. The second trend is a new kind of humanism which stresses the rights of underprivileged people, equality of gender, and protection against all forms of exploitation, injustice, cruelty, etc. Another mega-trend is the globalization of human life and the awareness of the interdependence of peoples of the world especially with reference to environmental concerns.

The fourth and most significant mega-trend is the rise of a new wave of spiritual awareness, a general awakening of the spiritual consciousness of humanity which has been hailed as "spiritual revolution." Till recently, spirituality had been regarded as a part of religion. The present trend is to separate spirituality from religion resulting in what is known as "secular spirituality." This new spirituality is cutting across the barriers of religion, race, nationality, etc., and is creating a "global spirituality."

Some of the main features of this new spiritual movement are:

- religion or spirituality as a personal quest for meaning,
- faith in one's own inner resources,
- emphasis on direct experience,

- freedom from sin consciousness,
- view of human personality as a trichotomy of body-mind-spirit,
- emphasis on healthy life rather than austerity
- positive outlook on life, and
- religious pluralism and openness to the spiritual traditions of all religions.

There is now a growing awareness that mere increase of wealth and affluence is not enough. A spiritual perspective is necessary to make life meaningful and fruitful. It is also being widely understood that existential problems of modern man such as loneliness, sense of meaninglessness, ennui, unfulfillment, anxiety, love, etc., have only a spiritual solution. In brief, spirituality is now being recognized as the common ground of all religious traditions, and as the common chord uniting the followers of different religions. This "global spirituality" is quite similar to Swami Vivekananda's concept of "Universal Religion."

It is in the light of these modern mega-trends, especially in the light of the ongoing global spiritual movement, that we have to understand the true significance of the Ramakrishna–Vivekananda approach to the problem of religious diversity. Their approach is to emphasize spirituality as the common ground to world religions and as the proper way to attain ultimate peace and fulfillment, and the establishment of peaceful coexistence of the peoples of the world.

PRACTICAL SUGGESTIONS

Till now, we have been discussing the theoretical aspects of the phenomenon of religious diversity. We now come to the practical approach to the problem of religious diversity.

As far as the Ramakrishna Movement is concerned, diversity of religions does not pose any problem in the practical field. Community life in the Ramakrishna Movement is based on Sri Ramakrishna's doctrine of *dharma-samanvaya* or harmony of religions which, as we have seen, is the Indian version of religious Pluralism. The community of Ramakrishna Movement consists of people belonging to all the world religions and even tribal religions. The sannyasins or monks of the Ramakrishna Order, known as the Ramakrishna Math, form the mainstream of the Ramakrishna Movement. The Ramakrishna Order was the first indigenous monastic Order to open its doors to people belonging to all castes and religions. In our monasteries, monks belonging to different religions, sects, and nationalities, live together like children of the same parents, bonded together by the love of Sri Ramakrishna. Monks of the Ramakrishna Order are not dry *jnanis* or intellectuals. Love plays an important role in our monastic life. This love is based on the oneness of the Supreme Spirit immanent in all people.

Now the question is how far the views and ideas of Sri Ramakrishna and Swami Vivekananda discussed above can be applied at the social, national, and international levels to bring about mutual understanding, amity, and cooperation among people? How far can their message help in counteracting mutual distrust, prejudice, and ill will among religious groups and communities?

From the standpoint of Sri Ramakrishna and Swami Vivekananda, what is needed is a positive approach to the problems arising from religious diversity. Some of the practical steps in this approach are briefly stated here:

1. Ignorance of other religions is the main cause of distrust, hatred, or fear among the followers of different religions. Hence it is necessary to spread the right type of religious education which gives correct understanding (and not distorted knowledge) of other religions. This has to be done only by the government, and not by private agencies.

    This means there is a need now to redefine "secularism" especially in the light of Indian culture. Three characteristics of Indian culture are to be taken into consideration in this context: (a) Harmony of religions has always remained an undercurrent in Indian culture from very ancient times, (b) Indian religious consciousness is not limited to a monotheistic conception of Godhead; it has a pronounced impersonal dimension which is in tune with some of the conclusions of modern science, (c) the foundation and core of religions and sects of Indian origin is spirituality. This last point is the most important one and is, therefore, discussed further below.

    As was stated earlier, spirituality forms a common ground among all religions. Moreover, all over the free world there is now going on a spiritual movement. Since it is independent of traditional religions, this global spiritual movement is often called "secular spirituality." People belonging to all walks of life—doctors, lawyers, businessman, housewives—are beginning to understand the benefits of leading a spiritual life or developing a spiritual perspective on life. It is, however, the youths, especially the students who need spiritual guidance and spiritual orientation more than anybody else.

Youth is the time when men and women seek ideals. If youths do not get spiritual ideals or other higher ideals, they fall for lower or destructive ideals. This is how extremists, terrorists, fundamentalists, suicide bombers, etc., are created. This shows how important spiritual education of youths is.

"Secular spirituality" can be introduced in our schools and colleges in the form of "Value Education." Along with it, the spiritual treasures of world religions can also be made available to students. This will not go against the secular nature of Indian Constitution or the government's secular policies.

2. Another practical means of fostering the spirit of religious harmony in society is to bring together liberal-minded people of all religions through dialogues, Interfaith seminars, religious get-togethers, parliaments of religions, and similar gatherings.

3. It is a well-known fact that in modern society there is an alarming increase in social evils such as crime, violence, immorality, corruption, etc. Leaders of different religions have a joint responsibility in alleviating such social evils and protecting the youths from them. Religious leaders can evolve joint action plans and implement these plans pooling together the resources of different communities.

4. On the positive side, leaders of different religions can jointly undertake welfare programs such as providing food, clothes, medicines, etc., to poor children, destitute people, and helpless women. Many religious organizations are conducting such welfare activities at present, but there is hardly any cooperation among them.

5. A most important factor in ensuring communal harmony is the role of the family, especially the part played by mothers. A good deal of distrust and ill will towards other religions can be eliminated if the parents, especially the mothers, take the initiative of inculcating the spirit of friendship, love, sympathy, and cooperation in the minds of their children from childhood.[10]

---

[10] See the article, "Can Mothers Stop Terrorism," by Nona Walia in the *Times of India*, Sunday Supplement, LIFE, May 12, 2013, which describes the views and work done by an Austrian social activist Dr Edit Schlaffer through her organizations, Women Without Borders (WWB) and Sisters Against Violent Extremism (SAVE).

6. Lastly, what is important is to make people get over medieval attitudes and mind-set. The awareness that we are at the dawn of a new age, and immense possibilities for a prosperous, peaceful, and creative life are open to all people without any distinctions of religion, sect, caste, or race, and the awareness that interreligious hatred and violence are ultimately self-destructive and obstruct the progress of one's own religious community—this twofold awareness must spread among the common people belonging to all religions. Mass media has an important role to play in this field.

5

Globalization, Judaism, and Its Diversity

Rabbi Ezekiel Isaac Malekar

Judaism is one of the world's oldest religions. Judaism is more than a religion. It is a way of life. Over the centuries, it has created standards of practice, most of which have been codified in the Shulchan Aruch (Code of Jewish Law). These laws spell out what the conduct of Jew should be from the moment he opens his eyes in morning until the moment his head touches the pillow at night.

The Jewish religion evolved over many centuries before the Common Era (referred to here as BCE, corresponding to the Christian BC) through the people known as the Israelites. It is necessary to know something about Jewish history in order to get a proper understanding of this ancient living faith.

HISTORY

Its origin goes back to Abraham (the Father of the people) who was born in Ur of the Chaldees (Babylonia—modern Iraq) approximately 4,000 years ago. His father was a maker of idols and Abraham spent the earlier part of his life in that moon-worshipping city. It was in response to a strong and persistent inner voice that he decided to leave Babylonia and go to a land that the Lord God was going to show him. In his old age, Abraham and his wife Sarah had a son, Isaac, as promised to them by God.

Abraham conceived the idea of Monotheism, the oneness of an invisible God (and the brotherhood of man), the Creator of heaven and earth, demanding absolute obedience to His will and to divine dictates for the good of mankind. It is recorded in the very first chapter of the Bible, the first five books of which are known in Judaism as the Torah (the way of life—the law) where it is said that man was created by God out of the dust of the earth. God made him in His own image and man became a living soul only when God breathed His spirit into that form, implying in other words that it is the divine breath that activates humanity.

And the Lord, God formed man of the dust of the ground
and breathed into his nostrils the breath of life;
and man became a living soul.[1]

Abraham's implicit faith in the Creator was put to stern test when he
was commanded to take his son Isaac up a mountain and offer him there
as a sacrifice to the Lord. Just as Abraham was about to fulfill this
injunction, the Lord God intervened.

The basic and overriding tenet in Judaism is the belief in the unity
and oneness of the Universal Creator. The most important prayer in
Judaism is the *Shema* (which is the Hebrew for hear)—"Hear O Israel
the Lord our God, the lord is one, Blessed be His name whose glorious
Kingdom is forever."

THE DOCTRINES

Judaism has many lessons to teach in addition to those about God. It has
a history, a culture, and at least one language of interest. It has a strong
ethnic dimension. Judaism gave the world the Torah—a vital source of
the Judeo–Christian Ethnic culture. The Torah has given the world a
vibrant part of the world culture.

The concept of the God of all creation including mankind carried
with it the corollary of the brotherhood of man, bound together by
mutual love. This was a revolutionary thought at a time when relations
between human beings were dictated almost solely by violence, fear,
envy, and rivalries. There are innumerable examples in history of Jews
who have died as martyrs, rather than choosing to give up their faith.
When after the destruction of the second temple in 70 AD, the Jews were
scattered throughout the world and lost contact with mainstream of their
faith, they retained their religion mainly by the daily recitation of the
divine formula contained in their prayer.

Unity

The fundamental principle of Judaism is its belief in the Unity and
Oneness of the Universal Creator. *"Heney ma tov u-ma-naim, Shevet*

---

[1] Genesis 2.7.

Akhim gamya-khad."[2] [How good and how pleasant it is for brothers and sisters to dwell in unity.]

Unity is the very essence of the Creative Being. From this very concept Judaism evolved throughout the ages and was codified by the Prophet Moses after Exodus from Egypt nearly 3,500 years ago in the shape of the Ten Commandments given by the Almighty to those who agreed to abide by them. These form the foundation of the Torah, the way of life and learning. The concept of the God of all creation and mankind carried with it the corollary of the brotherhood of man, bound together by mutual love. As said before, the central tenet in Judaism consists of the belief in the unity and oneness of the Universal Creator and its most important prayer is the *Shema*—"Hear O Israel the Lord our God, the lord is one, Blessed be His name whose glorious Kingdom is forever."

Ethics

Jewish ethics are closely tied to the idea of the unity of the human race. We all have one Father; one God has created us. In other words, we are all children of one God and, therefore, accept love to be the fundamental principle that binds us.

Underlying the injunction "Love Thy Neighbour as thyself" is the idea that there is no one who knows your many faults better than you yourself but still you love yourself, no matter how many faults you see in yourself. Similarly, you must love your neighbor as yourself.

When *Rabbi* (the word means a teacher or guide similar to a guru or *shastri* in India) Hillel was once asked by an agnostic to propound the Torah to him while he stood on one foot, the Rabbi replied, "What is hateful and hurtful to yourself do not do to your fellowmen." This is the advice demanding love and social justice.

Judaism forbids every sort of animosity, envy, or unkindness towards any one of whatsoever race, nationality, or religion. Judaism demands consideration for the life, health, powers, and possessions of others and injuring a fellowman by force, or cunning or in any other manner depriving him of his property. Again, Judaism teaches that a fellowman's honor is as sacred as one's own. It, therefore, forbids degrading him by evil reports, vexing him with ridicule, or mortifying him.

[2] Psalm 133.

Most importantly, Judaism commands respect for the religious convictions of others. It, therefore, forbids aspersion or disrespectful treatment of the customs and symbols of other religions. It recommends the practice of charity towards all, clothing the naked, feeding the hungry, nursing the sick, and comforting those that mourn. It, therefore, forbids limiting our care-giving acts only to our near ones and to our families while withholding our sympathy when our neighbors suffer.

Judaism commands respect for labor. Each shall strive for the blessings of life by worthwhile creative activity. It, therefore, demands the cultivation and development of all our powers and capabilities in consonance with absolute truthfulness. It, therefore, forbids the distortion of truth and deceit and condemns hypocrisy. Judaism commands that we walk humbly with God and in modesty while among men. It, therefore, forbids self-conceit, arrogance, and disparagement of the merits of others. Judaism commands chastity and the sanctity of marriage and forbids infidelity and lust. Judaism commands sanctification of the name of God through righteous living. It bids us to exert ourselves to hasten the time in which men shall be united in the love of God and the love of one another.

Four are the temperaments of men; easily provoked and easily appeased, his loss is cancelled by his gain. Provoked with difficulty but appeased with difficulty, his gain is cancelled by his loss. Provoked with difficulty and easily appeased, he is saintly. Easily angered and appeased with difficulty, he is a churl. Who is mighty? He who controls his anger.

Religion and Goodness

According to Judaism, the practice of religion is to be closely integrated with daily living and every ordinary human action must be invested with the realization that it is being watched and noted by the Almighty. If we separate goodness from religion or religion from goodness then we are denying God's role in our everyday life. Religion must never again be used for inspiring hatred and instigation for violence and neither as means for the pursuit of power. India has the right pride of being a land of religions.

Tolerance

Tolerance towards representatives of other religions, respect of human rights, and the rights of minorities must be the basis for peaceful coexistence between various religions and will defuse tension created by ignorance. It provides us with the opportunity to discover and remove stereotypes and social stigmas associated with perceived differences arising from nationality, religion, or background.

Tolerance is an inner strength, which enables the individual to face and transform misunderstandings and difficulties. A tolerant person is like a tree with an abundance of fruits, even when pelted with sticks and stones, the tree gives its fruits in return. Without tolerance, peace is not possible. Tolerance is integral and essential to the realization of human rights and the achievement of peace.

Peace

Peace is one of the most desirable fruits of salvation in all the world's religions. The peace that comes with reaching Ultimate Reality brings tranquility to the heart and clarity to mind. It is the absence of passions, desires, anxieties, and wondering thoughts; the heart becomes cool and content. The scriptures praise the peace and tranquility that come to the soul that is firm in faith. Peace is the foundation, the major building block upon which a healthy, functional society stands. Peace is the prominent characteristic of a civilized society and the character of a society can be seen in and through the response of the collective consciousness of its members to the demands of peace. A civilization can be heaven or hell depending on the character of the shared consciousness of its members.

The world today lacks peace basically because from core of our hearts we do not want peace. The major problem on earth is not the bomb or the presence of nuclear or chemical weapons. These are actually the products of the problem. The main problem is that human imagination has not yet expanded to the point where it comprehends its own essential unity.

Non-violence

The concept of Ahimsa (non-violence) against living form in Judaism finds expression in Chapter 20 of the Book of Exodus, "Thou shall not kill." In the same set of Commandments, there is another, "Thou shall not covet," which goes to the root of all forms of crime including murder, since inordinate desire for anything sets in motion in human heart the main principles of violence in all its forms. Although Judaism emphasizes the value and importance of peace and non-violence, it does not advocate passive reaction to any form of injustice and violence.

Universal Love

There are 613 precepts in Torah (first books in the Bible) to regulate the daily life of every Jew and this number is symbolized in the threads of the prayer shawl (*Tsisith*) that every male adult Jew is enjoined to wear at prayers, as a reminder of the obligations imposed upon him. Recall, when Rabbi Hillel was once asked by an agnostic to propound the Torah to him while he stood on one foot, the Rabbi replied, "What is hurtful to yourself do not do to your fellowman. That is the whole of the Torah and the remainder is but commentary." In other words, love and social justice are the mainsprings of ethical behavior and so important is it that in Judaism the cardinal daily prayer known as the *Shema* is immediately followed by these words:

> [A]nd thou shalt love the Lord thy God with all thine heart and with all thy soul and upon thy heart, and thou shalt teach them diligently unto thy children and shalt talk them when thou sittest in thy house and when thou walkest by the way and when thou liest down and when thou risest up, and thou shalt bind them for a sing upon thine hand and they shall be for frontlets between thine eyes and thou shalt write them upon the doorposts and upon thy gates.

Judaism lays great emphasis on the importance of leading a good and moral life at every living moment and does not advocate asceticism, celibacy, and self-imposed suffering, since salvation is obtainable only through good deeds. The observance of certain rituals and formalities, while significant if they are properly understood, cannot be a substitute for right living and it is only if such an attitude is adopted that religion ceases to be mere hypocrisy. In the Bible there is a constant dialogue between man and God, who is enjoined to be holy, because He says that "I the Lord thy God am holy." Hence there is a daily discipline of prayers to be said, apart from the prayers during feasts and on special occasions. In the morning prayers Jews are reminded to be thankful to the Creator for the great and wonderful gift of life, and if one follows this thought to its logical conclusion, one can achieve a spirit of peace and contentment by realizing and counting the blessing from day to day rather than by bemoaning what one does not possess.

TEN COMMANDMENTS

The importance of the Ten Commandments lies in the moral and ethical purpose with which it invests man's existence. And God spoke all these words, saying:[3]

1. I am the LORD thy God, who brought thee out of the land of Egypt, out of the house of bondage.
2. Thou shalt have no other gods before Me.
3. Thou shalt not take the name of the LORD thy God in vain.
4. Remember the Sabbath day, to keep it holy.
5. Honour thy father and thy mother.
6. Thou shalt not murder.
7. Thou shalt not commit adultery.
8. Thou shalt not steal.
9. Thou shalt not bear false witness against thy neighbour.
10. Thou shall not covet thy neighbour's house; thou shalt not covet thy neighbour's wife nor his manservant, nor his maidservant, nor his ox, nor his ass, nor anything that is thy neighbour's.

It must be noted here that when the Jews speak of their being chosen people, they mean chosen to receive and spread the divine commandments and not selected for special favors or privileges.

Another important commandment is the fifth which says "honour thy father and thy mother"—the value of which cannot be overemphasized. Love and respect of parents are the cornerstones for a healthy and happy family life and Judaism realized this thousands of years ago by making it a religious precept. In homes where this is strictly adhered to there is no room for that much-publicized present-day idea of generation gap.

JUDAISM IN PRACTICE

Prayers play a very important role in Judaism. They constitute an individual communal approach to God through meditation, pleas, requests, confession, supplication or expression of praise, and thanksgiving, whereby communication can be established between human beings and the Creator. After destruction of the temple and dispersion of the Jews,

[3] Exodus 20: 1–14.

the temple rituals were replaced by devotional prayers in the synagogue in the spirit of the sublime teachings of the prophets. The rabbis in course of time formulated three daily religious services—evening, morning, and afternoon—and each congregation was led by a professional or voluntary amateur cantor (termed *Hazzan*), since a major portion of the services is sung or chanted. The early morning prayer includes a sublime utterance of thankfulness to God for the divine gift of life.

There are also special and additional prayer services on the Sabbath and other holy days.

Observances

In Judaism, religious observances and rituals are of no value whatsoever when they do not lead to right conduct and moral behavior. The principles have to be put into practice at every moment if they are to be meaningful. Gratitude to the Supreme Creator has to be felt and expressed at every moment. Thus, a prayer of thankfulness has to be uttered every morning for the God-given gift of life. Blessings are recited on the occurrence of natural phenomena such as rain, thunder and lightning; thanks must be tendered for the pleasures and sustenance derived from pleasant sights, odors, good news, food of all kinds, and pleasant happenings.

Just as in the Bible there is a constant dialogue between God and man, so in the journey through life every good act is sanctified by its relationship with the Divine. This is the best antidote to envy, jealousy, and greed that play havoc with the human personality. The divine ties are emphasized at certain milestones of a Jew's journey from the cradle to the grave. On the eighth day after birth, the male child is circumcised in accordance with God's covenant with Abraham, when the child is named.

For girls, there is also a religious naming ceremony as well as *Bat Mitzvah* ceremony (Daughter of Commandment), at the age of 12, when she not only attains the age of puberty but she is also held morally and ethically to be an adult.

At the age of 13, the boy becomes a *Bar Mitzavah* (Son of Commandment) assuming the full responsibility of an adult and is called upon to read from the *Sefer Torah* in the synagogue congregational gath ring.

At the time of marriage, bride and bridegroom meet under the canopy (the *Chupah* on the Tebah/Bima) in the presence of the whole congregation in the synagogue, with rabbi or other leading members of the community officiating. The custom of the bridegroom crushing a tumbler towards the end of the ceremony is thought to be a solemn reminder for every Jew—even in the time of his highest joy—of the tragedy of the destruction of the Temple thousands of years ago. The ceremony ends with the recital of seven benedictions chanted by one of the congregants given this special honor. The couple then goes to the Holy Ark (where the *Sefer Torah*s are stored) and after paying their respects to the holy words of the Lord enshrined therein leave the synagogue amidst congratulations. Confetti and rice grains showered on the couple connote good wishes and fertility.

The Jew, if conscious, is enjoined to die with the recitation of the *Shema*—the fundamental article of faith in the unity and goodness of the Creator. After bathing the body and before the final ceremony, psalms and prayers are recited at the cemetery, then the body—draped in a white cotton garment—is lowered into a freshly dug grave with the head facing towards Jerusalem. In the case of a male, his *tallith* (prayer shawl) is buried with him. In accordance with the injunction in the Torah, "For dust thou art and unto dust shalt thou return," the body is interred without any coffin, or if there is a coffin, the lid is removed so that the dust with which the grave is filled touches the body.

A Jew generally covers his head in the synagogues and elsewhere during the various religious services. This is considered a sign of male piety and female modesty.

Dietary Laws

There are certain dietary laws laid down in the Torah such as the prohibition of meat from animals that do not have cloven hoofs and do not chew the cud (so banning pig flesh); of fish that leave neither scales nor fins; and the draining away of blood from all animal food before cooking or eating it and avoidance of any creatures that are scavengers. The meat eaten must be *Kosher* (ritually cleaned) from an undiseased animal which is slaughtered in a special way to minimize pain and make the blood flow out. Another example of a food restriction is the law prohibiting the consumption of meat and milk food at the same time; even the utensils and dishes used, therefore, must be kept separate.

Education

Education is given high priority in every family and children have to learn to read prayers when still quite small. The sanctity of family life is preserved by a number of home ceremonies and practices that bind the family together. For instance, the mother kindling the Sabbath lights before sunset on Friday (and they remain burning till sunset the next day) with a blessing sanctifying the weekly holy day, the refrain from lighting the fire and cooking, complete abstinence from the daily round of duties, the special festive meals, etc. All these make a deep impact on the children's mind and serve to knit the family close together.

Charity

Charity plays a very important role in the life of a Jew. The rabbis say that charity will save you even from death.

Kabbala and Jewish Mysticism

This word *Kabbala* originally meant "reception" and related to the oral Jewish tradition handed down by rabbis from generation to generation. The mainspring of the *Kabbala* is a deep-rooted belief in perpetual inter-relationship between God in the infinite power and man in the physical world as we know it. It is said that man can achieve closeness to God by subduing his own evil inclinations and by bringing about spiritual regeneration of mankind through prayers, meditation, and interpretation of the Divine mysteries hidden in the Torah. Kabbalists emphasize the importance of mystical formulas and the like in the recitation of prayers and psalms.

Shalom

In conclusion the infinite longing in Judaism for peace and goodwill finds expression at every time and on every occasion. For example, the form of greeting *Shalom Aleichem* (peace be unto you) figures not only when Jews meet one another but can be heard as a form of greeting by people of some other religions as well. There is hardly any prayer where the word *Shalom* (peace) does not occur; most of the prayers, be it noted, are not merely requests for personal favor from the Almighty but for blessings for all people and for mankind in general. Many of the prayers are contemplation of sublime truths and principles of ethical living. And thus it was that the prophet Isaiah in his vision of peace declared: "And it shall come to pass in the last days, that the mountain of the Lord's house shall be established in the top of the mountains and shall be exalted above the hills; and all nations shall follow into it."

And he shall judge among the nations and shall rebuke many people any they shall beat their swords into ploughshares and their spears into pruning hooks; nation shall not lift up sword against nation, neither shall they learn war any more. The wolf and the lambs shall feed together, and the lion shall eat grain like the bullock, and dust shall be the serpent's meat. They shall not hurt nor destroy in all my holy mountain, saith the Lord.

INDIA: A MULTIRELIGIOUS COUNTRY

India is perhaps the most pluralistic country in the world and, therefore, India is the land of religions. The Gandhian ideal about religions can be described as that of "republic of religions," and India is the home for all religions. The peaceful existence of the Jews in India for more than 2,000 years is a shining testimony to the complete absence of anti-Semitism in this country. Therefore, Jews here consider themselves as Indians first and then Jews. During the visit of Israel's Prime Minister Shimon Peres to Judah Hyam Synagogue, New Delhi, I was asked by the media to explain my feelings about Israel and I promptly replied that "Israel is in my heart but India is in my blood." I always remember the words of Revered Swami Vivekananda ji and I quote, "You may be born in any religion but you cannot die in it and therefore always follow your religion and respect other religions." Living with diversity is one of the greatest challenges facing societies in which our children are growing up. We always believed in *Vasudhaiva Kutumbakam* and *Athiti Devo Bhava*.

All minorities are a part and parcel of the National Fabric of India and they enjoy all rights and freedom provided under various provisions of the Constitution as citizens of India. Irrespective of their minority status, equal opportunities exist for all citizens without any discrimination.

The Indian Constitution guarantees absolute religious freedom to the citizens of India reflecting the well-known social traditions of tolerance and respect for all religions. Together these elements provide a strong framework for a secular and democratic polity in a country rich in cultural, lingual, and ethnic diversities. These rights are guaranteed by the Constitution and justifiable in accordance with laws of the land. They are also protected by the judiciary and effectively enforced by the executive authorities.

All the religions of the world, while they differ in other respects, unitedly proclaim that nothing lives in the world but truth. There should be truth in thought, truth in speech, and truth in action. In the words of Mahatma Gandhi, "My God is truth and non-violence is a means of realizing Him." Hence we know God as *Sat-Cit-Ananda*, one who combines in himself, truth, knowledge, and bliss.

Although people in their personal lives follow religions of their own, all religions are basically one. Religions could coexist without coming into conflict with each other like a rainbow. The rainbow is of seven colors but when it is merged we get only one color, i.e., white color. Cows are of different colors but we get milk which is white.

Like the bee, gathering honey from different flowers, a wise man accepts the essence of different scriptures and sees only the good in all religions, as said in the *Srimad Bhagavatam*. Therefore, we should visit all the Holy Places of worship of other faiths and also read and seek to understand the basic tenets/precepts of Holy Scriptures of other religions so as to get rid of the misconceived notions.

INTERFAITH DIALOGUE

The twentieth century has seen much bloodshed where religious differences have been a fundamental factor. But today a number of Interfaith movements exist with the explicit purpose of fostering a better understanding of religious differences and similarities. Through nurturing spirit of friendship and reconciliation, true dialogue can help us to overcome religious divisiveness and create better conditions for appreciating religious diversity and, thereby, make room for greater fellowship and deeper communion.

Interfaith dialogue refers to cooperative and positive interaction between people of different religious faiths and spiritual or humanistic beliefs, at both the individual and institutional level, with the aim of deriving a common ground. Focusing on similarities between faiths will augment our understanding of values and commitment to the world. This is distinct from any form of syncretism, or any alternative religion. Dialogue often involves understanding between different religions and it increases our ability for acceptance of others rather than to synthesize new beliefs.

The oft-quoted saying that "There will be no peace among the nations without peace among the religions. There will be no peace among the religions without dialogue among the religions," holds true.

This Interfaith dialogue will definitely boost interreligious cooperation in the struggle to eliminate hunger, poverty, ignorance, persecution, discrimination, and enslavement of the human spirit.

Tolerance towards representatives of other religions, respect of human rights and rights of minorities must be the basis for peaceful coexistence between two countries as well as within every society. In brief, peace, universal brotherhood, mutual respect, compassion, self-sacrificial love, and better understanding constitute the essence of communal harmony and world peace. Violence is the root cause of all miseries in the world.

Therefore, religion must never again be used for inspiring hatred and instigation for violence and neither as means for pursuit of power. All religions regard values such as love, tolerance, kindness, fraternity, and helpfulness as principles of their creed. Let us stop abusing each other. If there were no different religions, no one religion would survive. No one religion has ever been able to establish its superiority to all others. This essential truth is well expressed in the *Rig Veda*—(*Ekam sat vipraha bahuda Vadanti*) Truth is one, though the sages call it by various names. Similarly in the Bhagvad Gita, God manifesting as an incarnation, states: "As people approach me, so do I receive them. All paths lead to me."

It is imperative that we must live and let live. If religions of the world are to serve—as they must—humanity, they must respect and reinforce each other. They must reciprocate and work together for a global ethics, for ecology, for eradication of poverty, and for the reconstruction of human relations in a new international order. We have, therefore, to inculcate a new culture of peace, among religions. Religions must earn reverence through truth, tolerance, and humanity. Let the religions of the world unite for peace in common endeavor. As the ancient Indian seers put it, "Let us walk together with a common goal. Let us converse with a common purpose. Let our minds meet together in the quest of true knowledge."

All religions regard human values such as love, tolerance, kindness, fraternity, and helpfulness as principles of their creed. They have always aspired to bring and strengthen these commandments within the soul and conscience of each human being.

We should reaffirm and rededicate ourselves to the universal values of love, brotherhood, compassion, and selfless service. We must reassert the principles of peace, justice, and communal harmony so as to create a society that sustains and enriches life based on love, trust, and brotherhood.

6

Sacred Spaces: Interdependence, Not Dissension

Shernaz Cama

As a Zoroastrian steps out in the morning he bows to all four corners of the Earth and recites a little prayer called "The Homage to the Four Directions" (*Chaar-Deesha–no-Namaskaar*):

> I bow in reverence to the entire creation of Ahura Mazda, to the cities, the open fields, to the houses, the waters, the earth, the trees and the sky, the pure winds, the stars, the moon, the sun; all sources of bright light and to all men and women who tread the path of Truth. I bow to them all.

This reverence is of great significance to our times. Nature has always fostered interdependence while man has torn apart nature's creations through dissension: man against man, man conquering the earth, the waters, and the skies rather than respecting the interdependence that has enabled life to coexist for millennia. Today a lack of responsibility has led to the selfish exploitation of the Earth's fragile resources; thrift has become a negative casualty in a world where consumer is King. With Global Warming having become an ugly felt reality, there has been a realization that the consumerist creations of the Industrial Revolution have, within 300 years, actually caused the Polar Ice Caps to melt and apocalyptic floods to wreak havoc on regions as diverse as New Orleans and Phuket. When newspaper headlines and candlelight vigils both stress "saving the earth," it is time to look at how religions and cultures coexisted peacefully with the forces of nature before a time of exploitation, destruction, and greed.

While man dominates nature by an intellectual comprehension of the material world, humankind is paying heavily for living in ignorance of spiritual truth. Domination leads to strife and the mere quantitative accumulation of knowledge cannot reveal the secrets of the Universe. The telescope and the microscope have taught us to look only partially; this fragmentation of dimensions ignores the holistic approach of religion and philosophy. Science is not the only method of comprehension, it is a route map of the cosmos; it does not give us the whole picture of creation. If we do not take into account spiritual dimensions and traditional wisdom about the interrelationship of all life, we fragment our minds, our personalities, and ultimately the world itself.

Both philosophers and scientists attempt to understand the Universe and humankind. They hope to reach the Whole Truth, or as religions call it, the "One Truth." Each religion seeks to reach that "One," through whom all wisdom will be achieved. This is the essence and context of religious beliefs, practices, and institutions.

If we make an inventory of the types of beliefs and practices of religions from the Bronze Age till today we find a great deal of similarity in their concerns and values. All Prophets highlight interdependence and the unity of life. Man must learn that the religious experience unites humankind with a higher truth, providing a complete picture as opposed to the fragmentation of human experience, seen today. The symbol and the ritual in all faiths create a *Temenos* or Sacred Space; for most religions, this Sacred Space is our Earth.

The Interfaith movement has shown how there is One Truth though conveyed in different ways; one goal, through different roads. The Interfaith movement has worked to create harmony within religions and cultures. Today it is time to add to this a more crucial task: to create harmony with our environment. We all have only One Earth, just as we have only One Divine goal. Those who lead us to this goal may be called by various names, Muhammad, Christ, Krishna, Zarathustra, but their message to humankind is to protect that *Temenos*, which is our Blue Planet, for this Earth is the only one we will ever have. It is the greatest gift of the Creator and should be treasured with care.

The only way to conserve the environment is to obey and observe those sacramental duties enjoined by all faiths. At the present rate of destruction, the Amazon forest will become extinct as a rainforest by 2020 while 25 percent of all the earth species have already become extinct by 2010. Humankind, while proclaiming it is on a great path of progress, is actually facing terminal crises. Yet science has taught us the commonality between Physics and Spirituality. Both recognize the earth as a living organism. Today, String Theory and Quantum Cosmology are attempting to prove mathematically what mysticism has taught across millennia.

Zoroastrianism and Hinduism were religions of the ancient Aryans. These faiths shared a common original homeland and there are linguistic parallels in the meters of the *Rig Veda* and *The Gathas*. It is only to be expected that they share a great similarity of both symbols and ideas. In particular, the Hymns of the *Rig Veda* have several parallels with Zoroastrian teachings.

Hinduism as a religion is very close to nature. It asks its followers to see God in every object in the Universe. The worship of God in air, water, fire, Sun, Moon, Stars, and Earth is specially stressed. Earth is worshipped as the spouse of God, hence very dear and near to God. All that lives on Earth is considered the children of God and Earth.

The Vedic Hymn to Earth, the *Prithvi Sukta* in the *Atharva Veda*, is perhaps the oldest and the most evocative of environmental invocations. In it, the Vedic seer solemnly declares the enduring filial allegiance of humankind to Mother Earth: *Mata Bhumih Putroham Prithivyah*, "Earth is my mother, I am her son." A covenant is made that humankind shall secure the Earth against all environmental trespass; a prayer is sung in one of the hymns for the preservation and conservation of hills, snow-clad mountains, and all brown, black, and red earth.

The Vedic seers too regarded the Earth as *Temenos* or "Sacred Space" to fulfill the endeavors and aspirations of humankind as well as to learn the practice of restraint and responsibility. This view of the inviolable sacred space, both outside and within human consciousness, is integral to the Vedas and the Upanishads.

Just as in Hinduism, cosmic harmony can be understood in Zoroastrianism, through the concept of the doctrine of the interdependence and unity of man and creation. However, unlike the more metaphysical concepts of Hinduism, Zoroastrianism believes in actively working towards the protection of a *Spenta* or bounteous earth. Zoroaster's teachings can be compressed into three commandments every Zoroastrian child learns, "*Humata, Hukta, Huvarstha*," i.e., Good Thoughts, Good Words, Good Deeds; thoughts are the root of all actions and deeds are the ultimate result. Zoroastrianism is a religion of action, where work is a cardinal feature. The Zoroastrian girds himself up daily to be a worker of the Lord, the best service to God being service to his creation.

But it is seen that while the Earth is our prime concern, each world religion also centers around a physical *Temenos* or Sacred Space. Seen in tangible manifestations as temple, church, mosque, agiary or Fire Temple (Navsari Atash Behram), its intangible centers are the beliefs of the Prophets, the texts, and teachings of a faith. The Zoroastrian sacred book is the *Avesta*, literally meaning "Authoritative Utterance." All faiths teach compassion, empathy, charity, and recognize a universal interdependence because basic human values transcend historical time and geographical space. Their rituals, particularly those of the Indo-Aryan religions, also reflect a basic similarity.

This paper reflects upon both the physical and spiritual sacred space of the Zoroastrian religion (see Photograph 6.1). Preached by Prophet Zarathustra of Iran in the Bronze Age, around 1600 BC, Zoroastrianism gives great responsibility to man, who is seen as the *Hamkar* or fellow worker of the divinity Ahura Mazda, Lord of Light and Wisdom. With responsibility comes choice.

Photograph 6.1
Bronze Zarathustra Statue

Hear with your ears the Highest Truths I preach
And with illumined minds weigh them with care
Before you choose which of the Two Paths to tread—
Deciding man by man, each one for each.[1]

Zoroastrianism, one of the oldest of the revealed religions, is little known today. Once state religion of the mightiest Empire of the Ancient World it stretched from Europe to China. Today it survives primarily through the Parsis, a small group of refugees who found safety in tolerant and hospitable India. At its zenith Cyrus the Great of the Achaemenian Empire created what is today recognized by the UN as the First Bill of Human Rights. Encapsulated in the Cyrus Cylinder are the ethics of the Zoroastrian faith: equality, freedom of worship, and compassion to all. Cyrus, hailed as "Messiah" in the Bible (Isaiah 45: 7), liberated the Jews, allowed them to return to Israel, and gave them money to rebuild their Temple, while Darius his successor, completed its reconstruction. While the idea of Human Rights is unusual to any world conqueror, the ancient Zoroastrian religion goes even further, for it speaks at that early time of the rights of all Creation, or today, what we believe is the "modern" science of ecology.

Ecology, from the Greek word *oikos*, meaning home, is that branch of biology that deals with the interdependent relationship of organisms to their surroundings. In Zoroastrianism, respect for each aspect of creation is a cardinal tenet of the faith. The universe is *Spenta*, bountiful and good and the Avestan texts teach men and women to use their *Vohu Manah* or Good Mind so that all creation can move to perfection. Dissension has arisen in our world because man has tried to dominate nature and other human beings by the use of force; humankind as we can see, is paying heavily for ignoring eternal truths and spiritual wisdom. We are all interlinked life-forms on our One Earth. It is our Sacred Space. We need to work together in harmony to protect and preserve our *Spenta* creation.

In Zoroastrianism, the entire cosmos is united through the doctrine of the *Amesha Spenta*, Guardian Angels of all the Seven Creations. Through them, Zoroaster weaves together the material and spiritual, stressing the harmony that is the ultimate goal of life. The duties enjoined on Zoroastrians to protect man and the environment, nurture

---

[1] I. J. S. Taraporewala, *The Religion of Zarathushtra* (Bombay: B.I. Taraporewala, 1979), p. 116. All references to the *Gathas* will follow this text. (*Yasna* 30:2, *Ahunavaiti Gatha*).

trees and plants, care for animals, enrich the soil, and keep earth, water, and fire unpolluted can all be seen as stemming from the respect for the *Amesha Spenta*, protectors of all creation.

Zoroastrianism then makes the whole Creation the forum for one's conscience and choice. Wasting resources of any part of nature is regarded as a form of theft; waste, such as pollution, is an act of violence against the *Temenos* which is our planet. Zoroastrian man lives by the cosmic law of *Asha*, Righteousness or Truth, on which all depends. *Asha* is the only path to the divine, therefore creating cosmic harmony is a sacred duty.

When spirit and matter are so inter-assimilated, it is a *spiritual* duty to make this earth productive. For as the *Vendidad* says: "*He who sows corn sows righteousness.*"

All water, earth, plants, and fire must be kept pure, all life respected. The six holy festivals of the pastoral and farming year, later know as the *Gahambars*, remind man to celebrate and thank the elements while special birthdays in honor of Water and Fire recall to the Zoroastrian, the prime value of these creations even to this day.

The *Pahlavi Texts* have numerous stories that enjoin man's duty towards nature:

> *For when man commits sin against water and vegetation even when it is committed against merely a single twig of it and he has not atoned for it, when he departs from the world, the spirits of all the plants in the world stand up high in front of that man and do not let him go to heaven. And when he commits sin against water, even when it is committed against a single drop of it and he has not atoned for it that also stands up as high as the plants stood and does not let him go to heaven.*[2]

Care for and maintenance of animals, particularly cattle, sheep, and the dog is a virtue especially enjoyed by the Prophet of Iran. The Prophet's love of dogs is legendary:

> *It is declared, if a dog is asleep upon the road, it is not proper that (man) put a foot violently on the ground so that he becomes awake.*[3]

---

[2] F. Max Muller (ed.), *The Sacred Books of the East*, Volume V (Delhi: Motilal Banarsidass, 1977), *Shayast La Shayast*, p. 378. All references to the *Avesta* except for the *Gathas* will follow these texts.

[3] The *Sacred Books of the East*, Volume 24, *Pahlavi Texts*, III, *Sad-dar*, p. 293.

Compassion for life is the crowning glory of mankind and thanks-giving is an important part of faith, particularly giving thanks in appreciation of the Earth's bounties. In traditional Parsi homes the *Jamvani Baj* or Grace before meals thanks Ahura Mazda for his bounty and expresses gratitude each time a meal is shared. The first baked bread, *roti*, of the day is taken of the stove and saved for the neighborhood cow. Till today the "morsel for the dog," *Kutra no buk*, is solemnly placed apart in one's plate before man starts his meal, in gratitude to the dog who guards men's homes. To pluck a flower after sunset, when it is at rest, is a sin. To shield all life, to nurture all creation is the Zoroastrian creed.

How did Zoroastrian philosophy come into being? On the Central Asian Steppes, the Stone Age pastoralists worshipped water as the source of the nourishment and fire as the source of warmth. Zarathustra developed these prehistoric cults into a system of theology with the core message of caring for and conserving natural resources. All things flourish in Zoroastrianism according to the law of reciprocity—so the holy festivals of the pastoral and farming year, remind man to celebrate and thank the elements which make life possible.

The cosmos cooperates: Sun, moon, stars live together in harmony and according to Zoroastrianism this is what humans need to emulate. Like the cosmos, human life too, is a mutually interdependent enterprise. These ecological ethics highlight virtues of simplicity, patience, and generosity. Zoroastrianism also approaches life holistically. Because the world of matter is an emanation of the spirit, the material world is part of the divine plan and Zoroastrianism in no way reviles or ignores the material body to elevate the soul. A man is as responsible to his body and to this earth as to his soul and the hereafter.

Nature in its material form exhibits the archetypes of birth, life, death, and resurrection through its seasons. The Zoroastrian year starts with Navroze on March 21, the Spring Equinox, when after the cold of winter, life returns. On the ritual Navroze Table all aspects of creation come together in a sacred space. Fire, water, fruit, grain, the sweetness of sugar, the acidity of vinegar, plant and animal life (represented by fish in a bowl) are all present to honor and respect.

Similarly, the Zoroastrian life cycle journey starts at the Navjote or ceremonial investiture of the sacred shirt—the *sudreh*, denoting the righteous path, and *kusti*, the sacred girdle or direction finder. At an early age a child, boy and girl, through this ceremony chooses to become a Zoroastrian and a soldier on this Path of Truth wearing this sacred armor. Therefore, the Zoroastrian girds himself daily to be a worker of the Lord, tying the sacred girdle at the word *shyaothenanam* or action. Each day the *Kisseh-e-Kerfeh* or *gireban*, the Pocket of Good Deeds, must be filled with at least one good deed towards man or fellow creation.

While every religion speaks of goodness, Zoroastrianism is a religion of constant action, where doing good work is a cardinal feature. The phrase *Ushta-te* means "Happiness comes to him who gives happiness to others." So Zoroastrianism believes in actively working towards joy and harmony while fighting dissension and disharmony. This is necessary because opposed to the path of *Asha* or truth, is the destructive force of *Ahriman*. *Ahriman* stands for the Lie and hatred, the pollution of the mind and the earth. Because it negates, this force destroys. Evil is the antithesis of good but the conflict in Zoroastrian myth will end with the triumph of the Good spirit, *Spenta Mainyu*, when evil shall ultimately perish. Wisdom for the individual lies in choosing correctly, thus strengthening the path of *Asha* or Truth.

In Zoroastrian symbolism unity and interdependence are visually seen most clearly in the emblem of the Fravashi or Farohar. This winged figure has now become an emblem of the Zoroastrian faith. Originally seen in Egyptian and Assyrian art, the Persians made it their main symbol from the early Achaemenian period. These spiritual prototypes are protective guardian spirits; each aspect of creation, be it flower or stone, bird, animal or human, has its own Fravashi which existed before material creation and will continue to exist after death. Therefore, like Plato's Ideas, the Fravashi constitutes the divine element within. Symbolically it becomes a good example of the holistic doctrine of Zoroastrian scriptures. In Zoroastrian texts, every being has a *Menok* or spiritual aspect and a *Getik* or physical manifestation. The Fravashi, from the Avestan word *Fravarane*, "I choose," are those spirits who have chosen to enter this creation and protect it against the destructive force. Pictorially, the design represents the idea of unity—the exact circle at the centre, the sweeping outspread wings, suggest soaring heavenwards, while the figure in the physical form of a human being indicates the importance of material life. The Fravashi then unites universal spirit with universal matter, for matter is meaningless without spirit and spirit cannot act without matter. The function of both, united together, is to bring about the *Frashokereti* or perfected creation.

The term the Good creation often appears in Zoroastrian texts. Our earth is good, creative, and bountiful; evil is sterile, barren, and negative.

With wisdom comes spiritual illumination; with work and labor, the earth will blossom. Then there will be sharing in charity in place of personal greed, and a generosity towards all life. Man, blessed with intelligence, has been given a sense of responsibility towards fellow creation. It is his duty "to keep the waters, the earth, the trees and plants, pure and clean."[4]

When we turn from text to ritual, two core ceremonies of Zoroastrianism, the inner enactment of the *Yasna* and the outer ceremony of the *Jashan* also reiterate through prayer and offerings the Zoroastrian belief in an interdependent cosmic order. Here in a sacred ritual space material and spiritual worlds come together to be strengthened, blessed, and energized. By participating, the whole community is bonded together through *Hamazor* or spiritual energy.

So an ancient Bronze Age religion and culture continues to resonate in our postmodern world and has relevance even for the future. Its teachings are truly the need of the hour. When harmony returns to man and nature, and between man and nature, it will bring peace to each aspect of life on Earth—human, animal, insect, plant, water, and mineral. Only with harmony can the healing of dissension take place on an Earth, ravaged by man.

Zoroastrianism believes that Man will be judged after life at the *Chinvat Bridge*, or the *Bridge of the Separator*, where his good deeds and bad will be analyzed. He who has fulfilled his task of protecting this earth will enter Paradise, a sweet scented garden, full of flowers and gentle breezes and be blessed for all time. Man has choice and today more than ever before, the *Chinvat Paretu*, or Bridge of Choice, stands before us all. We can choose to protect the Ahuric life sustaining forces of peace and ecological development against the Ahrimanic life destroying forces of war, violence, pollution, and ecological degradation. We can teach our children to rejoice in:

> *This Earth which bears us*
> *The waters which are flowing and abundant*
> *The Fire of Ahura Mazda, His Most Holy Spirit*
> *The Souls of Animals*
> *Plants (which) flourish at the birth of primeval life*
> *The wind (which is) good, holy, might, swift.*[5]

---

[4] *Persian Rivayets.*
[5] *Yasnas* 38.1, 38.3, 36.3, 39.2, 48.6.

If Harmony is to be maintained on earth, humans must realize the interconnectedness of all living entities and take moral responsibility for oneself, one's society, and the world as a whole.

Whatever words and deeds are noblest, best,
Teach me, O Mazda, make my life express,
Through Love of Fellow-man, through Search for Truth,
The yearnings and the prayers of my heart;
Renew, Ahura, through the Strength to Serve,
My Life, and make it as Thou wishest—TRUE.[6]

Zoroastrianism gives man freedom of thought, speech, and practice but in the last link of interdependence man has to abide by his choices. It is by his choices in this life that he will be judged in the hereafter at the *Chinvat Bridge*.

The man or woman who has fulfilled the task of protecting the harmony of the world will enter Paradise, a sweet scented garden, full of flowers and gentle breezes to be blessed for all eternity.

The man or woman, Mazda, who doth bring
To life what Thou hast as the best decreed
Asha's best blessing, Vohu Manah named,
The strength to serve, that comes through Vohu Manah
All such I'll teach to worship Thee and Thine
With them I'll march across Thy Judgment Bridge.[7]

Across the Judgment Bridge lies *Garo Demana*, the House of Light and Song. It is this perfect goal which the human soul hopes to reach. Zarathustra's message has come to us from the Bronze Age; all Prophets and sages since have reiterated its truth. The paths to this cosmic truth may differ but all paths lead to a God of Truth and Enlightenment who blesses His followers with the same virtues. The Avestan *Tandarusti*, the prayer of blessings, also specifically asks for unity and peace.

May Harmony wipe out disharmony,
...so that, our lives be made perfect.

---

[6] *Ahunavaiti Gatha 7.15, Yasna 34.15.*
[7] *Yasna 46:10, Ustavaiti Gatha.*

This is truly the need of the hour. When harmony returns to man and nature, and between man and his own nature, it will bring peace to each aspect of life. Only with harmony can the healing of dissension take place. The words of the *Zamyad Yasht*, the ancient Zoroastrian Hymn, to Earth remind us of the great gift of this earthly life:

Numerous and good, numerous and beautiful, numerous and flourishing, numerous and splendid are the works that Ahura Mazda has made through His Glory.[8]

---

[8] *Yasht 19.*

7

Diversity of Religious Traditions— A Perspective from Baha'i Faith

A. K. Merchant

THE WINDS OF CHANGE ARE BLOWING

"A new life," Baha'u'llah, founder of the Baha'i Faith, prophetically stated, "is, in this age, stirring within all the peoples of the earth; and yet none hath discovered its cause or perceived its motive."[1] Today, more than one-and-half century later the implications of what He foretold has since taken place. Doomsday protagonists looking only at the dark side of world events and the physical aspects of human nature are inducing fear and panic, painting gruesome pictures of destruction, devastation, and divine chastisement. Way back in 1970 Alvin Toffler, well-known social scientist, wrote: "Change is the process by which the future invades our lives, and it is important to look at closely, not merely from the grand perspectives of history, but also from the vantage point of the living, breathing individuals who experience it."[2] Such perspectives have profound implications for the conduct of human affairs, healthy living, protecting the environment, and the way our belief systems have influenced us.

In 1893, the World's Columbian Exposition surprised even its ambitious organizers by giving birth to the famed "Parliament of Religions," a vision of spiritual and moral consensus that captured the popular imagination on all continents and managed to eclipse even the scientific, technological and commercial wonders that the Exposition celebrated.[3]

[1] Baha'u'llah, Gleanings from the Writings of Baha'u'llah, Section CXIX.
[2] A. Toffler. *Future Shock* (London and Sydney: PAN Books Limited, 1971, 10th repr. 1974), p. 11.
[3] The Universal House of Justice Message dated April 2002, "To the World's Religious Leaders."

The organizers went so far as to predict that the religions' Parliament "would awaken in the earth's long-divided religious communities a spirit of brotherhood that could provide the needed moral underpinnings for the new world of prosperity and progress."[4] Alas, today's tumultuous changes in every strata of human society portray a very disheartening picture. Rather, our very survival is at stake, there is an urgent demand for action on the part of not only the secular and religious leaders but that of every man, woman, youth, and child for determining the fate of our civilization.

For the spiritually minded, the transformation brought about by the period of history now ending does not negate the accompanying darkness that throws the achievements of present-day civilization into sharp relief: the deliberate extermination of millions of helpless human beings, the invention and use of new weapons of destruction capable of annihilating whole populations, the rise of ideologies that continue to suffocate the spiritual and intellectual life of entire nations, the damage to the physical environment of the planet on a scale so massive that it may take centuries to heal, and the incalculably greater damage done to generations of children taught to believe that violence, indecency, and selfishness are triumphs of personal liberty.

Darkness, the followers of Baha'u'llah believe, is not a phenomenon endowed with some form of existence, much less autonomy. It does not extinguish light nor diminish it, but marks out those areas that light has not reached or adequately illumined. In His elucidation of the concept of God or Ultimate Reality and the relationship of human beings to Him, Baha'u'llah wrote that God is unknowable and beyond any human attribute, such as corporeal existence, ascent and descent, egress and regress. No sign can indicate His presence or absence. This human inability to grasp the divine essence does not lead to agnosticism, since God has chosen to reveal Himself through His messengers. God is and has always been the Creator.[5] There was never a time when the cosmos did not exist. Human beings were created by God through His love. The purpose of human existence is to know and to worship God and to carry forward an ever advancing civilization. Sin does not exist, just as darkness does not exist. What we call darkness is the absence of light.

---

[4] The Universal House of Justice Message dated April 2002, "To the World's Religious Leaders."

[5] Baha'u'llah. Gleanings from the Writings of Baha'u'llah, Section VIII.

Similarly, what we call sin is the absence of righteousness. Much of the turmoil in the world is because 80 percent of the population is deprived, not only of material prosperity, but also of a voice in the decision-making forums.

The individual soul is immortal. The love and worship of God leads to spiritual progress, which is carried forward to the next level of existence. Body and spirit are joined together, just as an electric gadget is linked with the source of power. At the time of death, the spirit does not go anywhere or vanish. Only the connection is broken.

Heaven and hell are not designated places, and should not be taken literally. At the time of death, a person himself sees in a flashback a review of his life's journey on earth and whether he acted in accordance with the commandment of God and if his life has not been in alignment with the divine teachings he feels a deep remorse which is akin to experiencing "hell." Nearness to God results in good deeds and gives infinite joy, while remoteness from Him leads to "evil" and "suffering."

God is not only just but more importantly, He is merciful and has established Himself on the throne of mercy and compassion. Were He to be seated on throne of justice alone, none could escape punishment and wrath. While seated upon His throne of mercy He is still capable of dispensing divine justice. Rebirth is not of the individual body. When our children and grandchildren are born, they resemble us or our ancestors. So it is more a rebirth of attributes.

TRUE *DHARMA* (RELIGION) IS A CIVILIZING FORCE

Because it is concerned with the ennobling of character and the harmonizing of relationships, religion or *dharma* has served throughout history as the ultimate authority in giving meaning to life. Any unprejudiced observer will agree that in every age, it has cultivated the good, reproved the wrong, and held up to the gaze of all those willing to see, a vision of potentialities as yet unrealized. From its counsels the rational soul has derived encouragement in overcoming limits imposed by the world and in fulfilling itself. As the name implies, religion or *dharma* has simultaneously been the chief force binding diverse peoples together in ever larger and more complex societies through which the individual capacities thus released can find expression.

The great advantage of the present age, Baha'is believe, is the perspective that makes it possible for the entire human race to see this

civilizing process as a single phenomenon, the ever-recurring encounters of our world with the world of the Divine. Hence, I believe, there is
a great learning opportunity for all who are involved in the Interfaith
movement to appreciate and accept the initiative of Indian Council for
Cultural Relations as conceptualized by Dr Anindita Balslev in the context of the 150th birth anniversary celebrations of Swami Vivekananda.
Members of the Baha'i community are constantly reminded to appreciate the diversity that is intrinsic in creation mindful of the underlying
principle of unity and refrain from succumbing to the forces of dissension that have already done great damage to the human psyche. The
mystical experience provided by each one of the world's extant religions
repeatedly underscores the commonality of human aspirations. We are,
therefore, called upon to render the greatest service—a service that can
meaningfully contribute to healing the ills that afflict a desperate humanity. I appeal to all who are gathered at this Interfaith Conference to support my belief in the Oneness of the Divine Reality, the Oneness of
Humankind, and beyond all diversity of cultural expression and human
interpretation of the Oneness of Religion/*Dharma*. "The well-being of
humankind, its peace and security, are unattainable," Baha'u'llah urges,
"unless and until its unity is firmly established."[6]

Taking the 1993 Centenary of the Parliament of the World's Religions
held in Chicago as a landmark event, let me explore the journey of the
study of religious systems and the impact of the Interfaith movement
since that time. Here it may be apt to state that "religion" in the era of
globalization should be understood as a system of knowledge that would
complement another system of knowledge called "science."[7]

The dialectical process of disintegration caused by the forces of
superstitions, on the one hand, and that of integration produced by
enlightenment and active cooperation, on the other hand, has helped many
people belonging to different faith-based systems to strike a right balance and appreciate the spiritual side of the process of globalization. For,
therein lies the future success of promoting the comparative study of
religions.

The history of the study of comparative religions shows that bringing
together people belonging to different religions, more precisely belonging to various denominations in each of the extant religions, has been an

[6] Baha'u'llah. Gleanings from the Writings of Baha'u'llah, Section XV.
[7] The first time I learnt of the idea or concept of "religion" as a system of
knowledge that should complement another system of knowledge called "science" was in the writings of the Baha'i Faith.

ongoing activity since time immemorial. There are references to be found in most of the Sacred Scriptures of dialogue among peoples of different belief systems initiated by the Founders of the world's many religious systems.

Although religious communities still have a long way to go for achieving lasting peace and harmony yet the sense of proximity created through a dispassionate study of other's religion(s) and a certain willingness to work together on some of the issues of common interest is worthwhile and vital. The struggle challenges us to understand the triple mind-set. First, what happens when religious communities deny or resist the need for the larger unity; second, when the need of unity in diversity is admitted, but substitutes for true unity are attempted; and third, the spectacular turning point when all resistance and subterfuge are abandoned, and the spirit of real oneness with all the myriad forms of diversity is acknowledged and accepted.

We must raise a new generation of people that looks upon the current phase of the rapidly changing world in a hopeful way, and is aware of the anguish created by the present chaotic social dislocations but who sees these as a part of a long-term process of adjustment, the pain of which can best be alleviated by being conscious of its nature and direction. I firmly believe that the current period of human history is one of those axial periods understood best perhaps in the phrase "the coming of age of humanity."[8] The period of relative isolation of various peoples of the world has ended. We have now collectively entered a new world where boundaries, if they exist at all any more, are no longer impenetrable. The interdependence of humanity with all its diversity of cultures, religions, nations, and peoples will become more and more dominant. World travel for dialogue, trade, tourism, for higher study, for scientific research, for conservation and preservation of environmental heritage, for treatment of disease and holistic well-being is increasing.

The UN Alliance of Civilizations, created in 2005, is an initiative of former general secretary Kofi Annan and the governments of Spain and Turkey, which first met in Doha, December 11–13, 2005. Its primary mission is to improve the quality of dialogue between nations and people of different cultures and religions. There were over 2,500 participants including heads of state, foreign affairs ministers, NGOs, civil society representatives, media, academia, and the corporate sector. In

---

[8] Shoghi Effendi. Call to the Nations (Haifa: Baha'i World Centre, 1977), p. 14.

2011, on October 26–28, the then Pope Benedict XVI, recalling the
initiative of his predecessor, Pope John Paul II, convened a high-level
gathering of religious and spiritual leaders to celebrate the Silver Jubilee
of the "Spirit of Assisi" and World Prayer Day for Justice, Peace, and
Harmony holding conferences at the Vatican and at the monastery of St.
Francis in Assisi. Some 300 heads or representatives of all the religious
communities—ancient to modern—as well those who did not belong to
any religions including atheists responded to the Pope's invitation. The
purpose of citing these two examples is that today there is an enormous
awareness in the world of the role religious communities can play in the
shaping of human affairs.

What is the scenario in the Indian subcontinent? We are the cradle of
many civilizations with a mind-boggling diversity of cultural, social,
religious, and political milieu and an attractive source of energy and
admiration to enterprising leaders of men, be they Aryans, Greeks,
Arabs, Afghans, Mughals, Portuguese, French, Dutch, or English (the
Japanese advances during World War II in South Asia brought them
right up to the north-eastern states of India). It is possible to see the vast
span of India's several thousands of years of history as pieces of historical and cultural epochs. No clear demarcation is possible because
they overlap and cut into one another. For the description of the histori-
cal-cultural epochs, those who have not read A. L. Basham's *The
Wonder that was India* and Jawaharlal Nehru's *The Discovery of India*
are warmly invited to do so.

In the age of globalization, by any criterion whatsoever, India is in
the midst of a spiritual, cultural, and political shift like at no time before.
In his *A Study of History,* Arnold Toynbee, the British historian, identified 14 extinct and seven living civilizations (cultures). Two of them, the
Indic and the Hindu are from India. He says:

> In the struggle for existence, the West has driven its contemporar-
> ies to the wall, and entangled them in the meshes of economic and
> political ascendancy, but it has not yet been possible to disarm
> them of their distinctive cultures. Hard pressed though they are,
> they can still call their souls their own.[9]

For the sake of brevity one can only list out the several turning points
in India's past and present: (1) The Indus Valley Civilization, (2) The

[9] A. Toynbee. *A Study of History* (London: The World Classics, 1955), p. 213.

Aryan Civilization, (3) The Gupta Period of Indian History, (4) The Islamic Culture in India, (5) Western/British Cultural Era, (6) The post Independence Congress Era, (7) Late 1990s onwards—Age of Coalition/ Globalization. In *The Discovery of India,* Pt. Jawaharlal Nehru wrote:

> We might say that the first great cultural synthesis and fusion took place between the incoming Aryans and the Dravidians, who were probably the representatives of the Indus Valley Civilization. Out of this synthesis and fusion grew the Indian races and the basic Indian culture, which had distinct elements of both. In the ages that followed there came many other races: Iranians, Greeks, Parthians, Bactrians, Scythinans, Huns, Turkis or Turks (before Islam), early Christians, Jews, Zoroastrians. They made difference and were absorbed. "India was," according to Dodwell "infinitely absorbent like the oceans."[10]

It is a bitter truth that many of the world's conflicts can be, at least partially, attributed to religion, whether it is the India-Pakistan wars, the riots and struggles of Sikhs and Muslims against Hindus in India, or the Hindu Tamil rebellion against the Buddhist Sinhalese in Sri Lanka, the Catholic-Orthodox-Muslim wars in the former Yugoslavia, the Jewish-Muslim/Christian Arab conflict in the Middle-east. Additionally, there have also been many violent clashes within religions namely the Protestant-Catholic conflict in Northern Ireland, the Shia-Sunni killings from the very beginning of Islam to cite just two examples. In terms of human populations, these conflicts involve nearly every major religion in the world. On a less violent scale, the so-called culture wars in the US are partially based on a split between conservatively religious people, on the one hand, and the more religiously liberal and the secular, on the other. What does "religion" mean to those who profess a particular religion—Buddhist (Mahayana, Hinayana, Vajrayana), Christian (Catholic, Protestant, Orthodox), Hindu (Vaishnava, Shaiva, Shakta), Muslim (Sunni, Shia, Sufi), Jain (Digambar, Shwetambar), Sikh (10 Gurus and Dedhari gurus), Zoroastrian (orthodox and liberals), Jews (orthodox, conformists, neo-liberals)? In fact, none of the followers professing a particular religion belong to that religion rather they are adherents of one of its numerous denominations. The turmoil of the age has forced one

---

[10] Pt. Jawaharlal Nehru. *The Discovery of India* (Bombay: Jaico Publishers, 1975), p. 74.

scholar, Cantwell Smith, to write: "It is no longer possible to understand each 'religion' as a stable system."[11]

Let's look at how India as per the constitutional and United Nations provisions handles diversity. When India became independent, religious freedom was granted vide Articles 25 and 29 of the Indian Constitution; non-discrimination on the basis of race was included in Article 15. Later, India also joined and signed various United Nations adopted documents including the International Convention against Racial Discrimination. However, casteism and religious discrimination are rife in the country giving rise to numerous forms of dissension. Is the hoary caste system or the related obnoxious practice of untouchability (now banned vide Article 17 of the Constitutions) responsible for this? Even though caste system and untouchability are still living realities (though with subdued rigor and vigor, especially in cities) in this country, religious intolerance has become one of the biggest threats, at times endangering the unity of the nation-state. Here, I must admit, it is our unwarranted and over-the-top reaction which is responsible for creation of needless controversies sensationalized by the media.

When someone cracks a *Sardarji* or a *Mallu* joke, the idea is definitely not to denigrate one's religious belief, inflict insult or humiliation as both are supposed to be very successful members of the Indian society. But it becomes a problem once we take the same too seriously and start depriving each other of the deserved opportunities or social goodies or in allocation/distribution of societal values on the basis of such prejudiced opinions. The violence stemming from such opinionated prejudices can actually turn out to be serious enough as to break a nation, as happened to Pakistan during the 1970s. Our spiritual ethos of Unity in Diversity expressed in terms of "*vasudhaiva kutumbakkam*" (the world as one family) and "*ekam Sat Vipra Bahuda vadanti*" (truth is One, sages call it by different names) is still the dominant majority view. In Baha'i perspective this would translate as respect for all and goodwill towards all. For, Baha'u'llah proclaimed: "The earth is but one country and humankind its citizens."[12] If separatism in Punjab could not succeed, one reason for the same is said to be the *Roti-Beti Ka Rishta* (relationship of

---

[11] Cantwell Smith quoted in a talk by Professor Suheil Bushrui delivered at Landegg International University, Weinacht, Switzerland, for the classes on "World Order Studies" in 1992 (I was a student over there from 1991 through 1994).

[12] Baha'u'llah, Tablets of Baha'u'llah revealed after the Kitab-i-Aqdas, p. 183.

livelihood and matrimony) between the two dominant communities there. Similarly, as we go along and the society experiences more inter-caste, interreligious, intercommunity, interregional marriages, such notions and prejudices will slowly lose their sting, this is my sincere prayer.

FRUITS OF ONE TREE AND LEAVES OF ONE BRANCH

The Baha'i writings state,

> Anthropology, physiology, psychology, recognize only one human species, albeit infinitely varied in the secondary aspects of life. Recognition of this truth requires abandonment of prejudice—prejudice of every kind—race, class, colour, creed, nation, sex, degree of material civilization, everything which enables people to consider themselves superior to others.[13]

Let's then rise above our self-centered thought processes and look to the examples of great men and women and also into the faces of our innocent children (no one is born with any prejudices). Admittedly, as events of the twentieth century have already demonstrated, patterns of habit and attitude which have taken root over many, many generations are not abandoned either spontaneously or in response simply to education or legislative action. Whether in the life of the individual or that of society, profound change occurs more often than not in response to intense suffering and to unendurable difficulties that can be overcome in no other way. Just so great a testing experience, Baha'u'llah warned over a century ago, is needed to weld the earth's diverse peoples into a single people with all its myriad variety.

Earthmen landing on the moon have perceived what poets, philosophers, and prophets have proclaimed through the centuries—the oneness of the human family. At a time when there is talk of setting up a base on the moon let us recall what one astronaut reported:

> The view of the earth from the moon fascinated me—a small disk, 240,000 miles away. It was hard to think that that little thing held so many problems, so many frustrations. Raging nationalistic

---

[13] Cf. The Universal House of Justice. *The Promise of World Peace* (New Delhi: Baha'i Publishing Trust, seventh repr. 1999), p. 8.

interests, famines, wars, pestilence don't show from that distance. I'm convinced that some wayward stranger in a spacecraft, coming from another part of the heavens, could look at earth and never know that it was inhabited at all. But the same wayward stranger would certainly know instinctively that if the earth were inhabited, then the destinies of all who lived on it must be inevitably interwoven and joined. We are one hunk of ground, water, air, clouds, floating around in space. From out there it really is one world.[14]

"Ye are the fruits of one tree and the leaves of one branch," says Baha'u'llah.[15] We are all trustees of this planet, our common homeland. Thus we see again, from a Baha'i view, another dimension of the fundamental importance and significance of reciprocity. In fact, the parts of this infinite universe not only have their members and elements connected with one another but also influence one another spiritually, physically, socially, and materially. We must surmount the impasse of religious ethnocentricity. God has sent His messengers or "manifestations." They are one and all manifestations of His will and exponents of His word. Their message is, therefore, one and the same. At the same time, each manifestation has a distinct individuality, a definitely prescribed mission. Thus, each religion has special features that correspond to the needs of a time and place and to the level of civilization.

God's messengers are divinely inspired, occupying a level of existence well above ordinary men. They are to be revered, but not worshipped. Their messages have been given at different times and places, within an evolutionary paradigm of human history. Wide differences in their teachings can be explained by the alterations made by successive prophets and incarnations in order to meet the changing needs of society. Many of the teachings have been subsequently added by fallible religious leaders, resulting in dogma and misinterpretations.[16]

---

[14] View of the planet described by astronaut, Buzz Aldrin, 1972. How well it echoes what the Indian *Rishi*s (sages) envisaged thousands of years ago: *Ayam Nijaparoveti/Gananam Laghuchetasam/Udarcharitanam Tu Vasudhaiva kutumbakkam/*[This is mine, this yours, this sort of divisive intellect is the sign of people with small minds. For those endowed with larger vision the whole world is a family]. (A famous verse from the Hindu Scriptures).

[15] Baha'u'llah. Gleanings from the Writings of Baha'u'llah, Section CXXI.

[16] For an in-depth treatment of this and other related topics see Baha'u'llah's Book of Certitude (New Delhi: Baha'i Publishing Trust, 2001); the book can also be accessed through the Internet.

No religion teaches the unjust use of force. Those who advocate violence do so out of vested interest. These are gross distortions of the teachings of the founders of world's many religious systems. Religious truth, Baha'is believe, is not absolute but relative. Divine revelation is a continuous and progressive process. The teachings of different Faiths are facets of the same truth and represent successive stages in the spiritual evolution of human society.

Most religions carry the baggage of centuries' practices along with many aberrations. This baggage has first to be shed. We should also not confine our Faiths or God to the narrow confines of simply our planet knowing full well that billions of galaxies exist.

Interfaith meets should be a continuous process and should percolate down to the masses.

SAFEGUARDING THE RIGHTS OF THE INDIVIDUAL

One of the responsibilities which Baha'u'llah assigns to the Administrative Order instituted in His Writings is the protection of the rights of all persons. The equality of man and woman is a cardinal principle of the Baha'i Faith. They must coordinate and advance equally, for they are like the two wings of a bird. Boys and girls are to be given equal rights and opportunities and treated fairly. If resources are limited, more should be spent on female children, especially in the field of education.

The ultimate guardian of this vital principle is the Universal House of Justice, the supreme governing body of the Baha'i Faith itself, whose Constitution explicitly sets out the responsibilities "to safeguard the personal rights, freedom and initiative of individuals," for ensuring that no body or institution with the Baha'i Faith "abuse its privilege…" and "to be the exponent and guardian of that divine justice which can alone ensure the security of, and establish the reign of law and order in the world."[17] This belief stems from the guidance provided by Shoghi Effendi, the authorized interpreter of the Baha'i Revelation, in a letter that he wrote to the Baha'is of Iran:

> …they should have the most scrupulous regard to safeguarding the legitimate personal and civil rights of all individuals, whatever

---

[17] The Constitution of the Universal House of Justice released in 1972, produced in the Baha'i World (volume XV, 1970–75, Oxford, UK: Baha'i World Centre Publications, 1980).

may be their chosen career or station in life, and irrespective of their racial, religious or ideological backgrounds. It is not permissible in matters related to such rights to make distinctions and discriminations or show preferences. In all transactions and dealings that affect basic human rights, the standard required of the chosen supporters of Baha'u'llah—a standard that must claim their unhesitating and unreserved acceptance, and which they must meticulously and assiduously uphold—is that they should not make the slightest distinction between friend and stranger, believer and unbeliever, supporter and antagonist... If the friends were to act otherwise it would be tantamount to a reversion on their part, ... to the ways of those of a former age: they would re-ignite in men's breasts the fire of bigotry and intolerance: they would cut themselves off from the glorious bestowals and bounties of this promised Day of God: and they would frustrate the full revelation of God's grace and favour to men in this luminous age.[18]

THINK LOVINGLY, ACT UNITEDLY

Gandhiji once stated that one cannot create a system that is so good that people do not have to be good. In other words, it is impossible to create a system that is ethically strong without the people involved in it acting from moral principles and this is the *raison d'etre* of religion. Until we accept that all people, regardless of caste, creed, gender, class, or national status, are equal members of one human family, each with inalienable rights—and act out of that belief—we are likely to overlook the obscene disparities that now divide humankind. Therefore, the real purpose of religion is to promote the acquisition of praiseworthy virtues, betterment of morals, and the spiritual development of humankind. Which is the country willing to lead by example? If we look at the top five countries of the Human Development Index Report—Norway, Canada, Sweden, Finland, the US—are these model-nation-states?[19]

Arthur Koestler, the Hungarian-born British author and social scientist, writes that the great breakthroughs in science and art stem from "the

---

[18] Shoghi Effendi, letter dated July, 1925, translated from Persian, Baha'i World Centre.

[19] *United Nations Human Development Index Report* published annually.

sudden interlocking of two previously unrelated skills, or matrices of thought."[20] He defines this process as the "act of creation" and suggests that most of the great new theories and discoveries are born of this "biosociative pattern of creative synthesis."

Through comparative study of the religious systems of the world people need to develop the knowledge, values, attitudes, and skills necessary to participate confidently and constructively in shaping the world community, on all levels, so that it might reflect principles of justice, equity, and unity. Top-down models of community development can no longer adequately respond to present-day needs and aspirations. We must move toward more participatory, knowledge-based, and values-driven systems of governance in which people can assume responsibility for the processes and institutions that affect their lives. Democratic in spirit and method, the new mind-set must become visible at all levels of society, including the global level. Consultation—the operating expression of justice in human affairs—should become our primary mode of decision-making. Old ways of exercising power and authority must give way to new forms of leadership. Our concept of leadership (religious or secular) will need to be recast to include the ability to foster collective decision-making and collective action. It will find its highest expression in service to the community as a whole. In such a community, the fruits of science and technology will benefit the whole society, and no one will be jobless.

Nations that develop such an ethos will prove to be the pillars of a world civilization—a civilization which will be the logical culmination of humanity's community-building efforts over vast stretches of time and geography. Everyone has both the right and the responsibility to contribute to this historic and far-reaching collective enterprise whose goal is nothing less than the peace, prosperity, and unity of the entire human family.

In restoring the value system that stem essentially from the sacred scriptures and the exemplary lives of great men and women, legislators and law-makers will need to think in terms of curbing the rampant individualism that has come to characterize our culture, and seek instead to nurture the ideals of service and compassion. Unless the judiciary and legal institutions functioning in tandem with other branches of the state are able to reverse the present-day dangerous trends our civilization is doomed to perish. "The principal cause of the suffering, which one can

[20] A. Koestler. Wikipedia.

witness wherever one turns, is the corruption of human morals and the prevalence of prejudice, suspicion, hatred and untrustworthiness and selfishness and tyranny among men."[21] The increase in crime, the break-down of the institution of marriage, mental illness, and alcoholism, the dependence upon tranquilizers, the escape from reality into the drug experience, the breakdown of law and order, the corruption of political institutions, and the unethical practices of modern business and industry are all symptomatic of the decomposition of the civilization, as we know it.

Let me also share the following view expressed by a well-known Indian Muslim jurist, Professor Tahir Mahmood, whose perceptive understanding of the tensions among various religious groups in India I find to be very enlightening, very relevant in the context of our Conference:

India has always been and remains a deeply religious society. The present state of religious education in the country emanates from various provisions of the Constitution and law and sustained gov-ernmental and administrative policies—all of which, together, assure basic secularity of the State without undue sensitivity to society's religious sensitivities. The system partakes of two differ-ent channels—one accommodating religious education on an optional basis in institutions of a public nature, and the other mainly providing religious education in religion—specific private seminaries. The former works under State patronage and financing to varying extents, the latter under the sponsorship of various reli-gious communities. In a nutshell, religious education in India is a subject of public–private partnership and ordinarily does not face any serious problems.[22]

The reality of the Age in which we live is that no man is an island, no island is an island, no continent is an island. Our most fundamental problem is to think differently from the way we thought before, and to do

[21] The Universal House of Justice letter dated 1974 quoted in Baha'i Social and Economic Program by Holly Hanson Vick (Oxford: George Ronald Publisher, 1983), p. 38.

[22] Tahir Mahmood. *Religious Education in Modern India* (Report on India for a Russian Project: "Religious Education in the Modern World," 2008, quarterly of the Amity Law School, Noida).

so together. Nothing is more difficult. But we are perhaps beginning—almost imperceptibly—to do so. Followers of Baha'u'llah, wherever they reside, are firmly convinced that as the sweeping tides of consumerism, unfettered consumption, extreme poverty, and marginalization recede, they will reveal the human capacities for justice, reciprocity, and happiness.

8

Vedanta in the Nuclear Age

Karan Singh

Mankind today is in a major period of transition, as significant as the earlier ones from nomadic to agricultural society, from agricultural to industrial, and from industrial to post-industrial society. We may be too close to the event to grasp its full significance, but it is now quite clear that we are in the throes of a major change. Whether it is in the field of politics or economics, communications or culture, a powerful new globalism is developing. Indeed the outstanding feature of the second half of the twentieth century has been the collapse of the materialistic paradigm that has dominated world thought for many centuries. What may be called the Cartesian-Newtonian-Marxist paradigm has broken down, and with it the materialistic philosophies based upon that view, whether Marxist or Capitalist, can also be seen to have failed. With the impact of post Einsteinian physics, quantum mechanics, Heisenberg's uncertainty principle, and many other conceptual revolutions, the old structures have begun to crumble. Solid matter dissolves into "Waves of probability," and the new physics seems to be approaching the mystic vision of which seers and sages of all traditions have spoken.

The predominant consciousness of the human race reflects its evolutionary situation, and it would be true to say that at this crucial evolutionary crossroads mankind is groping for a new model, a new philosophy, a new paradigm, a new consciousness to replace the old. And it is no coincidence that this is happening at a juncture when mankind is in supreme peril; not from another species, not from outer space, but from itself. There has been a tragic divergence of knowledge and wisdom, and from deep within the human psyche there has developed a terrible poison that threatens not only our own generation or race but all life on this planet. We are perhaps like the fabled continent of Atlantis, rich and resplendent beyond compare but ultimately sinking below the waves, unable to survive its own technological ingenuity.

Ancient myths often illuminate the human predicament, and there is a powerful Hindu myth of the churning of the Milky Ocean (the *Samudra-Manthana*) which speaks to us today across the millenia, symbolizing as it does the long and tortuous evolution of consciousness on Planet Earth. In this great myth, the *Deva*s and the *Asura*s, the bright and the dark powers, both cooperated in the churning of the ocean. This went on for aeons, until at last the great gifts began to emerge, *Kamadhenu*, the all giving cow, *Ucchaishravas*, the divine horse, *Kalpavriksha*, the wish-fulfilling tree, and *Airavata*, the divine elephant. These and other gifts appeared, and were happily divided between the two sides. The churning proceeded as its ultimate objective was the *Amrita Kalasha*, the pot of ambrosia, the Elixir of Immortality for which even the gods crave.

Suddenly, without warning, the ocean started to boil with a deadly poison—the *Garala*—a new, malign dimension of which neither the *Deva*s nor the *Asura*s had any knowledge. Rapidly the poison spread through the three worlds—the water, land, and skies. The churners fled helter-skelter in terror, striving to escape from the deadly fumes, forgetting all the gifts that they had accumulated. And the Shiva-Mahadeva appeared, the great, primal divinity aloof from the avarice and materialism of the *Deva*s and the *Asura*s. He collected the poison in a cup and drank it, integrating, it into his being. Then the danger passed. Order was restored, and chanting hymns to the glory of Shiva the participants returned.

This myth vividly illustrates the human predicament today. Prolonged churnings have given many the great gifts of science and technology. There have been incredible breakthroughs in medicine and communications, agriculture and electronics, space travel and cybernetics. We now have enough resources and technology to ensure for every human being on earth the physical, intellectual, material, and spiritual inputs necessary for a full and healthy life. And yet surely the poison is also upon us. Billions of dollars and rubles, pounds and francs, rupees and yuans are spent every day on the manufacture of monstrous weapons with unprecedented power of destruction. It is estimated that there are now well over 50,000 nuclear warheads on planet earth, each a thousand times more powerful than the bombs that devastated Hiroshima and Nagasaki at the dawn of the nuclear age; each with more explosive force than used by both sides in the entire World War II.

There is overwhelming evidence to show that any kind of nuclear war would not only shatter human civilization as we know it, it would poison the air and the oceans and render Earth virtually uninhabitable, a charred and ravaged planet incapable of supporting more than extremely primitive life-forms. Whether this happens through political foolishness or an accident, a flight of geese or a malfunctioning computer chip, matters little. With all our tremendous knowledge, man has finally come to a single three-letter mantra—MAD—Mutually Assured Destruction. Thousands of years ago, at the dawn of human civilization, the Vedic seers had also discovered a three letter Mantra—AUM—as the symbol of the divinity that pervades the universe. Perhaps the time has come when we should revert from MAD to AUM, so that this greatest of all transitions, the transition to the global consciousness, can be safely completed and the earth becomes a crucible for the next major step in evolution.

Second great insight of the Upanishads, and the relationship between the *Atman* and the *Brahman* is the key point upon which the whole Vedantic teaching revolves. All the four *yoga*s are directed towards bringing about the union between the *Atman* and the *Brahman*—Gyana-yoga, the way of wisdom; Bhakti-yoga, the way of emotional rapport; Karma-yoga, the way of dedicated works; and Raja-yoga, the way of ecstasy. All of them are directed towards bringing about the union between the all-pervasive *Brahman* without and the immortal *Atman* within.

Flowing from this, we come now to another important Vedantic concept which is that all human beings, because of their shared spirituality, are members of a single, extended family. The Upanishads have a beautiful word for human beings, *"Amritasya Putrah,"* children of immortality. It is an extraordinary phrase. We do not look upon human beings as essentially sinners, weak and cringing, begging and supplicating some unseen being seated in some seventh heaven. Rather, we are children of immortality because we carry within our consciousness the light and the power of the *Brahman*, regardless of our race or color, our creed or sex, or any other differentiation. That is the basis of the concept of human beings as an extended family, *"Vasudhaiva Kutumbakan."* A famous verse points out that the division between "mine" and "yours" is a small and narrow way of looking at reality, indulged in by people with imma-ture minds. For those of the greater consciousness, the entire world is a family. This is another great insight of the Upanishads, peculiarly rele-vant at this juncture in human history.

We come now to a fourth major philosophical concept of the Upanishads, the essential unity of all religions, of all spiritual paths—*"Ekam Sadviprah Bahudha Vadanti"*—as the *Rig Veda* has it; the truth is one, the wise call it by many names. The Mundaka Upanishad has a beautiful verse which says that in the same way as streams and rivulets arise in different parts of the world but ultimately flow into the same ocean, so do all these creeds and religious formulations arise in different times and areas, but, if they have a true aspiration, ultimately reach the same goal. Here is a philosophy which cuts across barriers of hatred and fanaticism that have been built in the name of religion. The Vedanta is a universal religion; it accepts the infinite possibilities of movements towards the divine, it does not seek to limit or confine us to any particular formulation. It not only accepts but welcomes a multiplicity of paths to the divine, provided those paths are genuine movements towards divine realization and not merely intellectual gymnastics and disputations.

It is a little like climbing a mountain with several different starting places. If we keep arguing at those points we will remain miles apart, but when we actually start climbing and move upwards, then, as we approach the summit, our paths will begin to converge, and ultimately when we get to the top we will all meet there, because there is only one summit. Similarly, once we really start moving upwards in the field of spiritual endeavor, we will find all our denominations and intellectual differences gradually losing their importance, and as we rise to the summit we will realize the spiritual oneness of humanity.

The fifth Vedantic concept is the concept of the welfare of all beings, "*Bahujana Sukhaya Bahujana Hitaya Cha.*" The Vedanta seeks the welfare all creation, not only of human beings but also of what we call the lower creatures. In our arrogance and ignorance we have destroyed the environment of this planet. We have polluted the oceans, we have made the air unbreathable, and we have desecrated nature and decimated wildlife. Thousands of species have become extinct because of our hubris as human beings; and thousands more are on the verge of extinction. But the Vedantic seers knew that man was not something apart from nature, that human consciousness grew out of the entirety of the world situation and, therefore, they had compassion for all living beings. That is why the Vedanta constantly exhorts us that while we are working for our own salvation we must also shun the path of violence and hatred. We must seek to develop both elements of our psyche, the inner and the outer, the quietist and the activist. Indeed these are two sides of the same coin, so we must work not only for our own salvation but also for the welfare of the world. While working out our own destiny we also have social responsibility, and as long as we are embodied we have to continue to work for the welfare of all beings.

These five concepts from the Vedanta—the all-pervasive *Brahman*; the *Atman* which resides in all beings; the concept of the human race as members of *a* family regardless of all differences; the idea that all religions are essentially different paths to the same goal; and the concept that we must work for the welfare of society as a whole, for ourselves—when taken together provide a comprehensive worldview which can greatly help humanity in the process of globalization upon which it has embarked.

Gradually a world civilization is being born, and it has to be born if mankind is to survive in this nuclear age. Science and technology have given us tremendous power, and that power if used for benign purposes can abolish poverty and hunger, malnutrition and misery, illiteracy and unemployment from the face of this earth by the end of this century. It can be done; seven days' expenditure on world armaments can abolish hunger in Africa, 10 days' expenditure on world armaments can abolish the debt of Latin America. But instead, the equivalent of one trillion US dollars every year is going into the manufacture of weapons of mass destruction so awesome that it can hardly be imagined. We now have enough nuclear power to destroy the human race 40 times over, to commit not only *racial* suicide but terricide, the destruction of planet Earth.

We must never forget that power by itself is neither good nor evil; there is *Daivik Shakti* and there is the *Asurik Shakti*, the benign power and the malign power. The worship of power of science, is not enough, we also need to recapture wisdom, compassion, and understanding. We can now survive only if we have an alternative ideology to the one which has led mankind to this position, and if we boldly act in harmony with that ideology.

The Vedanta provides such an alternative ideology; and if even at this late hour we can imbibe some of its universal truths we can perhaps reverse the mad rush towards destruction and begin the long, slow climb bock to sanity. In the *Swetaswatara Upanishad* the seer says, *"Vedahametam Purusham mahantam Adityavarman Tamasah Purustat"*—I know that Great Being, shining like the sun beyond the darkness; it is only by knowing him that you can overcome death, there is no other way to immortality. The immortality of the Upanishads is not merely survival after death, which in any case is taken for granted. It is the transcending of birth and death; it means that our consciousness is raised to a state where we are not obliged to be reborn again and again in the cycle of Samsara.

Can you imagine what it is like when a caterpillar, and ugly, land bound worm, goes into a chrysalis and a miraculous metamorphosis takes place so that it emerges as a beautiful, radiantly colored butterfly?

That is the sort of metamorphosis that the Upanishads envisage for human consciousness, and that we need for the new global consciousness. We must change from our earthbound consciousness into this bright, multicolored, global consciousness which can still alight upon the ground like a caterpillar but can also fly into the air which the caterpillar could not do.

That, as I see it, is the true significance of the Vedanta, so ably expounded 12 centuries ago by Adi Shandaracharya. I will close with that immortal Vedic prayer that seeks to lead us from the untruth of ignorance into the truth of knowledge; from the darkness within into the light above; and from the cycle of birth and death into immortality. That is the highest achievement of the Upanishads; and that is the goal towards which we all must strive.

Asato ma Sadgamaya
Tamaso ma jyotirgamaya
Mrityorma amritam gamaya

PART II

Some Issues in the Context of Religious Diversity

9

Studying and Creating Peace

Steve Killelea

During the last 20 years humanity has entered a new epoch in its history. This has been brought about by a convergence of many factors, such as reaching finite environmental barriers that are now being faced on multiple fronts. World population recently reached 7 billion and in many places it's already at straining capacity. Additionally, technology is fueling change at an ever increasing pace which in many ways underpins the growth of globalization. The world is connected in ways that were unimaginable even 50 years ago. Wars are no longer economically viable and change is occurring so fast that nations are struggling to keep up with both the legal and social ramifications of these changes.

Global challenges call for global solutions and these solutions require cooperation on a scale unprecedented in human history. Peace is an essential prerequisite because without peace we will never be able to achieve the levels of cooperation, trust, inclusiveness, and social equity necessary to solve these challenges, let alone empower the international institutions necessary to address them.

All of the major religions have peace as a central core of their beliefs, but religion can be distorted when viewed as an absolute with judgments of good or evil being cast, depending on whether a person is a believer or not. The rallying call of interfaith tolerance not only appeals to the core spiritual doctrines of love which are expressed in all the major religions but also allows for a diversity of views and opinions to flourish. Diversity of views is central to enabling creative and peaceful societies to flourish because without these we will never be able to find solutions to global problems.

Peace lies at the center of being able to manage the transition, simply because peace creates the optimum environment in which the other activities that contribute to human growth can take place. In this sense, peace is a facilitator making it easier for workers to produce, businesses to sell, entrepreneurs and scientists to innovate, and governments to regulate.

But if peace is an essential prerequisite for solving our sustainability challenges and improving our economic and social well-being then having a good understanding of peace is essential. This poses the question "How well do we understand peace?" Fifty years ago peace studies were virtually non-existent. Today there are thriving Peace and Conflict Centers in numerous universities around the world. However, most of these are only centered on the study of conflict rather than on the understanding of peace.

A parallel can be drawn here with medical science. The study of pathology has led to numerous breakthroughs in our understanding of how to treat and cure disease. However, there is more to health than that. It was only when medical science turned its focus on the study of healthy human beings that we understood what we need to do to stay healthy: the right physical exercise, a good mental disposition, and a healthy diet. This could only be learnt by studying what was working. In the same way, the study of conflict is fundamentally different than the study of peace.

Over the last century we have moved from having departments of war to departments of defense and we are now seeing the emergence of organizations that are lobbying for the creation of departments of peace within governments. While these changes are beneficial in improving our understanding of peace, peace is not yet seen as germane to the major academic disciplines, nor is there a methodological approach to the cross-disciplinary study of peace. As an example, there is no university Chair of Peace Economics in any major Economic faculty, yet most business people believe that their markets grow in peace and that their costs decrease with increasing peacefulness.

The simplest way of approaching the definition of peace is in terms of harmony achieved by the absence of war, conflict, or violent crime. Applied to states, this would suggest that the measurement of internal states of peace is as important as those external factors involving other states or neighbors. This is what Johan Galtung defined as "negative peace"—an absence of violence. The concept of negative peace is immediately intuitive and empirically measurable and can be used as a starting point to elaborate its counterpart concept, "positive peace." Having established what constitutes an absence of violence, it is possible through statistical analysis to identify which structures, institutions, and social attitudes create and maintain peace.

MEASURING PEACE

Measurement is the key to understanding any human endeavor and peace is no different. If we do not measure peace, then how can we know whether our actions are either helping or hindering us in the achievement of a more peaceful world? Only by measuring and understanding the patterns of peace can we move to a better understanding of how it can be improved.

The Global Peace Index (GPI) was developed in 2007 by the Institute for Economics and Peace (IEP) as one of the first rigorous attempts to measure the relative levels of the peacefulness of nations. By aggregating and generating a comprehensive and reliable data set which measures direct violence, the GPI adds to the current stock of harmonized cross-country data. Since 2007 it has informed policymakers, academics, and civil society organizations about the objective state of direct violence in countries covering over 99 percent of the world's population. The purpose of this research is to better understand the cultural, economic, and political conditions associated with peaceful environments.

Up until now, the GPI has focused on measuring "negative peace," which was described by Johan Galtung as the "absence of violence" and the "absence of the fear of violence."[1] Hence the GPI utilizes 22 indicators of safety and security in society, militarization, and ongoing domestic and international conflicts to determine the multidimensional nature of negative peace in 162 countries. This means nations with a high ranking in the GPI are considered more peaceful because they are relatively safer and more secure than countries lower in the rankings.

In contrast to negative peace, Galtung described a second dimension called positive peace. Broadly understood, positive peace is derived from preventative solutions which are optimistic and facilitate a more integrated society.[2] According to Galtung, this results in "cooperation for mutual benefit, and where individuals and society are in harmony."[3]

---

[1] The definition of violence is adapted from the World Health Organization: "the intentional use of physical force or power, threatened or actual, against oneself, another person, or against a group or community, that either results in or has a high likelihood of resulting in injury, death, psychological harm, destruction of property, mal-development, or deprivation."

[2] J. Galtung (1985). "Twenty-Five Years of Peace Research: Ten Challenges and Some Responses," *Journal of Peace Research*, 22 (2): 141–158.

[3] Ibid.

From this conceptual basis, IEP defines positive peace as "*the set of attitudes, institutions and structures which when strengthened, lead to a more peaceful society.*"

This resulted in the development of the "Pillars of Peace" which is an eight-part taxonomy that categorizes the data sets statistically significant with the GPI. Conceptually, this emphasizes the importance of a holistic set of institutions which work together to systematically shape the environments that lead to peace. It is important to understand that this framework is not deriving causality between any of the attributes of the "Pillars of Peace," rather they work as an interdependent set of factors where causality and strength of a relation will change depending on the individual set of a country's specific political, economic, and cultural circumstances.

In order to derive indicators for the Positive Peace Index (PPI), IEP has compared over 300 cross-country data sets with the GPI to conceptualize eight factors strongly correlated with peaceful countries as measured by the GPI. Utilizing the eight-part "Pillars of Peace" taxonomy, a PPI has been developed with 24 indicators covering 126 countries. Under each of the eight domains of the index there are between two and three indicators which have weightings determined by the relative strength of the indicator's correlation to the GPI score. Further detail on this is provided in the methodology section below.

WHY A POSITIVE PEACE INDEX?

In contrast to negative peace, positive peace can inform our understanding of the appropriate attitudes, institutions, and structures which when strengthened, lead to a nation's capacity to harmoniously and non-violently resolve conflict. The approach in this work stands in contrast to the extensive quantitative conflict literature which is predominately focused on understanding the causes for outbreak of war or organized conflict as a key dependent variable.[4] The output of the PPI can be used for comparative studies which will further inform the understanding of the key economic, political, and cultural factors that can improve peace and resilience of all societies, not just fragile states.

By seeking to identify institutions which help a society move away from violence, it is hoped a more holistic picture of the key factors which drive peace can be identified. While focus on "trigger" factors

---

[4] Human Security Report 2009–2010, "The Causes of Peace and the Shrinking Costs of War, Human Security Report Project," Oxford University Press, p. 36.

or individual case studies is insightful they cannot reveal global or regional trends or help in identifying longer term causes of conflict. As the 2009–2010 Human Security Report identifies, there is still a "… remarkable lack of consensus in the research findings on the causes of war and peace…also the inability of conflict models to predict the outbreak of conflicts."[5] To date, there are only a small number of robust findings which have widespread consensus in the research community; according to Hegre and Sambanis[6] they suggest only three key findings have broad agreement on the causes of civil war:

- The lower a country's average income, the higher the risk of war.
- War is more likely if a country has already experienced a war, the more recent the war the more likely the risk.
- The risk of war increases as a country's size increases.

While some dispute the number of robust findings, it is clear there are conflicting empirical conclusions as to the causes of conflict. In contrast, by measuring positive peace it is possible to determine another way to better understand how to reduce violence, but more importantly how to build the resilience within societies so they are less likely to fall into conflict. It is hoped this research can influence debate on how international institutions can facilitate a more holistic and positive approach to peace and state building.

The composite index approach of the PPI was chosen because positive peace is a latent and multidimensional concept which is represented in different social, political, and economic forms. Defining positive peace as "*the set of attitudes, institutions and structures which when strengthened, lead to a more peaceful society*," it is clearly an unobservable variable that cannot be represented or embodied in any single factor.

WHAT IS PEACE?

While there are many nuanced definitions of peace, this article uses two concepts, both of which have a rich history in peace studies. These two concepts of peace are commonly referred to as "positive" and "negative."

---

[5] Human Security Report 2009–2010, "The Causes of Peace and the Shrinking Costs of War, Human Security Report Project," Oxford University Press, p. 35.

[6] Hegre and Sambanis (2006). "Sensitivity Analysis of Empirical Results on Civil War Onset," *Journal of Conflict Resolution*, 50 (3): 508–535.

Negative peace is the absence of violence or fear of violence, an intuitive definition that most people will agree with. This was used in defining the measures for the GPI which include indicators that measure both the internal peacefulness of nations as well their external peace in relation to other states.

This body of work by IEP is the only known quantitative approach to defining positive peace and as such occupies a unique position in peace studies. This work provides a foundation for researchers to deepen their understanding of the empirical relationships between peace, social development, and other development variables.

The empirical link between negative peace and the factors in the PPI appears to hold in developing and developed contexts. Both negative and positive peace can be seen as the producer and product of forms of trust and cohesion that are a prerequisite for well-functioning and prosperous societies. Countries higher in positive peace also tend to have many other fundamentally positive social and economic outcomes. For instance, IEP has found that high peace countries have:

- Higher per capita incomes
- More equitable distribution of resources
- Better health and education outcomes
- Improved trust between citizens
- Greater social cohesion
- Better ecological management

By moving countries away from direct violence and towards positive peace, this demonstrates that it is also possible to reap a significant social and economic dividend as a primary by-product of creating peace.

The PPI is similar to the GPI, in that it is a composite index attempting to measure a multidimensional concept. The PPI is the first known attempt to build an empirical derived index aiming to measure the latent variable of positive peace.

The starting point for developing the PPI was to correlate the GPI against over 880 cross-country harmonized data sets measuring a variety of economic, governance, social, attitudinal, and political factors. This aggregation of data attempted to cover every relevant quantitative and qualitative data set measuring factors at the nation-state level. Each data set, which was significantly correlated, was then organized under eight distinct headings or factors,[7] these have been previously referred to as the *Pillars of Peace* and become the eight domains of the PPI. These structures were derived by empirical inspection and from the large body of qualitative and quantitative literature highlighting the importance of these factors.

Under each of the eight domains, the data sources most closely cor-related with the GPI were then aggregated for each country. This resulted in the PPI having the following key features:

- 24 indicators under eight domains
- 122 countries covered in 2005
- 126 countries covered in 2010

The key domains of the PPI consist of the following:

- Well-functioning government
- Sound business environment
- Equitable distribution of resources
- Acceptance of the rights of others
- Free flow of information
- Good relations with neighbors
- High levels of human capital
- Low levels of corruption

Indicators

Table 9.1 shows all the 24 indicators used to build the PPI and the weight assigned to each along with their sources.

All indicators are scored between one and five, with one being the most "positively peaceful" score and five the least "positively peaceful."

---

[7] Significance (or significance threshold) is the qualitative level at which IEP considers that a relationship between two variables is meaningful. Statistical significance (significance level) indicates something that passes the appropriate statistical test (for correlation, the t-test which distinguishes the correlation from zero). All correlations presented, other than societal attitudes, have a determined level of significance > 0.5 or < -0.5. The threshold for a meaningful correlation from global surveys was considered more appropriate at > 0.4 or < -0.4.

Table 9.1

Positive Peace Index Indicators

PPI Domain	PPI Indicator	Weighting	Source
Well-functioning Government	Government Effectiveness	5%	World Governance Indicators, World Bank
	Rule of Law	5%	World Governance Indicators, World Bank
	Political Culture	5%	Sub-Index, Democracy Index, Economist Intelligence Unit
Sound Business Environment	Ease of Doing Business	4%	Ease of Doing Business Index, World Bank
	Economic Freedom	4%	Heritage Foundation
	GDP Per Capita	4%	World Bank
Equitable Distribution of Resources	Life Expectancy Index Loss	4%	Human Development Report, United Nations Development Programme
	Gini Coefficient	2%	Economist Intelligence Unit
	Population Living below $2/Day	5%	World Bank, IEP
Acceptance of the Rights of Others	Hostility to Foreigners and Private Property Rights	3%	Economist Intelligence Unit
	Empowerment Index	4%	Cignarelli-Richards Human Rights Dataset
	Gender Inequality	4%	Human Development Report, United Nations Development Programme
Good Relations with Neighbors	Satisfaction with Community	3%	Human Development Report, United Nations Development Programme
	Regional Integration	4%	Economist Intelligence Unit
	Intergroup Cohesion	5%	Indices for Social Development, International Institute for Social Studies

(Table 9.1 Continued)

(Table 9.1 Continued)

PPI Domain	PPI Indicator	Weighting	Source
Free Flow of Information	Freedom of the Press Index	4%	Freedom House
	World Press Freedom Index	4%	Reporters without Borders
	Mobile Phones Subs Per 1,000	3%	International Telecommunications Union
High Levels of Human Capital	Youth Development Index	4%	Commonwealth Secretariat
	Non Income HDI	4%	Human Development Report, United Nations Development Programme
	Number of Scientific Publications	4%	World Bank and United Nations Development Programme
Low Levels of Corruption	Control of Corruption	5%	World Governance Indicators, World Bank
	Factionalized Elites	5%	Fund for Peace
	Perceptions of Corruption	5%	Transparency International

Source: Institute for Economics and Peace (IEP), Global Peace Index 2012, p. 72 (http://economicsandpeace.org/wp-content/uploads/2011/09/2012-Global-Peace-Index-Report.pdf).

This means countries which score closer to one are likely to have *relatively* more institutional capacity and resilience in comparison to nations which score closer to five.

The weightings are between 0.5 and 0.8 and have been derived by the strength of the indicator's statistical correlation to the 2011 GPI score. The stronger the correlation to the GPI, the higher the weighting portioned in the PPI. The lowest weighting is given to the *Interpersonal Safety and Trust* indicator which accounts for 3.9 percent of the index. This is in comparison to the most heavily weighted factor of *Intergroup Cohesion* which is weighted at 0.80 and accounts for more than twice the portion of *Interpersonal Safety and Trust* at 6.2 percent of the PPI.

Results

Table 9.2 shows the rankings and scores of the 126 countries in the PPI.
Due to the small difference in scores between some nations the results
are best understood in groups of 10, as in the top 10, 11 to 20, and so on.

Table 9.2
Positive Peace Index Results

Rank	Country	Score	Rank	Country	Score
1	Denmark	1.25	64	Kazakhstan	3.00
2	Norway	1.28	65	Jordan	3.01
3	Finland	1.30	66	Moldova	3.03
4	Switzerland	1.32	67	Colombia	3.04
5	Netherlands	1.35	68	Turkey	3.04
6	Sweden	1.37	69	Armenia	3.05
7	Iceland	1.46	70	Morocco	3.08
8	Austria	1.50	71	Saudi Arabia	3.10
9	New Zealand	1.50	72	Ukraine	3.10
10	Australia	1.54	73	Guatemala	3.11
11	Ireland	1.54	74	Paraguay	3.12
12	Canada	1.54	75	Nicaragua	3.13
13	Germany	1.59	76	Honduras	3.16
14	Belgium	1.65	77	Vietnam	3.17
15	United Kingdom	1.67	78	Sri Lanka	3.19
16	Japan	1.79	79	Indonesia	3.19
17	Singapore	1.82	80	Russia	3.20
18	France	1.82	81	China	3.24
19	United States	1.83	82	Azerbaijan	3.25
20	Slovenia	1.87	83	Lebanon	3.26
21	Portugal	1.87	84	Ecuador	3.26
22	Czech Republic	1.91	85	Algeria	3.26
23	Estonia	1.91	86	Philippines	3.27
24	Spain	1.97	87	Bolivia	3.28
25	Chile	2.06	88	Senegal	3.28
26	South Korea	2.08	89	India	3.32

(Table 9.2 Continued)

(Table 9.2 Continued)

Rank	Country	Score	Rank	Country	Score
27	*Italy*	2.13	90	*Gabon*	3.33
28	*Poland*	2.14	91	*Egypt*	3.34
29	*Lithuania*	2.14	92	*Burkina Faso*	3.34
30	*Cyprus*	2.15	93	*Tanzania*	3.36
31	*Hungary*	2.16	94	*Swaziland*	3.36
32	*Uruguay*	2.18	95	*Malawi*	3.39
33	*Greece*	2.23	96	*Belarus*	3.40
34	*Latvia*	2.25	97	*Mozambique*	3.40
35	*Israel*	2.35	98	*Zambia*	3.41
36	*Costa Rica*	2.36	99	*Mali*	3.41
37	*Qatar*	2.36	100	*Cambodia*	3.41
38	*United Arab Emirates*	2.41	101	*Venezuela*	3.42
39	*Bulgaria*	2.49	102	*Syria*	3.44
40	*Croatia*	2.51	103	*Madagascar*	3.45
41	*Botswana*	2.58	104	*Bangladesh*	3.47
42	*Romania*	2.58	105	*Rwanda*	3.48
43	*Malaysia*	2.65	106	*Kenya*	3.51
44	*Panama*	2.68	107	*Nepal*	3.54
45	*Kuwait*	2.68	108	*Uganda*	3.55
46	*Bahrain*	2.71	109	*Laos*	3.60
47	*Oman*	2.72	110	*Iran*	3.61
48	*El Salvador*	2.73	111	*Republic of the Congo*	3.61
49	*Argentina*	2.73	112	*Liberia*	3.62
50	*Macedonia*	2.75	113	*Sierra Leone*	3.62
51	*Namibia*	2.77	114	*Mauritania*	3.66
52	*Albania*	2.81	115	*Cameroon*	3.68
53	*South Africa*	2.82	116	*Ethiopia*	3.68
54	*Brazil*	2.84	117	*Haiti*	3.73
55	*Ghana*	2.86	118	*Burundi*	3.73
56	*Mexico*	2.87	119	*Pakistan*	3.74
57	*Peru*	2.91	120	*Uzbekistan*	3.74
58	*Tunisia*	2.91	121	*Ivory Coast*	3.77

(Table 9.2 Continued)

(Table 9.2 Continued)

Rank	Country	Score	Rank	Country	Score
59	*Dominican Republic*	2.92	122	*Nigeria*	3.85
60	*Georgia*	2.92	123	*Central African Republic*	3.93
61	*Mongolia*	2.93	124	*Yemen*	4.00
62	*Guyana*	2.93	125	*Chad*	4.09
63	*Thailand*	2.95	126	*Democratic Republic of the Congo*	4.27

Source: Institute for Economics and Peace (IEP), Global Peace Index 2012, pp. 80–81
(http://economicsandpeace.org/wp-content/uploads/2011/09/2012-Global-Peace-Index-Report.pdf).

Key observations from the results are:

- Positive peace has slightly improved over the five-year period from 2005 to 2010 (by 1.7 percent).
- Five of the top 10 countries are Nordic.
- Twenty-eight of the top 30 countries are high income countries. The two exceptions, Chile and Lithuania, are both upper-middle income nations.
- Of the top 30 countries, 70 percent are full democracies while 27 percent are flawed democracies.
- France, Slovenia, Chile, Italy, Poland, Lithuania, Cyprus, and Estonia are the flawed democracies in the top 30.
- The only one country in the top 30 with a hybrid regime is Singapore.
- Six of the bottom 10 countries are Sub-Saharan African nations. The other four are Yemen (MENA), Uzbekistan (Russia and Eurasia), Pakistan (South Asia), and Haiti (Central America and Caribbean).
- North America and Europe rank highest on the PPI.
- South Asia and Sub-Saharan Africa rank lowest on the PPI.
- Six pillars of peace improved: *equitable distribution of resources, levels of human capital, free flow of information, levels of corruption, acceptance of the rights of others,* and *well-functioning governments.*
- The other two pillars, sound business environment and good relations with neighbors, recorded little notable change.
- Unlike the GPI, scores in the PPI are slow moving with most countries' 2010 score remaining within five percent of the 2005 score.

- The top 10 countries in the PPI perform largely better than the world average on *levels of corruption and well-functioning government.*
- The bottom 10 nations lag most on the *equitable distribution of resources.*

The importance of this analysis is that it enables conceptualizing a nation's multidimensional institutional capacity and resilience to deal with external shocks and avoid conflict. Perhaps unsurprisingly, the nations at the top of the PPI tend to be high on the GPI, in the high income category, and full democracies as defined by the Economist Intelligence Unit (EIU) Democracy Index. On an average, North America and Western Europe are the most positively peaceful regions, with Sub-Saharan Africa clearly well behind on positive peace. Interestingly, the average positive peace score is very similar for Central and Eastern Europe, the Asia Pacific, Latin America, and the Middle East and North Africa. This suggests that these diverse regions on an average face similar challenges in terms building resilience and institutional capacity.

The lower ranked nations in the PPI tend to be lower income nations with hybrid or authoritarian regimes. Despite the fact that hybrid regimes are on an average slightly less peaceful than authoritarian regimes on the GPI, they tend to have the same average PPI score. Evidently, the countries facing governance or economic constraints will have ongoing challenges in boosting their levels of positive peace. Additionally, with the available trend data showing purported declines in intergroup cohesion, slight increases in corruption, and declines in press freedom, there may be future challenges to boosting positive peace.

India ranks lowly in both the PPI and the GPI despite being the largest democratic nation on Earth. In terms of the GPI, India performs poorly in the following indicators: perceptions of criminality in society; political terror scale; terrorist acts; and number of external and internal conflicts fought. Furthermore, its formal institutions score poorly on corruption.

For humanity to grow and prosper in a world that is facing finite resource constraints, global threats, and the potential of economic devastation through warfare there needs to be a new paradigm for managing international affairs. Much of the interaction of nation states is based on competition and win/loss outcomes. Although some level of competition is healthy the current inability to reach agreement on many critical issues demonstrates the failures of the current system. A focus on peace can create a paradigm shift simply because the attitudes, institutions, and structures that create peace also create by-products. By-products such as resilience, economic prosperity, and international cooperation are at the heart of a viable future. Therefore, peace is a prerequisite for the survival of society as we know it in the twenty-first century.

THE ROLE OF BUSINESS IN PEACE

The great Scottish economist Adam Smith once said that there are some activities which are for the benefit of all members of society but are too expensive for any individual or group of individuals to afford. These activities became known as public goods and encompass services such as railway infrastructures, roads, and social security.

Peace is the preeminent "public good," its value is undeniable and is beyond the scope of any group of individuals to afford. Therefore, our governments are empowered with the sole control over activities dealing with violence, examples being policing and defense. This then raises a fundamental question regarding the role of business in creating peace.

Certainly the principle of *do no harm* is an excellent starting point. A business which sees itself as ethical would certainly not be involved in creating war for profit nor would it be investing in industries that create violence for a purely monetary motive. This brings into sharp focus industries such as the defense or prison industries. However, in the case of the defense industry there is a strong case for justifiable defense expenditure. We do not live in a peaceful world and many nations maintain their peace through appropriate levels of defense, additionally humanitarian interventions undertaken by defense forces have saved countless lives.

Therefore, the detail of the business opportunity must be known before making an ethical judgment. There are certain industries that thrive in peace and there are certain industries that thrive in war but which one has the higher moral ground is dependent on circumstance. Most businesses do, however, thrive in peace.

If business thrives in peace then there is a self-interest in improving peace but how does business quantify this self-interest and what actions can it take to promote peace?

Research carried out by the IEP clearly demonstrates that the biggest economic benefits for business relating to peace arise from small decreases in violence in their major markets; notably the US and Europe. In fact the cost of containing violence in the US in 2010 was calculated by IEP to be approximately 15 percent of Gross Domestic Product (GDP). This is the equivalent of $15,004 per annum for each taxpayer. For the purposes of this study violence containment encompasses all expenditures related to violence, including but not limited to medical expenses, incarceration, police, the military, insurance, homeland security, the private security industry, cyber security, CCTV cameras, etc. This grouping of industry is termed the Violence Containment Industry and is the largest industry in the US. Although likely not to be as high as the US, it is safe to assume that most developed countries spend a substantial percentage of their GDP on the containment of violence.

While there are some flow-on benefits from the violence containment industry; the majority of expenditure is "sunken money." Consider, for example, the cost of building a jail compared to the same amount of money being spent on a rapid transit system. The flow-on effects of the latter are far superior. Therefore, the 85 percent of the US economy that is not engaged in containing violence has a considerable benefit from shifts in expenditure away from containing violence, providing that it does not increase the levels of violence within society.

Some societies are more peaceful than others and these societies share a common set of attitudes, institutions, and structures which create and sustain their levels of peacefulness. It is this "set of attitudes, institutions, and structures" that embody the public good known as *Peace*. The creation of these attitudes, institutions, and structures is beyond the capability of any individual, organization, or company; however business can play a pivotal role in helping to create the societal conditions for improvements in peace through its influence on government and through its marketing skills. For business this is simply *selfish wisdom*, but how well does business understand this simple self-interest?

Although peace is one of our most cherished ideals, how much do we really know about peace, its economic benefits, and its impact on business? The truth is not much. In fact the national accounts for all nations do not account for their Violence Containment spending, which as we found to be the case in the US, is spread through many different sets of accounts and is difficult to find. The good news is that this issue is now starting to get attention. Future research will enable a better understanding of the relationship between peace and consumer demand, violence and its impact on company cost structures. As well as precisely what role improvements in peace will have on overall economic development. It is hard to argue that violence in a shopping mall does not affect the number of customers that attend the shopping center, nor that a company's cost structures are not related to the violence in the environment in which they operate. Or that government expenditure on containing violence, if directed to other areas of the economy, would not be more beneficial for business.

Therefore, it would be in any ethical businesses' self-interest to support the study of peace economics, for lobby governments through their industry associations to improve the levels of peace in the markets in which they operate. And to have at the forefront of their Corporate Social Responsibility (CSR) agendas a policy of *do no harm*.

CALCULATING THE COST OF VIOLENCE TO COUNTRIES AND THE GLOBAL ECONOMY

Calculating the cost of violence to the global economy is notoriously difficult. In the past, IEP has adopted a methodology developed by Tepper-Marlin and Brauer. This methodology reviewed existing literature on the cost of violence, conflict, and war and then used multiplying factors to estimate the additional economic flow-on effects if these costs were not sustained. It demonstrated that the impact of violence on the global economy in 2011 was estimated to be US$9 trillion.

To complement this approach IEP has adopted a new and novel method of calculating the cost of violence to the global economy through placing an economic value on 12 different dimensions of conflict, violence, or protection against violence. This process also facilitates a bottom-up approach whereby the cost of violence can be estimated for each country. To do this, pro-rata rates referred to as "scaling" were used, and are based on a country's per capita income. In both the US and the UK detailed estimates have been made on the cost of various types of violence and crime. Given the robustness of these studies they were used to form the baseline of costs associated with different types of violence. These costs were then adjusted depending on the per capita income of a country so that the human capital costs would be appropriate for the society. A simple example of this is the cost of a homicide. The total costs of homicide were determined by multiplying the cost per homicide, as mentioned above, by the number of homicides which occurred in 2012 for each country. For countries where cost estimates per homicide did not exist, available estimates were used from the US and "scaled" according to their GDP per capita relative to the US per capita income.

Using the above methodology the total cost of violence to the world economy in 2012 was estimated to be US$9.5 trillion or over 11 percent of the world's Gross World Product per year when calculated on a purchasing power parity (PPP) basis (see Table 9.3).

Table 9.3

The Worldwide Costs of Violence

Violence Type	Total Cost (Billions US$)	Percent of Total
Internal security	650	13.7
Homicides	715	15.1
Incarceration	190	4.0
Terrorism	5	0.1
Internal conflict	40	0.9
Military expenditure	2,425	51.2
IDPs and Refugees	3	0.1
External conflict	1	0.0
Violent crime	300	6.3
UN Peacekeeping	5	0.1
Fear	20	0.4
GDP losses from conflict	80	1.7
Private security	295	6.2
Total	*4,729*	
Total (including multiplier)	**9,458**	

Source: Institute for Economics and Peace (IEP).

If the world were to reduce its expenditure on violence by half it could end world poverty, cancel the debt of the developing world or provide enough money to solve the European debt crisis in one year.

The methodology used in the study is conservative due to the fact that the analysis has only included what could be counted. Therefore, many items that are related to violence containment spending have not been included. Future studies by IEP will aim at including as many of these items as possible. Some examples of items not included are:

- The costs related to property crimes of motor vehicle theft, arson, household burglary, and larceny/theft as well as rape/sexual assault.
- Some of the costs associated with preventative measures are also excluded such as insurance premiums or the business cost of surveillance equipment.
- Direct costs of domestic violence in terms of expenditures and costs to providers. Also, the indirect costs such as lost wages (lower productivity and absenteeism from work) and inability to perform household and other tasks.

One of the easier items to count is military expenditure. If items that aren't counted were included, then the percentage of military spending compared to the total would drop considerably. The results from this study show that by far the largest cost, at just over 50 percent of the world's expenditure, is a result of government expenditure on the military. For the purposes of comparison, the world's expenditure on the military is more than 15 times the amount of expenditure on aid, when measured in the form of Official Development Assistance (ODA). Homicides represent the next most significant cost at US$1.43 trillion or 15.1 percent of the world's violence containment costs. The third largest contributor was found to be internal security, representing 13.7 percent on the global costs of violence containment or US$1.3 trillion (see Figure 9.1).

Although it is a utopian vision to expect a world free of violence, the results suggest that even a 30 percent reduction in violence would have a substantial impact on global GDP, thereby allowing for resources to be diverted back to more productive uses such as investments

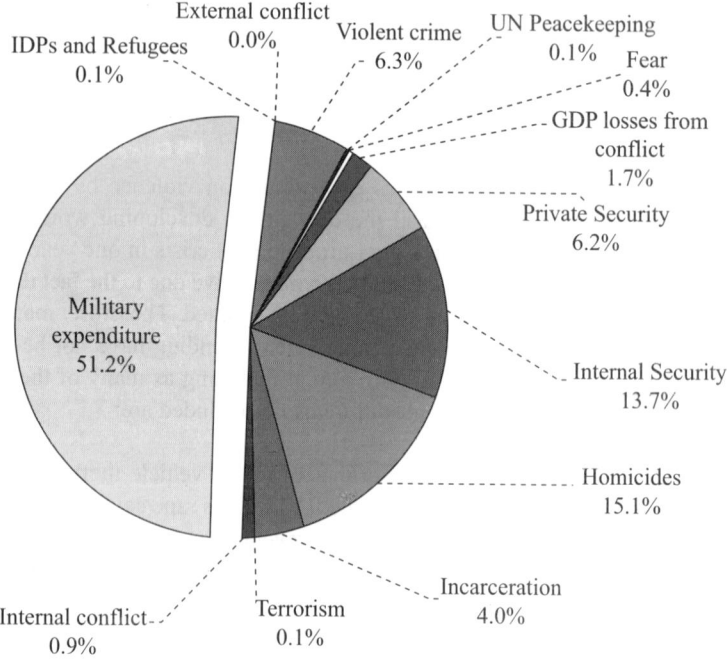

Figure 9.1

Cost of Violence by Category

Source: Institute for Economics and Peace (IEP).

in infrastructure, education, or health care. This goal may seem aspirational but given the steep drops in violent crime in many Western countries in recent years and the reductions in military spending in Africa and Latin America, it is achievable with the appropriate level of international goodwill and policies.

The three countries to have the largest percentage of their GDP spent on violence containment are North Korea, Syria, and Liberia (see Table 9.4). For North Korea this is chiefly a consequence of their high levels of military expenditure, accounting for over 70 percent of their costs of violence. Homicide costs and internal security were also significant, at approximately 10 percent of the country's violence costs. For Syria, it was found that over 50 percent of violence costs are related to deaths from internal conflict, this was followed by military expenditure and internal security which account for 16 percent and 14 percent, respectively.

The countries with the biggest violence burden in raw numbers are the US, China, and Russia; together these three countries account for almost half of the world's violence costs. In all three cases the majority of costs are related to expenditure on the military. In particular, in the US, military expenditure constitutes approximately 70 percent of violence cost, followed by homicide and incarceration expenditure which is 8 percent. Similarly, for China the military was found to be the major contributor of violence-related expenditure, however, in China's case this is followed by expenditures on internal security and private security. For Russia, the biggest component of violence costs after military

Table 9.4

Top 10 Countries by Violence Costs as a Proportion of GDP

Top 10 (as a proportion of GDP)	%
North Korea	27
Syria	24
Liberia	23
Afghanistan	21
Libya	20
Somalia	18
Zimbabwe	18
Honduras	17
South Sudan	17
Iraq	15

Source: Institute for Economics and Peace (IEP).

Table 9.5
The Individual Costs of Violence (US$ PPP)

Top 10	Cost of Violence Per Person
United States	$5,483
Oman	$3,610
Qatar	$3,576
Kuwait	$3,277
Israel	$3,242
Singapore	$3,177
Libya	$3,176
Bahrain	$2,747
Trinidad and Tobago	$2,535
Saudi Arabia	$2,359

Source: Institute for Economics and Peace (IEP).

expenditure is expenses relating to internal security and homicides, each accounting for 22 percent.

The potential for reductions in violence containment to materially contribute to the welfare of society has been examined below where the per capita expenditure by per capita expenditure has been calculated for the 10 countries with the highest per capita expenditure.

On this basis, the US was found to have the highest cost of violence per person, followed by Oman and Qatar. This is illustrated in Table 9.5. As previously explained, the majority of these costs were found to be attributed to military expenditure and the costs of maintaining internal security forces.

Given that many of the items used to calculate the cost of violence for an economy are also used as measures to calculate the GPI, it would be expected that a close relationship would exist between changes in peacefulness and changes in the percentage of GDP spent on dealing with or containing violence.

In summary, through highlighting the costs associated with violence containment, businesses have a better way of understanding the lost potential from violence of the markets within which they operate. Similarly, through monitoring changes in these costs structures and combining them with an understanding of how the savings are redirected back into the economy will help better inform business investment decisions. Small reductions in violence in the world's major markets are significant for most global companies.

10

The Emotional Psychology of Religious Diversity

John A. Teske

The universe is made of stories, not atoms.[1]

As a foreigner to Indian culture, and to the Dharma traditions born there, I was honored and humbled to be part of the celebration of the 150th birth anniversary of Swami Vivekananda. This "lion among men" helped us move toward understanding that we must accept, not merely tolerate, the multiple expressions of this potent force that molds the destinies of us all, the manifestation called religion. He helped us to understand that there can be no unity which suppresses the diversity of these traditions. His vision helps to encourage both the presence and the continuation of diverse religious traditions, despite their differences in metaphysical views, mythologies, and rituals, and that, if nurtured by all of us, these can grow into huge blossoming trees that can keep multiplying, not destroying anyone's individuality but showing a point of union with others. What I hope to sketch here is a view of the emotional psychology of religious diversity which both draws attention to the universalities of human emotional life, but respects the human variety of their developed expression, the envelopes within which we function as members of diverse traditions, both shaped by them and underwriting our preferences in doctrine, belief, and practice. Perhaps we can come to understand that each tradition has emphases by which we may all be enriched, even where those emphases produce different patterns of expression in the religious lives of human beings.

---

[1] Muriel Rukeyser.

EMOTIONAL DEVELOPMENT AND
THE DRAMATICS OF NARRATIVE

Much of human uniqueness is produced by an *extended childhood* (documented extensively by Konner).[2] This means that our emotional physiology requires several decades to be shaped and channeled by the close and interdependent relationships we have with others. Much of our religious belief and practice is well established in our childhood years, much of it in pre-linguistic and mimetic patterns of interaction,[3] but certainly well before affirmations of belief, or other "coming of age" rituals in many traditions. What is likely to be solidly in place by this age are a number of emotional scripts, resulting from extensive early experience and conditioning, which are below the level of awareness, difficult to counter-condition, and likely to underwrite our belief preferences and resonances with divergent traditions.

A better understanding of such emotional patterns, their sources, and their role in our engagement with different religions might help uncover some of their commonalities, as well as unpack some of their tensions. The present thesis is that regardless of which ideology, metaphysical system, or religious doctrine to which one gives, or withholds, one's assent, one's deeper orientation to, and embodiment within the world is shaped by a biologically basic neural affect system which is the *sine qua non* for the construction of meaning, relationship, morality, and purpose. These neural components undergird the dramatic and compelling emotions from which come our divergent religious experience.

The shaping of narrative content over the course of development is central to understanding our emotional engagement in narrative, our own development of a narrative self, and the embedding of human meaning and identity in broader narrative and religious traditions. Jerome Bruner, distinguishes between the "paradigmatic," synchronic understanding of logical proof, empirical observation, theories and causality, and the "narrative," diachronic understanding of the "vicissitude of human intention" organized in time, of human actors striving to do things over time, which requires believable

---

[2] Melvin Konner, *The Evolution of Childhood: Relationships, Emotion, Mind* (Cambridge, MA: Harvard University Press, 2010).

[3] Merlin Donald, *A Mind So Rare: The Evolution of Human Consciousness* (New York: Norton, 2002).

accounts (by virtue of their fit to available traditions of understanding) about motivational acts and meaningful ends.[4] Theories of cognitive development, like that of Piaget, have focused largely on the paradigmatic understanding of scientific reasoning, which emerges in early adolescence. Storytelling is learned earlier, and even children are aware that stories are about people-like characters trying to do things over time, that they have a beginning, a middle, and a "how it's going to turn out," and that what makes it a story is narrative tension, a protagonist who could be defeated, or a conflict needing resolution, including the stories of our gods, and of human redemption or enlightenment.

This narrative tension is what I believe to be central to a narrative self, including our religious progression. Phenomena such as infantile amnesia (the difficulty of accessing pre-linguistic memory), the difficulty of remembering dreams that are not put into storied form, and the ease with which students remember a good illustrative story, suggest that we encode events into a story form *in order to remember them.* Indeed, given the evidence of the role of long-term potentiation in the hippocampus (an important part of our mammalian emotional system), the reactivation of such memories during sleep,[5] the relationship of arousal to memory,[6] and the common experiences of rehearsals and retellings of stories over time,[7] it may well be that there are crucial dependencies of human episodic memory upon narrative form. The difficulty of remembering dreams, unattended disjoint events, and even traumatic ones, may be in their absence of narrative structure. This is particularly due to the arousal-producing qualities of narrative tension, conflict, and resolution, of which the religious stories by which we are acculturated to a particular tradition are full. We all share traditions of acculturation, and the emotional patterns out of which stories are built, even if the emotional particulars of those patterns, and the contents of the stories may vary widely.

[4] Jerome Bruner, *Acts of Meaning* (Cambridge, MA: Harvard University Press, 1990).

[5] N. McNaugton et al. 1994. "Reactivation of Hippocampal Ensemble Memories During Sleep." *Science* (July 19): 676–679.

[6] Yadin Dudai, *The Neurobiology of Memory: Concepts, Findings, Trends* (NY: Oxford University Press, 1989).

[7] Elizabeth Loftus, *Eyewitness Testimony* (Cambridge, MA: Harvard University Press, 1979).

WHAT WE SHARE

Out of what do we build the emotional sequences which are needed to produce dramatic narratives, religious and otherwise? A neural affect system is shaped into emotional patterns by the social scripts from our lengthy period of developmental dependency, including second-order emotions, the development of independence, autonomy, and relations of intimacy and power. There are certain basic emotions which are universal across traditions, including surprise, happiness, anger, fear, disgust, and sadness, which are also biologically adaptive. Other emotions sometimes added to the basic six include interest, pride, shame, embarrassment, contempt, relief, hope, frustration, love, awe, boredom, jealousy, and regret. Hindu subjects also include as "basic" heroism, amusement, wonder, and peace.

Basic emotions are the products of biological adaptations, are universal, typical of a species, and reliably developed, for which there are distinct expressions and specific physiology. There are at least six biologically primary human affects, found cross-culturally, each linked to particular facial expressions.[8] According to Tomkins, these primary affects provide the amplification, the urgency to our biological drives.[9] Each of these affects is innate, with different neural pathways, and links to specific facial responses, which provide both sensory feedback and social information. The affects move from mild to intense levels (e.g., interest-excitement, shame-humiliation), and have a particular response profile, but provide no information about the environmental source (e.g., sobbing does not tell us whether it is from hunger or loneliness). Our personal dramas are based on the scenes and scripts produced by regular patterns of emotions, and their recall, which will depend heavily upon the domestic dynamics within a particular religious tradition or cultural context. Despite the innateness of the basic affective equipment, our early emotional patterning is likely to shape our extremely plastic and immature nervous systems in ways that may be irrevocable or difficult

---

[8] Paul Ekman, "Universals and Cultural Differences in Facial Expressions of Emotion." In J. Cole (ed.), *Nebraska Symposium on Motivation 1971* (Lincoln, NE: University of Nebraska Press, 1972); Carroll Izard, *Human Emotions* (NY: Plenum Press, 1977).

[9] S. Tomkins, "Script Theory: Differential Magnification of Affects." In H. E. Howe and R. A. Dienstbier (eds), *Nebraska Symposium on Motivation*, 1979, 26: 201–236.

to change. For example, this is true in the case of early fear learning, which may be tied to moral and religious strictures of varying severity, and to anticipated punishments and rewards.[10]

Facial Expression

Darwin recorded similarities across species when threatened, angry, sad, or excited, and across human groups in the open-eyed expression of surprise, the frown of the puzzled or perplexed, the tightly closed mouth of determination, the shrugs of helplessness, and the embarrassed use of hands to cover the face that appears even in the blind.[11] Eibl-Eibesfeldt photographed expressions found across cultures, adding the raised-eyebrow greeting and the turned and raised shoulder and lowering head of coyness.[12] Research beginning with Ekman and Izard in the 1960s has extensively documented high levels of cross-cultural agreement in identifying standard faces showing the six basic emotions, and matching them with the appropriate emotion words.[13] Regardless of our religious traditions, we understand each other's feelings from our faces.

Emotion-specific Physiology

Ekman, Levenson, and Friesen measured baseline-to-trial changes in heart-rate, finger temperature, skin conductance, and muscle tension.[14] Anger and fear showed the biggest heart-rate change, followed closely by sadness; happiness and surprise both showed small increases, disgust a slight *decrease*. Anger showed large finger temperature changes, with happiness a distant second, and sadness a small but positive change. Surprise, fear, and disgust showed *decreases*, in that order. Controlling

[10] A. Ohman and S. Mineka, "Fears, Phobias, and Preparedness: Toward and Evolved Module of Fear and Fear Learning " *Psychological Review*, 2000, 108: 483–452.

[11] C. Darwin, *The Expression of Emotions in Animals and Men* (New York: Oxford University Press, 1998; original work was published in 1872).

[12] I. Eibl-Eibesfeldt, *Human Ethology* (New York: Aldine de Gruyter, 1989).

[13] Paul Ekman, "All Emotions Are Basic." In P. Ekman and R. J. Davidson (eds), *The Nature of Emotion: Fundamental Questions* (1994, pp. 15–19). New York: Oxford University Press.

[14] Paul Ekman, R. W. Levenson and W. V. Friesen, "Autonomic Nervous System Activity Distinguishes Among Emotions." *Science*, 1983, 221: 1208–1210.

for differences in elicitation techniques, Cacioppo and colleagues showed that: (1) arousal was lower with happiness than with the negative emotions of anger, fear, sadness, and disgust, (2) heart rate accelerates more during anger, fear, and sadness than disgust, and (3) blood pressure was higher with anger than fear, but heart rate and stroke volume were smaller with anger, and finger pulse volume and temperature were greater with anger.[15] There appears to be little physiological effect of happiness, though positive emotion may help recover from the arousal of negative emotions.[16] Levenson, Ekman, Heider, and Friesen compared two widely divergent cultures, from the US and from the Minangkabau society in Sumatra (which follows strict Islamic gender roles but is matrilineal).[17] They found no differences in the pattern of responses, save a lower magnitude of facial responses and skin conductance for the Minangkabau. This suggests shared emotional patterns across diverse religious traditions, differing only in arousal level.

EMOTIONAL DEVELOPMENT AND RELIGIOUS TRADITIONS

The basic affects emerge in a common developmental sequence, from newborn distress patterns, through the enjoyment of early attachment, the fear and sadness of separation, loss, and novelty, and finally with self-consciousness, the second-order emotions of shame and guilt. Along with pride, these second-order emotions constitute the contraction and expansion of self-boundaries (e.g., "swelling with pride"). According to Nathanson, healthy pride is the triggering of the enjoyment upon achieving an interesting or exciting goal.[18] The concomitant

---

[15] J. T. Cacioppo, G. G. Berntson, J. T. Larsen, K. M. Pohlmann, and T. A. Ito, "The Psychophysiology of Emotion." In M. Lewis and J. M. Haviland-Jones (eds). *Handbook of Emotions* (2nd ed.) (2000, pp. 173–191). New York: Guilford.

[16] B. L. Frederickson and R. W. Levenson, "Positive Emotions Speed Recovery from the Cardiovascular Sequelae of Negative Emotions." *Cognition and Emotion*, 1998, 12: 191–220.

[17] R. W. Levenson, P. Ekman, P. Heider, and W. V. Friesen, "Emotion and Autonomic Nervous System Activity in the Minangkabau of West Sumatra." *Journal of Personality and Social Psychology*, 1992, 62: 972–988.

[18] Donald Nathanson, *Shame and Pride: Affect, Sex, and the Birth of Self* (New York: Norton, 1992).

experiences of competence or efficacy become integrated into personal identity. We are built such that these experiences are infectious when shared socially, a process that can be encouraged or discouraged during socialization. Hence, diverse religious traditions may vary in the degree to which competence or efficacy may be integrated with identity. Pride is affiliative, it makes us public. Shame, on the other hand, attenuates enjoyment, when a pattern-mismatch is detected during interest or enjoyment, and it includes withdrawal, gaze-avoidance, blushing, and incapacities for speech. Shame is alienating. Mutually positive affect powers sociality. Shame is the modulator; it is what draws boundaries between us, and between different religious traditions. Failure is embarrassing, and the memories and associated affects of these experiences are what we want to hide. Shame separates us, it isolates us and makes us private, but it is what gives us an interior. Shame molds character, from the shameless, to the cautious, to the paranoid. Diverse religious traditions will mold character differently; though all may encourage the observation of particular boundaries, what the boundaries are, and the consequences of violating them, will vary. Where socialization emphasizes experiences of incompetence and failure, identities are based more on shame than pride.

These emotional dynamics are, of course, central to the power of our religious stories, our rituals, and our experiences. Indeed, if these dynamics are so deeply rooted, they are likely to shape and drive our religious yearnings. How great a difference between religious communities in which shame and judgment seem to dominate and ones in which, regardless of what one may think about the doctrines in which the practices are putatively grounded, one can feel "the spirit move," and feel the power of the positive emotions. Social shame produces an abject isolation mitigated only by a community of love. These are the poles of the social matrix of adult life, from the sharing of communion to exile, excommunication, or disgrace (which probably adds disgust, repulsion, and stronger forms of rejection). Under diverse religious systems, one is never alone, but one can be with God quite differently, and one's emotions can be shaped accordingly.

Religions shape human emotions in ways that reflect both similarities and diversities in the deeper values and preferences they express. Particular religious traditions favor distinctive patterns of emotional dynamics, and it is the dynamics of emotional life that forge our human identity. Emotion is, therefore, central to understanding religious traditions and providing a model of the branching tree of their functions.

Douglas Davies provides an in-depth study which shows how different traditions emphasize preferences for particular patterns of emotion, both engendering and shaping them at both individual and community levels.[19] For example, rituals may enhance social values through the emotional engagement which they provide, both selecting and intensifying the repertoire of emotions. Our experience and understanding of love, mercy, humility, and even betrayal are shaped by a "personal religious career." Hope, despair, and suffering provide somatic experience to moral categories. Davies asks us to consider religious iconography as paradigmatic, and I can reflect upon religious images in my own home, from a sculpture of the Buddha on a shelf, to a Crucifix on the wall. Such images are always, whether explicitly or not, embedded in some kind of narrative structure, or the myths by which we make sense of the world: the enlightenment of the Buddha, the sayings of Confucius, the sacrifice of Christ, the words of Muhammad. We all share the components by which such dynamics are shaped, but may differ on what specific components are emphasized, and how they are combined.

For example, from my own Christian tradition: Prior to his arrest and crucifixion, Christ prays all night in the garden of Gethsemane, asking God to "take this cup from me" as his disciples sleep. He is deathly afraid of what he knows must come, but he knows it must, what sacrifice is needed and why, and he gives himself over to God's will, despite the cross he must bear. For me this is an important dynamic, knowing that one must do what is right regardless of the consequences, and trusting in a deeper reality into which one pours oneself. I have a Hodgell woodcut of this image of Christ as I descend from my bedroom every morning; it was behind my father's study door which he would close to work on his tearful anti-war sermons. I think of this image sometimes before I take on some challenging or threatening task, when I know why I was selected to do it, and that I had willingly committed myself to it. It captures the fear and anxiety that *passion for what is right* must sometimes overcome; we sometimes have no choice, and we surrender to what is greater than us.

There are equivalent but different emotional dynamics in the Dharma traditions, which reflect a value of Peace, of *namaste*, over the Passion of much of the Christian (Abrahamic) traditions, but which also include

---

[19] Davies Douglas, *Emotion, Identity, and Religion: Hope, Reciprocity, and Otherness* (New York: Oxford University Press, 2011).

willingness to sacrifice things one values for greater realities than one can even fully know. From my Jain scholar colleague and friend Jeff Long (personal communication), a great example sprang to mind from the Buddhist tradition:

> In the *Buddhacharita*, there is the scene in which Prince Siddhartha, having resolved to renounce the world and find the path to freedom from suffering for all beings, looks back upon his sleeping wife and newborn son. Parting from them is devastating to him, but he must do so in order to find the path to freedom from suffering, not only for himself, but for them as well. Like Rama, he calmly accepts his duty and goes into voluntary exile to seek the path to nirvana. One of my favorite paintings is by Abanindranath Tagore (brother of Rabindranath). One cannot tell just from looking at the painting, but the Buddha is here departing for his great renunciation and looking back one last time at his sleeping wife, Princess Yashodhara, and his newborn son, Rahula. And Jeffery D. Long overcomes the loss of his father and the limitations of small-town Missouri to talk about dharma from Elizabethtown to New Delhi. The Hindu deities are heavenly kings and queens who reach down to lend a helping hand to us struggling mortals. This is very different from the "suffering servant" or the righteously angry prophet of justice. This is why I found the Dharma traditions more empowering than Christianity. The emphasis is on recalling a forgotten divinity, rather than on being crushed and wounded and in need of redemption. *Both, of course, are true; but they speak to different needs.*

HOW WE DIFFER

Biological universals can have diverse expression. How we appraise situations and express emotion may be very similar; events conducive to our goals make us happy; unpleasant, external, or unfair intrusions upon them make us angry. Nevertheless, given different norms and experiences, we may still *interpret* situations differently, e.g., a barking dog as dangerous, badly trained, or friendly, producing different responses: fear, anger, or a smile. Traditions encourage some interpretations, discourage others, and set different *display rules*.

Differences in the Language for Emotion

Some basic emotion *words* are absent in some cultures. English has 2,000 emotion words, Taiwanese 750, and Chewong (Malaysia) has seven.[20] There are also emotion words English doesn't have, such as the German *schadenfreude,* the enjoyment of another's suffering, or, alternately, the word *mudita,* in Pali and Sanskrit, which is vicarious joy in other people's well-being. These are clearly differences which are reflected in patterns of religious practice. The Japanese have *amae*: pleasurable feeling of passive dependency without an obligation to reciprocate. Doi calls this the foundation of Japanese social structure.[21] There is a 2nd Century CE Indian treatise on emotion, the *Natyashastra,* which describes emotions corresponding to English anger, fear, sadness, and disgust, but not to happiness or surprise, though it does include love, amusement, enthusiasm, and wonder.[22] The language differences allow us to make sense of and communicate about experience. Emotions more important in a culture are often *hypercognized*, with much more elaborate concepts and distinctions[23]: there are 46 words for anger in Tahitian, none for our "sadness." Emotions described by *amae* or *mudita* are *hypocognized* in English, as well as in religious traditions which diverge on the importance of dependency, or in the sharing of joy.

Differences in Intensity

Intensities of expression are strong in the US, but other cultures are more subtle, differences which correlate with physiological intensity. Blood pressure is higher with African samples, followed by European, and then by Asian. Americans report feeling emotions longer and more intensely than Japanese,[24] Japanese being about three times more likely to report

[20] R. A. Shweder and J. Haidt, "The Cultural Psychology of the Emotions: Ancient and New." In M. Lewis and J. M. Haviland-Jones (eds), *Handbook of Emotions* (2000, Second edition, pp. 397–414). New York: Guilford.

[21] T. Doi, *The Anatomy of Dependence* (J. Beste, trans; Tokyo: Kodansha International, 1973).

[22] R. A. Shweder and J. Haidt, "The Cultural Psychology of the Emotions: Ancient and New." In M. Lewis and J. M. Haviland-Jones (eds), *Handbook of Emotions* (2000, Second edition, pp. 397–414). New York: Guilford.

[23] R. Levy, *The Tahitians* (Chicago: University of Chicago Press, 1973).

[24] D. Matsumoto, T. Kudoh, K. Scherer, and H. Wallbott, "Antecedents of and Reactions to Emotions in the United States and Japan." *Journal of Cross-Cultural Psychology*, 1998, 19: 267–286.

they'd *not* been feeling an emotion.[25] It is harder for interdependent groups to function if anger is expressed, especially by those of lower status, and religious traditions can differ in their degree of interdependence. European-Canadians were more likely to openly express anger; Chinese-Canadians were more likely to reappraise or distract than express anger.

Display Rule Differences

There are rules about where and when (and to whom) we can express freely and when to show control. To whom can you show anger, do you try not to laugh at stupidity, or politely laugh at bad joke, and can you show more sorrow than you feel? Matsumoto and Ekman found that Japanese rated posed negative emotion and happiness as less intense; for photographs of *weak expressions* Japanese rated *stronger* emotion.[26] Japanese display rules are to try to inhibit expression, so a weak expression is seen as emotion someone is inhibiting. Americans trust stronger displays as authentic, Japanese distrust them, which is consistent with an emphasis on passion in the Abrahamic traditions. In some Arab populations, it is dishonorable not to show great anger at an insult.[27] Display rules in the US include men not crying in public. Public laughter is acceptable but restrained in Spain. Ekman and Freisen found that Americans showed the same disgust face whether alone or with high-status person, Japanese suppressed it in the presence of the latter.[28]

Differences in Appraisals of Unfairness and Immorality

There are also distinct cultural variations in the tie between negative emotions and appraisals of unfairness and immorality. Violations of different moral norms may be responded to with anger, contempt, or even moral disgust. In Sherer's study of emotions in other cultures (in 37

[25] B. Mesquita and M. Karasawa, "Different Emotional Lives." *Cognition and Emotion*, 2002, 16: 127–141.

[26] D. Matsumoto and P. Ekman, "American-Japanese Cultural Differences in Intensity Ratings of Facial Expressions." *Motivation and Emotion*, 1989, 13: 143–157.

[27] L. Abu-Lughod, *Veiled Sentiments* (Berkeley: University of California Press, 1986).

[28] P. Ekman and W. V. Friesen, *Unmasking the Face: A Guide to Recognizing Emotions from Facial Cues* (New York: Prentice-Hall, 1975).

countries, across five continents), participants were asked to remember experiences of joy, anger, fear, sadness, disgust, shame, and guilt, describe the experience, and then appraise it on dimensions of: Expectedness, Unpleasantness, Goal Obstruction, Unfairness, External Causation, Coping Ability, Immorality, and Self-Consistency. Ratings differed only for "unfairness" and "immorality."[29] Situations eliciting negative emotions Africans found to be the *most* immoral, Latin Americans the *least*. On all other dimensions, the appraisals were nearly identical. The actual events remembered and described might be different, but the appraisals mostly agreed, except for *moral appraisals*. What this means is that the relationship between moral judgment and emotion is likely to show variation across different traditions, religious diversity encouraging some rein on passion.

EMOTIONAL DIFFERENCES IN MORAL JUDGMENTS

The dimensions of moral differences between traditions are likely to be one of the important areas requiring our attention if practitioners of different religions are to understand each other. Jonathan Haidt, well known for his research on cultural differences in moral judgment points out, in his book *The Righteous Mind: Why Good People Are Divided by Politics and Religion*, that there are actually *five* innate psychological systems which ground diverse moralities.[30] Along with the liberal systems of attention to (1) harm/care and (2) fairness/reciprocity, there are also (3) ingroup/loyalty, in which group membership is more important than overall utility, (4) authority/respect, in which hierarchical authorities have a responsibility to establish and sustain order and stability, and (5) purity/sanctity which urges the cultivation of a higher, spiritual nature over carnal pleasures and petty concerns. Most culture-war battles are over the legitimacy of the latter three systems. But *none* of these moralities see society as a social contract made to benefit *individuals*, and the latter three are *moral* in how they constrain individuals from pleasure-seeking individualism by binding them into larger groups. Perhaps what our religions are about is not a contest between belief

---

[29] K. R. Scherer, "The Role of Culture in Emotion-Antecedent Appraisal." *Journal of Personality and Social Psychology*, 1997, 73: 902–922.

[30] Jonathan Haidt, *The Righteous Mind: Why Good People Are Divided by Politics and Religion* (Vintage, 2010).

systems, but differing sets of unifying social practices. People need to be part of something larger than themselves in order to flourish, but this may make the struggle between "for" and "against," between *us* and *them*, to be the mind's worst disease, and righteousness the fuel of conflict. Its resolution may be in seeing, within all our religious diversity, a planetary, human *us* that is shared, and enriched rather than enfeebled by our diversity.

Moral Disgust and Purity/Sanctity

Disgust is one of the basic emotions, and as we have seen, the tie between negative emotions and morality varies across traditions. Evolutionarily, disgust is about protecting ourselves from consuming unhealthy or dangerous foods, the revulsion we feel at taking offensive objects into our mouths.[31] But merely *disliked* tastes are not *disgusting*; animal products, human bodily fluids and wastes, as well as signs of death and decay, often are. Disgust can also produce a rejection of even *touching* the offensive material. Our *core disgust* at the prospect of eating feces or rotten meat protects health, but *disgust* is also extended to more abstract moral judgments.[32] It is associated with a prototypical facial expression,[33] associated with specific appraisals,[34] and may evoke physical feelings of nausea. It is also a response that is hard to "reframe," to "think our way out of it," hence it is experienced as irrevocable. It also isn't about the sensory quality itself. We can respond quite differently to the same smell when described as "vomit" versus "strong cheese."[35] Sometimes it is the *thought* of the object, not any sensory or objective realities at all: Would you put rubber vomit in your mouth? Drink from

[31] P. Rozin and A. Fallon, "A Perspective on Disgust." *Psychological Review*, 1987, 94: 23–41.

[32] J. Haidt, P. Rozin, C. R. McCauley, and S. Imada, "Body, Psyche, and Culture: The Relationship between Disgust and Morality." *Psychology and Developing Societies*, 1997, 9: 107–131.

[33] P. Ekman, W. V. Friesen, M. O'Sullivan, A. Chan, I. Diacoyanni-Tarzlatzis, and K. Heider, "Universals and Cultural Differences in the Judgments of Facial Expressions of Emotion." *Journal of Personality and Social Psychology*, 1987, 51: 712–717.

[34] K. R. Scherer, "The Role of Culture in Emotion-Antecedent Appraisal." *Journal of Personality and Social Psychology*, 1997, 73: 902–922.

[35] P. Rozin and A. Fallon, "A Perspective on Disgust." *Psychological Review*, 1987, 94: 23–41.

a brand new toilet bowl? Drink your own spit? Sometimes an animal or animal part resemblance can be sufficient, as can things that remind us of our animal nature, hence we *hide or make private* urination, defecation, and sex, and find it disgusting in animals. We also extend influences of disgusting objects, e.g., the "sympathetic magic" of things being "tainted" by contact: once touched always fouled, from a fly on food, to the concept of wearing a sweater worn by Hitler or Bin Laden. We can also show aversions to things that *remind* us of disgusting objects, extending disgust to the idea or representation of an object, and effects are contagious, e.g., discussions of bodily functions at the dinner table. One of the deepest and most troubling tensions between diverse religious traditions may be about the irrevocability of what is "dirty."

Moral Disgust

Haidt et al. catalog a number of categories of disgust, which also include socio-moral violations.[36] People who feel more disgust are also likely to feel more antipathy to criminal behavior (e.g., vote guilty on a jury).[37] People also make stronger moral judgments after a disgust elicitation,[38] and weaken them after a "cleansing" manipulation.[39] Think of metaphors such as "you make me want to puke," or spitting to show moral judgment. Haidt and his colleagues have argued that the relationship between disgust and moral judgment is about violations of *moral purity*.[40] For many judgments which include the moral dimension of purity and sanctity, including bodily and sexual acts, the emotional substrate can be strongly felt as a bodily reaction of disgust, which can extend widely by similarity and contagion, and is difficult to change and counteract. These become some of the more troublesome emotional differences between different traditions, where an object or event that

[36] J. Haidt, P. Rozin, C. R. McCauley, and S. Imada, "Body, Psyche, and Culture: The Relationship between Disgust and Morality." *Psychology and Developing Societies*, 1997, 9: 107–131.

[37] A. Jones and J. Fitness, "Moral Hypervigilance: The Influence of Disgust Sensitivity on the Moral Domain." *Emotion*, 2008, 8: 613–627.

[38] S. Schnall, J. Haidt, G. L. Clore, and A. H. Jordan, "Disgust as Embodied Moral Judgment." *Psychological Bulletin*, 2008, 34: 1096–1109.

[39] Chen-Bo Zhong and K. Liljenquist, "Washing Away Your Sins: Threatened Morality and Physical Cleansing." *Science*, 2006, 313: 1451–1452.

[40] J. Haidt, P. Rozin, C. R. McCauley, and S. Imada, "Body, Psyche, and Culture: The Relationship between Disgust and Morality." *Psychology and Developing Societies*, 1997, 9: 107–131.

produces a powerful and bodily negative emotion in one group may be quite incomprehensible to another.[41]

The Self-conscious Emotions and Authority/Respect

One of the important dimensions on which cultures and traditions can vary is that of the organization of power distance, the *vertical* emphasizing hierarchy and status differences, the *horizontal* minimizing and privatizing these differences.[42] Under such variations, shame, pride, and other second-order "self-conscious" emotions play roles in the construction and maintenance of quite different self-boundaries, and motivations to self-improvement and/or saving face. Hindu Indians show greater attention to class differences than do Americans, even using titles within a family, the young showing gestures of respect to the older, and never calling people of higher status by their first names.[43] American culture is more horizontal, and authority tends to be limited to domains (e.g., a boss at work *versus* over dinner). More vertical cultures can show emotions not present in horizontal ones, like *hasham* in Bedouin, a combination of embarrassment, shame, admiration, shyness, and gratitude displayed to show respect.[44] Those of higher status *display* more anger, but less sadness or fear.[45]

Motivation: Self-esteem versus "Face"

What motivates people? What makes them pursue what they want and avoid what they don't? We all want things that improve the quality of our lives, such as material advantages, good relationships with others, and public respect, but our cultural environment can have a huge influence on how we go about doing these things. Our values are also reflected in how we manage the desire and motivation for competing

[41] A. B. Cohen, A. Malka, P. Rozin, and L. Cherfas, "Religion and Unforgivable Offenses." *Journal of Personality*, 2006, 74: 85–117.

[42] D. Matsumoto, *Unmasking Japan: Myths and Realities about the Emotions of the Japanese* (Stanford, CA: Stanford University Press, 1996).

[43] N. C. Much, "A Semiotic View of Socialization, Lifespan Development and Cultural Psychology: With Vignettes from the Moral culture of Traditional Indian Household." *Psychology and Developing Societies*, 1997, 9: 65–105.

[44] L. Abu-Lughod, *Veiled Sentiments* (Berkeley: University of California Press, 1986).

[45] D. Matsumoto, *Unmasking Japan: Myths and Realities about the Emotions of the Japanese* (Stanford, CA: Stanford University Press, 1996).

outcomes, and we may differ in needs for self-esteem, perceived control, and the acceptance of others.[46] Japanese versus European-Canadians show 55 percent versus 93 percent high self-esteem. European-Americans believe self-esteem should be cultivated, Taiwanese that it might lead to frustration; schools are also less likely to focus on self-esteem. "Face" is more important than self-esteem in much of the world, and is not well understood by Westerners.[47] It is the amount of social value given by others if you live up to standards of position. What matters is not how positively you think of yourself, but how positively others do. It is *easier to lose than to gain face*. Therefore, a *Prevention Orientation* leads to a cautious approach, making sure others do not reject you. Opportunities to avoid loss are more important than opportunities to win. This is opposed to a *Promotion Orientation:* to advance oneself, and aspire for gains, one is likely to take more risk. Gain is important, loss is not as worrisome, it is "better to have tried and failed." The focus of the prevention orientation is to overcome shortcomings; the focus of the promotion orientation is to do what you do well, and avoid what you do poorly. Japanese persist longer after failure than success, Westerners do the reverse.[48] *Face involves others' evaluations.* These differences in self-esteem versus "face" are also moral: members of one tradition may view another as selfish, disrespectful, and self-aggrandizing versus shy, unfriendly, and self-deprecating, with clear manifestations in religious diversity.

Anxiety, Empathy, and In-group/Loyalty

Individualism versus Collectivism

Markus and Kitayama, in one of the classics of cultural psychology, identify one of the best known distinctions between cultures, that of *individualism* versus *collectivism,* the dimension with the most bearing on the issue of in-group loyalty as a moral dimension.[49] Individualism

[46] S. J. Heine, *Cultural Psychology* (second edition) (New York: W. W. Norton, 2012).

[47] D. Y. F. Ho, "On the Concept of Face." *American Journal of Sociology*, 1976, 81: 867–884.

[48] S. J. Heine, *Cultural Psychology* (second edition) (New York: W. W. Norton, 2012).

[49] H. R. Markus and S. Kitayama, "Culture and the Self: Implications for Cognition, Emotion, and Motivation." *Psychological Bulletin*, 1991, 98: 224–253.

focuses on (a) uniqueness, (b) personal rights, (c) being true to oneself, and (d) being *independent*. Collectivism focuses on (a) values the group over the individual, (b) involves strong group identification, (c) encourages deference, (d) emphasizes the harmony of the group, and (e) being *interdependent*. North Americans, for example, tend to talk more about how *they feel*, Asians more about how *others think they feel*.[50] Responding to the prompt "I am…" Chinese were three times more likely than Americans to list group membership. One of the clearest findings is from the simple task of interpreting a picture of one fish in front of a group of others. Americans interpret the fish in front as *leading* the others, and being *happy*; Chinese participants see the front fish as being *chased* by the others, and feeling *fear*.[51] The effect on emotional *expression* is the collectivist tendency to inhibit negative emotion to preserve the harmony of the group. The effect on emotional *experience* is that collectivist cultures facilitate and individualist ones discourage self-conscious emotions such as pride, shame, and guilt. So, the American "self" is more tied to individual accomplishments, where collectivist cultures tie it to group membership and relationships, therefore emphasizing responses to others actions. Some traditions see an assertion of individual freedom as heroic or even holy, others as selfish or even immoral.

In-group loyalties also produce out-group denigration. The gulf that divides groups begins with simple cognitive strategies that make perfect sense and appear even in minimal groups,[52] like randomly assigned discussion groups in a college classroom. Such strategies reduce information overload by (1) paying attention to and differentiating members of the in-group, and treating members of the out-group as more alike, (2) seeing the differences between groups as greater than they are, and (3) seeing members of the in-group more positively, the out-group more negatively. Such processes, in limiting attention and contact, are also likely to substantially reduce empathy, freeing us to project what we most fear in and for ourselves. Even socially splintered high-schools can

---

[50] D. Cohen and A. Gunz, "As Seen by the Other: Perspectives on the Self in the Memories and Emotional Problems of Easterners and Westerners." *Psychological Science*, 2002, 13: 55–59.

[51] Y. Hong, M. W. Morris, C. Chiu, and V. Benet-Martinez, "Multicultural Minds: A Dynamic Constructivist Approach to Culture and Cognition." *American Psychologist*, 2000, 55: 709–720.

[52] H. Tajfel, "Social Psychology of Intergroup Relations." *Annual Review of Psychology*, 1982, 33: 1–39.

produce "outsider" groups whose lives are sufficiently hellish to result in violent response, such as occurred at a Columbine, Colorado high school in the US in 1999. Interreligious conflicts, as between Muslims and Jews in the Middle East, Hindus and Muslims in India, or even between groups with hugely overlapping belief systems such as Catholic and Protestant Christians in Northern Ireland, or Shia and Sunni Muslims in Iraq, are so endemic as to suggest rather more serious problems with this particular moral dimension.

Harm/Care and Fairness/Reciprocity

I have less to say about the two moral dimensions which, Haidt acknowledges, are shared, but there are some differences in emotional emphasis which may be relevant.[53] We can uncover and understand the differences in basic emotional scripts, regardless of explicit and conscious beliefs, across diverse religions, on many dimensions. The preferences for peace versus passion might also suggest differences in strategies for promoting care, a preference for peace suggesting the importance of doing no harm, that for passion encouraging more active intervention, *compassion* meaning to suffer with, and suggesting, again, the importance of empathy. In the case of fairness, it may be important to recognize that there are different norms for fairness, from equal distribution, through principles of *equity*, which would distribute depending upon *merit*. Davies points out that *merit* is one of the most common concepts across different religions, which vary widely on the ability to obtain merit and the consequences of doing so or failing to do so.[54] In the Christian system, original sin suggests that we do not deserve salvation, but mercy trumps justice in the gift of grace. In the Dharma traditions, a cycle of reincarnation and a doctrine of *karma* suggest both perfect justice and perfect mercy.

Passion or Peace

The kinds of *positive* emotions desired may vary cross-culturally. Some positive emotions, such as excitement and elation, are related to arousal, others, such as feeling calm or peace, are not. Jeanne Tsai and colleagues

[53] J. Haidt, *The Righteous Mind: Why Good People Are Divided by Politics and Religion* (New York: Pantheon, 2010).
[54] Davies Douglas, *Emotion, Identity, and Religion: Hope, Reciprocity, and Otherness* (New York: Oxford University Press, 2011).

found that the Americans preferred high-arousal and East-Asians pre-ferred low-arousal emotions.[55] Classic Christian (Gospels of the Bible) and Buddhist (Lotus Sutra) texts, as well as contemporary self-help books from these traditions show high-arousal states encouraged more in the former than the latter; Christian sects include enthusiastic (*en-theos*) practices such as jumping, shouting, and applause, whereas Buddhist practices tend toward meditation and calming the mind; and European-Americans prefer fast-tempo and exciting music over the calmer music preferred by Chinese.[56] Latin-Americans may have an even greater preference for high-arousal positive emotions than North Americans.[57]

Linear or Dialectical Epistemology

There is a final dimension of cultural difference that is highly relevant to our project here and that is about how we know our epistemology.[58] Linear knowing, like Aristotelian logic, involves knowing what is con-stant, how things are differentiated, what is true versus false. Dialectical knowing, as in the analects of Confucius, involves knowing that every-thing changes, that everything is interrelated, and is willing to accept paradox. One of the findings about emotional life is that Americans experience fewer "mixed emotions," and experience emotions in *mutual exclusion*. East Asians more likely than Americans report positive and negative emotion at the same time.[59] Shiota et al. had Asian-American versus European-American dating couples have a number of conversa-tions targeting particular emotions.[60] The conversations were similar, but European-Americans reported *either* love or the target emotion (shame,

[55] J. Tsai, F. F. Miao, and E. Seppala, "Good Feelings in Christianity and Buddhism: Religious Differences in Ideal Affect." *Personality and Social Psychology Bulletin*, 2007, 33: 409–421.

[56] Ibid.

[57] S. J. Heine, *Cultural Psychology* (second edition) (New York: W. W. Norton, 2012).

[58] K. Peng and R. E. Nisbett, "Culture, Dialectics, and Reasoning about Contradiction." *American Psychologist*, 1999, 54 (9): 741–754.

[59] C. N. Scollon, E. Deiner, S. Oishi, and R. Biswas-Diener, "Emotions across Cultures and Methods." *Journal of Cross-Cultural Psychology*, 2004, 35: 304–326.

[60] M. N. Shiota, B. Campos, G. C. Gozanga, D. Keltner, and K. Peng, "I Love You but…: Cultural Differences in Emotional Complexity during Interaction with a Romantic Partner." *Cognition and Emotion*, 2010, 24: 786–799.

anger, contempt) while Asian-Americans were more likely to report both, and the more love expressed, the more negative emotion was also. Some traditions are more likely and willing to accept "mixed emotions" than others, and may be far more willing to accept such diversity.

It seems to me that one of the advantages of building a common pool of emotional dynamics rooted in different religious traditions is not merely to collect a set of concepts, experiences, and themes that are shared, though there are universals, but to understand the tensions and differences that are not. But it is a difference in epistemology that provides one of the best clues, and that is of how to understand these different experiences not as mutually exclusive, in opposition and contradiction to each other, but as mutually inclusive, as part of the complexity and variety of human options. In doing so, we may each be able to learn from the other about the possibilities and advantages present in traditions not our own, but which can bring out a fuller range of the human experience in which we all take part.

11

Hybridity in Meaning-making Practices
Planetary Values for a Multiperspectival Context

Whitney A. Bauman

The apple tree should not be judged by the standard of the oak, nor the oak by that of the apple...unity in variety is the plan of Creation.[1]

To put it briefly, the central question which remains before us is: how must a multicultural global society deal with the question of religious pluralism?[2]

The world that we find ourselves in at the beginning of the twenty-first century is one marked by globalization, hybrid identity formation, and rapid change. Few people adhere to what we might call a single religious tradition in the contemporary globalized/globalizing world: Christians practice Yoga; people of many religious faiths take components of modern cosmology and other sciences to be part of their "worldviews"; and prophetic voices such as those of Martin Luther King, Jr., Gandhi, and the Dalai Lama all have influences upon people well beyond their geographic and historical locations. In other words, we are always-already hybrid meaning-making creatures. From such a starting point, how do we begin to understand "interreligious" or "multireligious" dialogue? How do we understand the flows of information between religious and scientific beliefs and values? How do apple and oak trees inhabit one world? Or, how do we deal with a plurality of meaning-making perspectives on a single planet? In an attempt to foster some dialogue on these

---

[1] Swami Vivekenanda, *The Complete Works of Swami Vivekananda*, Volume 1 (Hollywood, CA: Vedanta Press and Bookshop, 1947), p. 38.
[2] Anindita Balslev, "On Religious Pluralism: Diversity Not Dissension," on *Here Now 4U Online Magazine*. Available at: http://www.here-now4u.de/eng/on_religious_pluralism__divers.htm, last accessed on May 16, 2013.

issues, this chapter will argue that we have to identify a few key ingredients if we are to respect the nature of peoples' lived meaning-making practices. The question then becomes not how we "come together as one," but more of how our multiperspectival and polydox realities can coexist on a single planet. For the very paradox of becoming a planetary community is that our meaning-making practices are at once contextualized and spread across the face of the planet. In other words, as the forces and technologies of globalization uncover hidden and secret foundations to thought-systems once thought to be universal, so the space-time crunch of globalization spreads meaning-making practices far beyond their contexts and reveals all meaning-making practices as hybrid. But more on this phenomenon is explained in the following paragraphs.

The key ingredients or ground rules for meaning-making, as theologian Catherine Keller and sociologist of religion Laurel Kearns remind us, are precisely not foundations or binding forms into which all religions must fit.[3] The foundational method of approaching "religion" points to a western, Jewish and Christian theological approach to other religions based upon the idea of orthodoxy.[4] Such foundational thinking is more accurately described as "singularization": "abstraction means singularization above all else, an operation that exploits the singularity of what it deals with in constructing new forms of definition."[5] Rather than this, ground rules or key ingredients ought to be thought of more as part of a recipe for analyzing meaning-making practices. Such recipes can be amended, modified, and evolved differently in different contexts, times and depending upon various and changing tastes. In this brief chapter, I begin to identify what some of the ingredients of contemporary meaning-making practices are. In order to do so, I first refer to a few of the culinary rules by which we will be constructing our recipes, *viz.* that a good recipe adheres to our evolving planetary contexts, which are marked by multiperspectivalism, agnosticism, and polydoxy. After laying out these ground rules, I turn to the various ingredients by which one might construct and identify contemporary meaning-making practices. Think of the end result, the meal, as meaning-making practices, and the

---

[3] Catherine Keller and Laurel Kearns, *EcoSpirit: Religions and Philosophies for the Earth* (New York: Fordham University Press, 2007), pp. 1–20.

[4] Talal Asad, "Genealogies of Religion," in Scott Elliott and Matthew Waggoner (eds), *Readings in the Theory of Religion: Map, Text, Body* (Sheffield, UK: Equinox, 2010), p. 42.

[5] Isabelle Stengers, *Cosmopolitics I*, translated by Robert Bononno (Minneapolis, MN: University of Minnesota Press, 2010), p. 96.

various ingredients that make up such practices as the variation in cuisine that one might find over time, place, and context.[6] Though the actual ingredients might differ, the steps of the recipe for meaning-making might be the same. Thus, I will identify at least the following steps along the way to identifying good meaning-making practices: the planetary context, the existential context, the aesthetic context, and the ethical context. In closing, I suggest that the rules and steps for making-meaning fall into three basic types of pluralistic cuisines. Emerging out of the three ground rules, three basic contexts, and three types of pluralism, is the beginnings of a meaning-making menu.

GROUND RULES FOR MAKING GOOD MEANING: MULTIPERSPECTIVALISM, AGNOSTICISM, AND POLYDOXY

Preadaptations unstateable in advance, intersections between partially open systems of multiple kinds, and novel capacities for self-organization within a system triggered by infusions from elsewhere periodically operate in and upon each other, generating turns in time out of which a new equilibrium emerges, transcending our ability to articulate it in advance.[7]

As American political philosopher William Connolly notes in the opening quote of this section, the world to a great extent is a conglomeration of multiple forces, entities, and emergent possibilities that cannot be predicted or controlled in advance of their emergence. This is not to say that every moment is radically disjointed and new as if created "out of nothing," but rather that it is impossible to predict the full consequences of one idea or action. It is impossible to predict in advance how multiple perspectives and actants coming together will emerge in a given moment to create new possibilities for the becoming of life.[8] As such, we must

---

[6] In: *Map, Text, Body*, p. 42.

[7] William Connolly, *A World of Becoming* (Durham, NC: Duke University Press, 2011), p. 20.

[8] For a discussion of actants, which are assemblages of agency that break down the divide between humans and the rest of the natural world and suggest that human beings are actants among many other actants, see, e.g., Bruno Latour, *Reassembling the Social: An Introduction to Actor-Network-Theory* (New York: Oxford University Press, 2005).

always understand the world as in a constant state of becoming. Such a state of becoming, according to non-equilibrium thermodynamics and theories of emergence, is neither becoming toward any ultimate goal (as many cultures and religious traditions have suggested) nor is this becoming cyclical in nature (as some religious traditions and cultures have suggested). Both of these options do not allow for emergent new-ness, and both do not lead to ultimate concern for the emerging bodies and processes along the way. In the linear model, everything is swept up to some sort of final fulfillment and in the circular model, all is merely recycled for the next round. Though these models are somewhat carica-tures of time, they do represent the spectrum between which many models of time have been articulated.[9] What we need, is something more like what Catherine Keller identifies as "spiraling recapitulation," or fol-lowing Deleuze and Guattari, "origami-like" time.[10] From such a per-spective, time is more like a rhizome that can shoot off into many directions,[11] which means that life can never be predicted by any thought system, rationality, scientific theory, theology, or revelation in advance. In fact, process thinker John Cobb suggests that all religious figures and movements in their inception are secularizing movements in that they break their adherents out of religious ideas that have become dogma or uncritically accepted.[12] Uncritically accepted dogma creates injustice that keeps certain people in these ossified religious structures on top, and others rejected or at the bottom. From this perspective, whatever else meaning-making is about, it is about paying close attention to the emerg-ing here and now rather than ideas that take us far away from the world and from our own becoming embodiments.[13] Meaning-making, in other words, calls us to pay radical attention to the immanent emerging con-texts of which we are a part. It calls for what Isabelle Stengers identifies

[9] See here, for example: Anindita Baslev, J. N. Mohanty (eds), *Religion and Time* (Leiden, Netherlands: Brill, 1993).

[10] Catherine Keller, *Face of the Deep: A Theology of Becoming* (New York: Routledge, 2003), pp. 121–123; 177.

[11] The metaphor of the rhizome is of course taken from Gilles Deleuze and Felix Guattari, *A Thousand Plateaus: Capitalism and Schizophrenia* (Minneapolis, MN: University of Minnesota Press, 1987), pp. 3–25.

[12] John Cobb, *Spiritual Bankruptcy: A Prophetic Call to Action* (Nashville, TN: Abingdon, 2010).

[13] Bruno Latour, "Thou Shalt Not Freeze Frame: Or How Not to Misunderstand the Science and Religion Debate," in Bruno Latour, *On the Modern Cult of the Factish Gods* (Durham, NC: Duke University Press, 2013), pp. 99–123.

as an "ecology of practice." She writes, "Ecology is, then, the science of multiplicities, disparate causalities, and unintentional creations of meaning."[14] Such an understanding of reality, calls for new rules of meaning-making that go beyond and work outside of comparative models of religious studies that deal with religious pluralism. Three such rules or key ingredients include: attention to multiperspectivalism, epistemological agnosticism, and polydoxy in hermeneutics or interpretations.

Attention to Multiperspectivalism

The study and practice of religion, as I understand it study and practice are not separate, is all about paying attention to meaning-making practices. It is much less about authority, dogma, and truth than it is about helping to co-create what one identifies as the best possible worlds, given what one knows about the world. As Swami Vivekendanda notes, "The Hindu religion does not consists in struggles and attempts to believe a certain doctrine or dogma, but in realizing—not in believing, but in being and becoming."[15] Such an understanding, given that we have multiple contexts in which we exist and multiple possibilities for the future ways in which we might become with the rest of the planetary community, depends upon some acknowledgment of interconnected multiperspectivalism. Two concepts very near the context of the traditions of India are dependent co-arising (or *paticcasamuppada*) and multiperspectivalism (or *anekantavada*). These two concepts get to the heart of what I mean by an embrace of multiperspectivalism.

In this becoming process that we call life, "I" will never know fully what it means to be any other, just as no other will ever know fully what it means to be "I." We are each a unique conglomeration of bio-cultural or natural-historical flows, assemblages of plant, animal, mineral, and technology.[16] My perspective is very much located within these flows and can never exhaust the reality of any other. Furthermore, the human perspective, even the coveted scientific perspectives of human beings, can never exhaust the reality of what it means to be a dog, a cat, a cow, or a tree, much less the fullness of the earth or cosmos. We are but located perspectives on an ever-expanding journey. As such, it becomes

---

[14] Stengers, *Cosmopolitics I*, p. 34.

[15] Swami Vivekananda, *The Complete Works of Swami Vivekananda*, Volume 1, p. 14.

[16] Cf. Deleuze and Guattari, *A Thousand Plateaus*, pp. 232–309.

hard to justify one perspective as the objective perspective (whether that perspective is based in "the sciences," in some sort of religious "revelation," or in some combination thereof). In other words, studying religion, theology, and philosophy is much more an exercise in hermeneutics than in metaphysics or ontology. It requires what Vattimo and Caputo call a "weak" understanding of god or ultimate reality. Though they speak of Christianity here, I think the following statement can be used for meaning-making practices in a globalized world: "The essence of the Christian revelation is its own fulfillment in nihilism, that is, the weakening of its strong truth into hermeneutics; the liquidating of its own and every other foundationalism."[17] This multiperspectival, evolving reality, then calls for another rule when it comes to meaning-making practices: a viable agnosticism.

A Viable, Epistemological Agnosticism[18]

The experience of meaning-making in the globalizing and climate-changing world, in which we live, calls for a good dose of negative or *apophatic* thinking. In other words, whatever else it means to be a living human, we exist in a context of time that is not linear or chronological but rather emergent. From where we stand, even with our technological extensions, we can only see so far into the past before things shade off into mystery: personally, this has to do with our own birth and lack of experience beforehand; cosmologically this has to do with the mystery of what happens seconds after and before the big bang. Furthermore, we can only see and predict so far into the future: we cannot see beyond tomorrow much less beyond our death or beyond the boundaries of our ever-expanding universe. We exist in between two mysteries and it is in this space that meaning-making emerges. Robust theisms that claim universal truth or robust atheisms that do the same both close off this emergent space of mystery and reify life into their own images.[19] Thus,

---

[17] Clayton Crockett, *Radical Political Theology: Religion and Politics After Liberalism* (New York: Columbia University Press, 2011), p. 147.

[18] I have written about this at length elsewhere. See, for example, Whitney Bauman, *Theology, Creation, and Environmental Ethics* (New York: Routledge, 2009), pp. 126–153.

[19] This is also the insight of William James and the pragmatists. See, for example, William Connolly, *Pluralism* (Durham, NC: Duke University Press, 2005), p. 71.

some form of agnosticism is the only viable way to remain existentially and creaturely true to our becoming existence.

Religions of all sorts have strands within them that acknowledge this existential reality: negative and apophatic theologies, mysticisms of all stripes, *syadvada* and *anekantavada*, and the concept of *neti-neti* are but a few examples. Furthermore, philosophies (another important tool for making-meaning) have also acknowledged this: from the Death of God Nietzsche spoke of so long ago to the deconstructive moves of Jacques Derrida. An active embrace of this unknowing is called for in contemporary meaning-making practices. From this position, "you absorb the agony of having elements of your own faith called into question by others and you fold agonistic contestation of others into the respect that you convey toward them."[20] Such unknowing begs the final ingredient essential to contemporary meaning-making practices: hermeneutical or interpretive polydoxy.

Hermeneutical Polydoxy

Polydoxy is something that is not new to any tradition, but it has been difficult to embrace in most forms of monotheism, and thus for the heirs of monotheism: Western liberalism and scientific materialism. Such closure of the world into a single truth (or orthodoxy) has never been possible, but is much less possible in an era of mass communication and transportation. In other words, though at one time it may have made some amount of sense to confuse one's meaning-making practice with the only meaning-making practice, or to assume that one's meaning-making practice was on a quest for the one truth, this no longer makes sense in a 13.7 billion-year process of cosmic expansion and in a geo-cultural context in which our localities are everyday crisscrossed by global connections. Thought systems of universality break under the pressure of such immense understandings of time and such rapid paces of information exchange and change.

From within this context, it is now much easier to see that there has never been an orthodox position on anything. Women have pointed out sexism within traditions and offered alternative readings and historical voices, racial and ethnic minorities have pointed out racism and ethnocentrism within traditions and offered alternative readings and historical voices, non-heterosexual people have pointed out the existence of homophobia and alternative sexualities in virtually every culture/society

---

[20] Connolly, *Pluralism*, p. 123.

of the world, and environmentalists have pointed out the anthropocentrism inherent within traditions and provided earth and animal-based
interpretations of doctrines, ideas, and scriptures. These polydox perspectives are beginning to show us that there has never been something
close to orthodoxy.[21] On the one hand, we can look to multicultural
exchanges along the Silk Road, or to the time of the *Convivencia* in
Southern Spain, or the era of colonization to understand how there are
no pure traditions but rather that meaning-making practices are always
created through exchange with many others. On the other hand, we can
look within what have been identified as single traditions and we can
begin to hear the multiple perspectives within those traditions at any
given time. Both of these interpretive strategies make it hard to claim
any sort of orthodoxy on any grounds other than that of brute force and
political power. In fact, the claim to orthodoxy is always and already a
political, power play. Indeed attention to the politics of meaning-making, including claims of orthodoxy, is perhaps the only way to resist
totalitarianism. As Creston Davis and Santiago Zabala suggest in a
recent article, "The only hope of a democratic politics is to form citizens
who articulate their own practical needs, freely and unencumbered by
the pressures of simplistic and lazy metaphysical systems."[22] Far from
being relativistic, the multiperspectival, agnostic, and polydox conditions for meaning-making in a globalizing world call for some version
of radical democracy that the world has not yet seen. Liberal democracy
with its foundational individualism does not do justice to the evolving,
planetary contexts that we find ourselves in. Multiperspectivalism,
agnosticism, and polydoxy highlight the deep pluralism which constitutes any given moment of our becoming realities.

THE CONTEXTS OF MAKING MEANING: PLANETARY, EXISTENTIAL, ETHICAL, AND AESTHETIC

At this point in the chapter, I have identified three key ingredients that
go into a deep, planetary version of pluralism: multiperspectivalism,

---

[21] A great volume discussing contemporary polydox interpretations of theological traditions is: Catherine Keller and Laurel Schneider, *Polydoxy: Theology
of Multiplicity and Relation* (New York: Routledge, 2010).

[22] Creston Davis and Santiago Zabala, "The Logic of Democracy" (in
Aljazeera, May 15, 2013). Available at: http://www.aljazeera.com/indepth/opin-
ion/2013/05/20135138427260651.html, last accessed May 16, 2013.

agnosticism, and polydoxy. Without these three ingredients monological thinking seeps in and we are left with old, local/parochial tendencies to impose sameness upon the entire face of the planet. What might it mean to embrace these three ingredients of planetary meaning-making practices? Though, again, it is not the task of this chapter to identify the content of meaning-making practices *per se*, I do want to identify a few contextual varieties in meaning-making now that I have identified some of the ingredients. The actual forms and variations that take place within these contexts will vary from time to time, place to place, and person to person. But, the final meaning-filled product should pay attention to at least the following four contexts: the planetary context, the existential context, the ethical context, and the aesthetic context. It is to a discussion of these contexts for meaning-making that I now turn. I should note here, again, that people will approach these contexts in different orders, and with some variation, but the important thing is that each context gets addressed lest an understanding of meaning-making practices be left undone. Further, I would argue along with many pragmatists, that the ethical and aesthetic contexts drive our understanding of the planetary and existential contexts; they are the lures toward which we move and co-create the latter, rather than *vice versa*. It is not that we create our own realities, but that reality itself, as James notes, is pluriform, or deeply pluralistic.[23]

The Planetary Context: Or our Creaturely Condition

There is good reason to start with our context as planetary creatures. First and foremost, starting with such a context acknowledges that mutliperspectivalism, agnosticism, and polydoxy extend well beyond the boundaries of Homo sapiens. In other words, we find ourselves in a 13.7 billion-year expanding universe (possibly in a multiverse) and a 4.5 billion-year process of geo-evolution. One of the paradoxes of such knowledge is that this displacement of the human existential experience comes as a result of the very knowledge known as "western science" that seeks to control the world.[24] Rather than develop here a universal

[23] William James, *A Pluralistic Universe: Hibbert Lectures at Manchester College on the Present Situation in Philosophy* (1909).

[24] Mary Midgley, "The End of Anthropocentrism?" in David Keller, *Environmental Ethics: The Big Questions* (Malden, MA: Blackwell, 2010), p. 140.

story or narrative into which all other stories must fit,[25] the point in starting with a planetary context is to realize our embeddedness in evolving systems of multiple other earth-creatures. Just as many trans- or posthumanist thinkers have noted, we are in a process of becoming beyond our very humanity: always becoming plant, mineral, animal, and cyborg.[26]

From a planetary context, whatever else meaning-making means it must always acknowledge our embeddedness or our entanglement with many earth or planetary others. Too often our dominant modes of making meaning place the human at the center stage or assume that humanity is the boundary of moral concern: this includes narratives of human salvation from religious traditions and narratives of progress in scientific and economic traditions. Whether we make meaning via religious traditions, scientific materialisms, or some combination thereof, we help to create the conditions of ecocide and planetary decline when we continue to treat human beings as exceptions to the rest of the natural world. It is only from our embeddedness in planetary contexts of becoming that we can address the second context from which we make meaning: the existential.

The Existential Context: Or a Planetary Humanism

As the feminist, environmental philosopher Val Plumwood has pointed out, there is a huge difference between epistemic anthropocentrism and ethical anthropocentrism.[27] In other words, part of being located, eco-contextual creatures is recognizing that our own identities and agencies are located in human bodies in certain times and places. We can't, therefore, think like any other person than who we are, much less like a mountain or another animal. Our existential context is such that we are evolving planetary creatures, and in this respect we share in the evolving contexts of many other planetary creatures. Yet, we each have a unique, human perspective on the planet in which we live. Each of us is an

[25] This is something which I think "The Universe Story" made popular in the world of religion and ecology by Brian Swimme and Thomas Berry is partly guilty of. See, Brian Swimme and Thomas Berry, *The Universe Story: From the Primordial Flaring Forth to the Ecozoic Era* (New York: HarperCollins, 1992).

[26] Donna Haraway, *Simians, Cyborgs and Women: The Reinvention of Nature* (New York: Routledge, 1991), pp. 149–182.

[27] Val Plumwood, *Environmental Culture: The Ecological Crisis of Reason* (New York: Routledge, 2002), pp. 123–142.

intersection of a unique set of planetary flows. From this intersection we see, experience, and know things about the world. From this intersection we act in the world and add to the world. This constitutes one part of our existential context.

Another part of our existential context involves our seemingly hyper (if not unique) ability to want to imagine many future possibilities in the face of an unknown future. In other words, we are constantly assessing the world from our point of view and our location in life, and acting in ways that we imagine or decide to be better or good. "Time is not linear ... it is projected toward the future as it faces and grasps the past in the present moment."[28] The unique existential stature of the species Homo sapiens seems to be tied up in this ability to strive toward the realization of multiple possible futures emerging out of past conditions in the present moment. This open-ended living is ultimately marked off (as stated earlier) by the darkness of unknowing before we were born and after we are dead. It is important to house this existential context within the larger planetary context, and not *vice versa*. Too many religions and meaning-making systems have made the human system the context into which the ecosystem and planetary systems must fit. "We seek to transform the world, not to exchange it for another one that conforms to our desires."[29] If we are going to do justice to our creatureliness, we must begin to resituate our own existential context within the planetary out of which it emerges and into which it shall return. Only once these two contexts have been identified is it possible to begin talking about the more complex contexts of meaning-making practices: the ethical and aesthetic. It is to a discussion of these two contexts that I now turn.

The Ethical Context

It may be a bit of a surprise to discuss ethical implications of meaning-making only here toward the end of the chapter as many (including myself) argue that meaning-making is primarily about ethical actions. However, my argument has not been that these contexts are sequential or somehow separated. My argument is that if we are going to have room for multiple meaning-making practices in a planetary context then we must have the three key ingredients of multiperspectivalism, agnosticism, and polydoxy if monological thinking is to be resisted, and further that our

---

[28] Crockett, *Radical Political Theology*, p. 130.
[29] Ibid., p. 165.

creatureliness must be placed into a planetary context of becoming. Without critical attention to the key ingredients of meaning-making and the planetary and existential contexts from which we make meaning, then ethics and ethical action are next to impossible. Ethics that don't acknowledge our epistemic limitations are absolutist; ethics that don't acknowledge our planetary context are anthropocentric; and ethics that don't acknowledge our human existential striving are not likely to be persuasive.

What the specifics of a given ethical system might look like will depend upon the many different value-laden contexts out of which we approach the world. However, here I suggest that ethics should persuade us toward possible ways of becoming rather than close off possibilities for future becomings. The function of ethics, then, is aporetic,[30] or keeping spaces open for evolving multiple others to become. Such an ethical system keeps us focused on the abject, or that which is "othered" by any system of meaning-making.[31] In this way, we might think of ethics as experimental actions toward co-creating spaces for future becomings. Such experimental actions will indeed involve closure in a given moment, as all moments must, but perhaps it will also mitigate the violence rendered by ultimate closure when an ethic becomes absolute. Finally, meaning-making must also be at least in part about envisioning the possible worlds toward which our practices aim.

The Aesthetic Context

Empirically convincing metaphors must be the basis of the principal metaphysical concepts, and those concepts must order and interpret the actual facts of experience in a convincing way. However, despite these empirical features, the metaphysical task is most fundamentally the constructive and imaginative one of creating an overarching conception of reality or the world within which all the dimensions and elements of experience can be seen, both in their unique individuality and in their interdependence and interconnection with each other.[32]

[30] Michael Anker, *The Ethics of Uncertainty: Aporetic Openings* (New York: Atropos, 2009).

[31] On the process of abjection and how abjection opens space for political action, see Judith Butler, *Bodies that Matter* (New York: Routledge, 1993), pp. 65–98.

[32] Gordon Kaufman, *The Theological Imagination: Constructing the Concept of God* (Philadelphia, PA: Westminster, 1981), p. 249.

Though the opening quote of this section is from within a Christian, theological perspective, its author, Gordon Kaufman, is much more of a viable, agnostic thinker. He represents a type of radical materialism (similar to that of the pragmatists) from within the context of the euro-Christian west. In other words, he recognizes that though he has moved from what he calls "first order" or naïve belief to that of "third order" or imaginative co-construction in terms of meaning-making, he does so always and already from within the bio-historical context of Western, European, Christianity.[33] Though our bio-histories will have shifted in another thousand years, from our context in the twenty-first century, it is hard to deny the influence of the extant major world religions on our various cultures. Thus, it is important that we continue to struggle with their meanings, truths, practices, and metaphors—hybrid though we may be. In other words, our imaginings toward possible planetary futures will at least partially be located within extant world religions. These imaginings are what I am calling the aesthetic contexts of meaning-making.

It is at once this aesthetic context that provides the final touches on our meaning-making practices and brings us full circle: for the aesthetic nature of our meaning-making practices highlights their very co-constructed nature, and the nature of meaning-making as imaginative lines of flight, or what we might call truth regimes.[34] In other words, though I began this chapter with three ingredients without which we cannot make meaning in the early twenty-first century, those very ingredients were gleaned from the aesthetic context of globalization and global climate change. Multiperspectivalism, viable agnosticism, and polydoxy are all part of the imaginative co-construction of our experience as planetary creatures in a globalizing, postcolonial, postmodern, post-secular world. This aesthetic would then constitute the common grounds of our experience. Common grounds are precisely not universally imposed foundations for some type of genuine or true experience, but rather they are cobbled together through millennia of bio-historical sedimentations.[35] Furthermore,

---

[33] The distinctions between first, second, and third order theology can be found in Gordon Kaufman, *An Essay on Theological Method* (Atlanta, GA: The American Academy of Religion, 1995).

[34] The language of "lines of flight" is taken from Deleuze and Guattari and that of "regimes of truth" is taken from Michel Foucault.

[35] Keller and Kearns, *Eco-Spirit*; Cf. on "bio-history," Gordon Kaufman, *In the Beginning ... Creativity* (Minneapolis, MN: Augsburg Fortress, 2004), p. 44.

these grounds, unlike universal foundations, are tectonic: they shake, shift, and move over time. Finally, the terrain of these common grounds can look quite different depending upon where one stands.

It is in the context of imagining from different terrains that we find most of our planetary conflicts when it comes to meaning-making practices. The struggle is located in something like the following: we mistake our temporary shifting grounds for ultimate foundations. Such a mis/taking of the penultimate for ultimate is precisely what many religious traditions associate with suffering, idolatry, and/or sin. When we mistake our own ground as foundation, we experience the world as if our own perspective is without eco-social context or objective. We then seek to reify the world into the image of our own self-making. Again, as Swami Vivekananda noted, we often mistake our own wells for the entire world. He wrote:

> I am a Hindu. I am sitting in my own little well and thinking that the whole world is my little well. The Christian sits in his little well and thinks the whole world is his well. The Mohammedan sits in his little well and thinks that is the whole world.[36]

Such absolutism, whether of the religious or scientific type, is nothing more than the imaginative projection of one's own bio-historical, existential location onto the entire becoming planetary community. It is an attempt to stop the worlds becoming by placing the world into the image of the "I"; it is, in other words, an attempt to step in the same river twice. Such certainty, as Keller notes, has created more violence than any uncertainty ever will. She writes, "For in every age the wounds inflicted by certainty—and perhaps in ours more totally, more globally—will be better healed by a discourse of uncertainty than by just another sure truth."[37]

Here at the end, then, we find ourselves at the beginning of what it means to be a particular human being in an evolving planetary community articulating imaginative possibilities for future becoming. We are always stuck to some degree in this context of unknowing, in this context of acting and thinking toward a future that is open-ended. Dealing with the radical other, the abject, the unknown, the stranger, is indeed at the

---

[36] Swami Vivekananda, *The Complete Works of Swami Vivekananda*, Volume 1, p. 7.

[37] Keller, *God and Power: Counter-Apocalyptic Journeys* (Minneapolis, MN: Fortress, 2005), p. 150.

heart of many of our meaning-making values and practices. Whether we want to talk about hospitality, enemy love, loving the outcast other, taking on the abject, or about prophetic voices who aim to redistribute wealth and resources in such a way that every other has the space for living—our daily bread—the diverse forms of planetary meaning-making might find common grounds in articulating imaginative ways to ever-widen circles of moral concern to include as many planetary voices as possible.[38]

A BRIEF ENDING NOTE: PLURALISMS ON THE MENU

Articulating a method for understanding our pluralistic contexts does not necessarily mean that there are not other methods. I do not expect that all readers will agree with my analysis of pluralism much less my value-laden assumptions that pluralism ought to be embraced. However, no one can disagree that dealing with pluralism is part and parcel to living in the world today. As such, we ought to at least be able to talk about varieties of pluralism. Here, at the end of this chapter, I locate my own understanding of pluralism in a threefold typology of pluralism in the hopes that such a pluralistic menu will at least provide some type of nourishment for all those gathered around the planetary table. The concept of pluralism, I argue, can roughly be divided into three different types or waves. Though I am hesitant to use the term waves because it suggests linear succession in a world that is temporally fluid, the image of thoughts as waves that wash over our minds and that have lives of their own is quite helpful. So think as you will of the following as types or waves that are not mutually exclusive.

Pluralism 1: Many Paths, One Mountain

This idea of pluralism is at the heart of perennial philosophy as well as at the center of liberal philosophy. It suggests that though our experience of truth is multiple and polydox, and though we experience multiplicity in the material world, in the end, all of these paths or truths are just aspects of the one truth. This way of thinking is found in strands of

---

[38] This is in line with what Anindita Balslev calls for in terms of looking at the insights into the "other" in other traditions and finding out how various religious traditions deal with difference. See, "On Religious Pluralism: Diversity Not Dissension," 1998.

religious thought that are considered to be "Eastern" and "Western," and even among some indigenous religions. Furthermore, such thinking is behind ideas of equality based upon sameness, viz. ideas of liberal individualism that suggest "we are all the same." A common form of this way of thinking suggests that cultures (including philosophies, values, religions, and ethical systems) are many, while nature (what science gives us) is one.[39] Such a narrative is found even at the heart of the Enlightenment mentality that suggests modern, Western science is uniting us under one single truth about the world in which we live and, thereby, waking us up from religious dogmatic slumber. Obviously, I find many problems with such a universal way of thinking as do many "post" thinkers. However, from foundational, universal, or transcendent metaphysical perspectives, this is the best form of pluralism that we can hope for and it deserves a place at the table just as much as its counterpart, often thought of as relativism, does.

Pluralism 2: Many Paths, No Mountains

The second form of pluralism suggests that there are just multiple perspectives. This is often thought of as relativism and many forms of materialism, atheism, and immanent thought find a home in this type of pluralism. This type of pluralism is in direct opposition to the colonizing tendencies of belief in some underlying universal truth or oneness. Though I am more sympathetic to this type of pluralism than I am to Pluralism 1, in my own thinking it too has significant challenges. While claiming ultimate respect for multiple perspectives, it offers little in the way of how these perspectives might interact with, affect, and change one another. In other words, its multiplicity relies paradoxically on the same type of liberal individualism that suggests "my" truth is "the" truth. Here, however, rather than enforcing one truth over the many bodies of the evolving planetary community, one simply asserts an individual truth in isolation. Again, I won't hide my disagreements with this type of pluralism, but it deserves a place at the table.

Pluralism 3: Many Paths, Many Mountains

Navigating between Pluralisms 1 and 2, in a similar way that Donna Haraway navigates between universalism and relativism, is a form of

[39] Bruno Latour, *The Politics of Nature: How to Bring the Sciences into Democracy* (Boston, MA: Harvard University Press, 2004).

contextual pluralism that holds in dynamic tension the experience of globalization as both transcending context and as radically contextual. She writes,

> The alternative to relativism [is not universalism but] is partial, locatable, crucial knowledges sustaining the possibility of webs of connections called solidarity in politics and shared conversations in epistemology…Relativism and totalization are both "god-tricks" promising vision from everywhere and nowhere equally and fully.[40]

This form of pluralism recognizes our radical contextuality, our hybridity, and a radically open future that might take multiple directions. It is this type of pluralism that provides the means by which Pluralism 1 and Pluralism 2 can dialogue with one another. Far from all-inclusive (which would entail the misplaced concreteness of closure in thought), Pluralism 3 recognizes our radical contextuality and the co-constructed nature of all meaning-making claims and practices. "The constructivist ambition requires that we accept that none of our knowledge, none of our convictions, none of our truths can succeed in transcending the status of a 'construction'."[41] As such, and again following Stengers, the task of understanding pluralism should be about an ecology of ideas or understanding how our meaning-making practices affect one another and other planetary bodies rather than searching for some metaphysical or ontological truth. We are, in the end, ethical and aesthetic planetary creatures within a planetary community rather than universal or isolated gods that determine the fate of the entire universe.

---

[40] Donna J. Haraway, *Simians, Cyborgs, and Women: The Reinvention of Nature* (New York: Routledge, 1991), p. 191.
[41] Stengers, *Cosmopolitics I*, p. 38.

12

Weak Faith

How to Manage Religious Diversity without Dissent

Santiago Zabala

Europe, instead of a "union" of different religions, faiths, and sects, has become a "container," that is, an indifferent storage device. While a lot of effort is put toward conserving and implementing the financial markets, the multicultural and religious differences of the Old Continent are ignored, allowing new racist and fundamentalist groups to emerge. The recent slaughter perpetuated by Anders Behring Breivik in the name of a fundamentalist interpretation of Christianity is a symptom of the Union's disinterest in this problem, similar to its court's inability to decide upon such marginal issues as the display of the crucifix in state schools. Nevertheless, the Breivik terrorist attack and the European court's deadlock should not be interpreted as a rigid attitude against foreigners but rather as an inability to interpret. The same holds true for the failure of referendums about the European Union's (EU) constitution a few years ago. This disappointment gave a clear signal that the EU is run by a group of technocratic rationalists uninterested in the interpretations of others, that is, indifferent to the diverse cultures, politics, and also religions that constitute the continent. If they had been considerate of others' interpretations, a deal would have been reached and several other important social issues would also have finally been addressed. In sum, thought in the EU, like Breivik's ideology, is submitted to metaphysics, that is, a rationalistic description of how finance, religion, and many other vital components of our lives ought to function. These matters must be urgently addressed if Europe wishes to improve the peace it has managed to maintain since the end of the war in the Balkans. But how can a continent with so many cultures, religions, and languages manage the different faiths of its citizens? As we all know, the answer to this question is not straightforward, simple, or even certain of success, but rather only possible within a philosophical stance whose starting point is the recognition of the possibility of failure.

The aim of this brief chapter is to indicate how the philosophy of interpretation, that is, hermeneutics, must become the main intellectual approach for Europe if we wish to manage the diversity of religions in Europe and others parts of the world. The fact that harmony among religions still remains merely a goal, as Swami Vivekananda foresaw, should not be seen as a problem for hermeneutics but rather as a sign of the possibility that it can succeed. The space left after the deconstruction of metaphysics has opened the way for a nondogmatic practice and understanding of religion where "faith" is not defined anymore in contrast to rationalism but as an alternative to such rationalism, that is, by its weakness.[1] Hermeneutics offers to Europe the possibility to apply this weak faith because it has radically changed our way of understanding not only the world but also ourselves. Given the existential nature of our meeting, I believe the best way to present the weak faith of hermeneutics is to expose the ontological constitution of hermeneutic Being (in both the subjective and objective meanings of the term), which will indicate how weak faith can live in diversity without dissent.

Although hermeneutics, which today has become the *koine* of contemporary thought,[2] has its etymological origins in the Greek god Hermes, the reputed messenger and interpreter of the gods, it first developed systematically as biblical exegesis and then in a theoretical framework to

[1] On the relation between science and religion, see Hans-Georg Gadamer, "The Relation of Religion and Science," in *Hermeneutics, Religion, and Ethics*, trans. J. Weinsheimer (New Haven, Conn., and London: Yale University Press, 1999).

[2] Evidence that hermeneutics has become the common language of contemporary philosophy can be found in G. Vattimo, "The Age of Interpretation," in *The Future of Religion*, ed. Santiago Zabala (New York: Columbia University Press, 2005), pp. 43–54; and G. Vattimo, *Beyond Interpretation: The Meaning of Hermeneutics for Philosophy* (Stanford, Calif.: Stanford University Press, 1997); and the recent A. Ortiz-Oses and P. Lanceros (eds), *Diccionario de Hermeneutica* (Bilbao: Universidad de Deusto, 2006). Recent series dedicated to hermeneutics thought include Joel Weinsheimer (ed.), Studies in Hermeneutics (Yale University Press); Hermeneutics: Studies in the History of Religions (SUNY Press); Studies in American Biblical Hermeneutics (Mercer University Press); The Interpretations Series (Melbourne University Publishing); and Hermeneusis (Anthropos Editorial); these make a large library not only of Heidegger, Pareyson, and Gadamer but also contemporary authors such as J. Grondin, K. Eden, J. Sallis, J. Risser, and others.

govern such exegetical practice.[3] But starting in the eighteenth and early nineteenth centuries, theologians and philosophers extended it into an encompassing theory of textual interpretation in general, regardless of the subject matter, which could be God, the Bible, nature, science, or even art. From the narrow interpretation of sacred texts hermeneutics moved to the modern concern of interpretation in general. This primarily occurred through Friedrich Schleiermacher's and Friedrich Nietzsche's theories of interpretation. For them, there are no things (facts) "out there" that could subsequently receive a certain shape by our (subjective) understanding of them; that is, neither the interpreter nor the interpreted depend on pre-established agreements but only on an involvement that occurs during knowledge's natural interpretive process. Schleiermacher recognized that one always understands a work "at first as well as and then even better than its author," but Nietzsche instead insisted that "there are no facts, but only interpretations, and this is also an interpretation." Both found in hermeneutics the "ontological dimension" that Heidegger would then transform in the "ontological relation," that is, in Dasein.

Heidegger, in order to avoid the traditional partition of a person into body, soul, and spirit—that is, in order to avoid locating Being's essence in a specific faculty, in particular that of Reason, of the rational animal—coined the term "Dasein," which is not the world nor the subject nor a property of both but the relation, the in-between, which does not arise from the subject coming together with the world, but is already itself. The central feature of Dasein, along with "thrownness" and "fallenness," is "existence"[4] because it has to decide how to be. It's this essential characteristic that makes Dasein not a rational being but, more profoundly, a relationship to Being through which humanity must decide if it wants to exist as "a metaphysical describer of objectivity" or a

[3] A fine study on the historical grounding of modern hermeneutics is Kathy Eden, *Hermeneutics and the Rhetorical Tradition: Chapters in the Ancient Legacy and Its Humanist Reception* (New Haven, Conn.: Yale University Press, 1997).

[4] "Thrownness" refers to the fact that Dasein always finds itself already in a certain spiritual and material, historically conditioned environment; hence, in the world, in which the space of possibilities is always historically limited. It represents the phenomenon of the past as having-been. Dasein's "fallenness" characterizes its existence in the midst of beings that are both Dasein and not Dasein. Existence means that Dasein is potentiality-for-being, *"Seinkonnen"*; it projects its being upon various possibilities, especially the phenomenon of the future.

"postmetaphysical interpreter of Being." The classical example of the describer of objectivity is Descartes, for whom the world consists of objects that are already there *as such* even before they are investigated, that is, as if Dasein could only "understand its own being in terms of that being to which it is essentially, continually, and most of all closely related—the 'world'…in terms of what is objectively present."[5] If this were the case, our thought would only have to re-present objects in order to find objective accounts, but such a philosophy would imply that we all have an impossible God's-eye view for which the truth of things exists in the form of a timeless presence. In sum, Dasein is the in-between that does not arise from the subject coming together with the world, but in a relationship with its own Being; as Heidegger says, Dasein "is in a hermeneutical relation,"[6] an involvement in the world that takes the form of an interpretative process. If Heidegger insisted that this hermeneutic relation represents the world not as it is but rather as it could be; that is, it questions the fact that it exists because, in contrast to the rest of the objects of the world, Dasein has a relationship with its own Being, called "existence." It is a self-relationship, hence, a Being-relationship.

If, as Heidegger explained, when we speak of Being, we also speak of the people and the creative force of the people, which, through its poets, thinkers, statesmen, and theologians, performed the greatest assault on Being that has ever happened in Western history, then philosophy will also consist in returning to the main creative force that inspired these thinkers. But if we assume (as we should) that this creative force is religion, then the work of philosophy today is to clarify "what being signifies in the present situation" through the most important cultural figures that have conditioned Western civilization. This is why philosophers are best understood when confronted with the classical ontological question as to "why Being *is* and why there *is* not rather nothing" and also "why it is such as it is." But the importance of both classical thinkers such as Karl Jaspers, Martin Heidegger, and Hans-Georg Gadamer and contemporary philosophers such as John Caputo, Jean-Luc Nancy, and Gianni Vattimo does not lie in the fact they have reminded us that we do not have an answer to the question of what "Being" really means or in the fact that philosophers have always tended

---

[5] M. Heidegger, *Being and Time* (1927), trans. Joan Stambaugh (Albany: SUNY Press, 1996), p. 16.

[6] M. Heidegger, *On the Way to Language*, trans. Peter D. Hertz (1959; New York: Harper & Row, 1982), p. 32.

to assimilate all entities to the present-at-hand, but in the fact that philosophers should be "aware that objective knowledge is subject to conditions rooted in the structure of Being as it is given to us."[7] These philosophers have provided the answer not to this classical metaphysical question but to the ontological presupposition that sometimes Being "is actually given to us"; it is our capacity to recognize "when" and "how" it is "given to us" that is important, not what it really is.[8]

As we can see, the hermeneutic Being is the "postmetaphysical interpreter of Being," interested in entering into dialogue with reality instead of recognizing it as representing a static perfection. Heidegger's destruction of metaphysics together with the hermeneutics that followed have not only allowed us to "question of the very *fact* of objects," but most of all have demanded an *interpretative process* to enter into dialogue with reality. In this process, where reality becomes a point of departure rather than a point of arrival, we can finally stop asking what reality means, what it refers to, or even if it is beautiful in order to begin to ask what it wants to say. Exposing the ontology of hermeneutics has delineated the hermeneutic constitution of the weak faith we are interested in because it showed how, after metaphysics, Dasein must institute a relationship with the world that is not simply an acknowledgment of reality as it is but a true recreative interpretation. This implies the interpretative nature of all existence, and most of all the religious obligation of Dasein to practice a weak faith. Gianni Vattimo was the first to outline such a faith in a 1979 article later reprinted in various edited and authored books such as *Belief, After Christianity*, and, with Richard Rorty, *The Future of Religion*. But what is weak thought?

[7] Karl Jaspers, "Myth and Religion," in Karl Jaspers and Rudolf Bultmann, *Myth and Christianity: An Inquiry Into the Possibility of Religion Without Myth*, trans. Norbert Guterman (New York: Noonday Press, 1958), p. 44.

[8] For a systematic account of Being's event in actuality, see S. Zabala, *The Remains of Being: Hermeneutic Ontology After Metaphysics* (New York: Columbia University Press, 2009). Heidegger also explained this when he said that

> Only a god can save us. The sole possibility that is left for us is to prepare a sort of readiness, through thinking and poetizing, for the appearance of the god or for the absence of the god in the time of foundering (*Untergang*); for in the face of the god who is absent, we founder.

("Only a God Can Save Us: Der Spiegel's Interview" [September 23, 1966], in M. Heidegger, *Philosophical and Political Writings*, Manfred Stassen (ed.) (New York: Continuum, 2003), p. 38.)

Weak thought is the knowledge, acceptance, and recognition that philosophy, after the deconstruction of metaphysics, cannot capture the ultimate essence of its objects but must comply with a multiplicity of interpretations. In other words, weak thought understands the end of metaphysics as an emancipation from the objectivistic-representational thought that limited man's creations. This emancipation allowed all disciplines to contribute to liberating our culture from oppression: psychology in science, women's rights in political thought, and even liberation theology in Christianity. But Vattimo found a surprising paradigmatic example to present the weakness of faith.

Vattimo found the model of weak faith in Nietzsche's "*Ubermensch*," a person capable of living the end of metaphysics not only without resentment but also as a possibility for the future. Although Nietzsche is the first to have used this expression, he did not systematically explain its constitution. The only place he indicated its autonomy is in a very famous fragment of "European Nihilism" where, responding to the question, who will be the strongest once the will to power will conflict between each other? He affirmed that the strongest will be the:

> most moderate, those who have no need of extreme articles of faith, who not only concede but even love a good deal of contingency and nonsense, who can think of man with a considerable moderation of his value and not therefore become small and weak: the richest in health, who are equal to the most misfortunes and therefore less afraid of misfortunes—men who are sure of their power and who represent with conscious pride the strength man has achieved.

Thus, the dialogic nature of interpretation reveals the nature of weak faith, the interpretive position of the individual who does not need extreme articles of faith but only a sense of moderation in all actions. The cultural pluralism in which we live is precisely the locus of the end of metaphysics and the emergence into visibility of the interpretative nature of all existence. This is why, as Vattimo said, "whoever does not succeed in becoming an autonomous interpreter, perishes, no longer lives like a person but like a number, a statistical item in the system of production and consumption."[9] To be weak is to be not only moderate or tolerant but also capable of considering one's own interpretation and

---

[9] G. Vattimo, *Dialogue with Nietzsche*, p. 130.

practice of faith without needing to believe it is objectively true. Hermeneutics is the philosophy of the *weak* because it implies a plurality of interpretations and also since it describes our way of being in a world without foundations. Such a world requires constant dialogue, a dialogue that becomes the recognition that only by being weak can we overcome our own most immediate and brutal self-interest.

The EU must rely on hermeneutics not only because it shows how literal interpretations of sacred text are always inadequate to understanding the spiritual meaning of God's words but also because it can become an important tool to prevent fundamentalist terrorist attacks such as Breivik's. If the literary interpretation of Christianity allowed Breivik to return to what he thought of as a "pure Christianity," contemporary philosophical hermeneutics will help us proceed toward the richness and diversity of Europe's own religious tradition.

13

Democracy, Pluralism, and Conservative Religion

Zainal Abidin Bagir

Echoing Alexis de Tocqueville's observation of his time, "the organization and the establishment of democracy in Christendom is the great political problem of our times," Nader Hashemi regards that the great political problem of our time is the establishment and organization of democracy in the Muslim world.[1] There has indeed been quite some rethinking in theorizing democracy and religion in recent years, which makes thinking about "democracy among Muslims" more understandable, amidst so much mass-media as well as scholarly skepticism about the possibility of reconciling democracy and Islam. In any place where religion plays an effective role, the rethinking of secularism itself and the questioning of old assumptions about its necessity for democracy have opened up new possibilities to think about religion and democracy.

A related issue in this rethinking is what kind of religion is compatible (or not) with democracy. When religion is said to be compatible with democracy, does it refer only to the liberal kind? Can democracy live with a conservative religion? If diversity is a mark of today's democracy, what kind of pluralism is required by a pluralist democratic polity—should it be a theological pluralism that accepts the equality of religions and as such requires the weakening of particular religions' truth claims?

In countries that have been democratic for a long time but also relatively religiously homogenous, the challenge is to accept that secularism did not manage to marginalize religion from the public—or, more seriously, to accept the new diversity of religions effected partly by strangers. The US and Europe are the examples. But these are also concrete questions for many countries now that are aspiring to be democratic yet at the same time host a population with strong religiosity. A number of Muslim countries would fit in with this description. Indonesia is one

---

[1] N. Hashemi, *Islam, Secularism and Liberal Democracy: Toward a Democratic Theory for Muslim Societies* (Oxford: Oxford University Press, 2009).

such example which I will use as an illustration throughout this chapter in addressing these questions.

DEMOCRACY WITHOUT SECULARISM?

Following the success of three general elections in the past 15 years, and the fact that more than 200 millions of its population (87 percent) are Muslims, Indonesia has been called as the largest "Muslim democracy." This description may not be fully accurate. While Indonesia is a country with the largest Muslim population—larger than the Muslim population of all Arab countries combined—yet religious diversity runs deep in its history up to now. Many world religions as well as indigenous religions have had a history of hundreds or even thousands of years. Moreover, in terms of its Constitution, Islam does not occupy a privileged space.[2]

Before the popular pro-democracy movement known as *Reformasi* in 1998, which marked a break with the previous regime (1966 to 1998), the authoritarian regime was acknowledged to be successful in boosting economic development and crafting an Indonesian national identity to overcome diverse religious and ethnic identities. After 1998, with the proliferation of religious and ethnic groups which demand recognition of their own identities and the rise of local actors due to the decentralization, the question of how to acknowledge the diversity and at the same time build unity has become one of the main challenges for the new democracy.

As such Indonesia has been used as an example of the coexistence of public religion (especially Islam) with democracy. The prominent scholar Alfred Stepan mentions Indonesia together with India and Senegal as exemplifying a democracy which is not founded on a kind of secularism known in Western countries;[3] Nader Hashemi uses Indonesia

---

[2] As will be discussed later, Islam does have marked influences in many sectors; yet the Constitution does not single out this or any other religion. Going deeper into history, this statement refers to a complex reality that will require a different writing. For a good summary of the history of religions in Indonesia see, R. Hefner, "Religion: Evolving Pluralism" in Donald K. Emmerson, *Indonesia Beyond Suharto: Polity, Economy, Society, Transition* (New York: M.E. Sharpe, 1999), pp. 205–236.

[3] A. Stepan, "The Multiple Secularisms of Modern Democratic and Non-democratic Regimes," in *Rethinking Secularism*, Craig Calhoun, Mark Juergensmeyer, and Jonathan VanAntwerpen (eds) (Oxford University Press, 2011), pp. 114–144; A. Stepan, *Arguing Comparative Politics* (New York: Oxford University Press, 2001), pp. 213–253.

and Turkey to base his theory on how democracy may develop in Muslim-majority countries and the role of indigenized theory of secularism;[4] similarly, Mahmood Ayoob takes Indonesia and Turkey as Muslim democracies "to show that there is no inherent and irreconcilable contradiction betweem Islam and democracy."[5] What are the conditions of such possibility?

Twin Toleration

Alfred Stepan argues that democracy (understood, for example, in Robert Dahl's eight principles of electoral democracy) does not require the concept of secularism. However, an alternative description, also based on empirical observation in democratic countries, could be that while democracy may require secularism, we need to grant that different concepts of secularism are available, as in Stepan's formulation of the concept of "multiple secularisms." Stepan himself prefers to use his own term, which is "twin toleration": "democratic institutions do need sufficient political space from religion to function, just as citizens need to be given sufficient space by democratic institutions to exercise their religious freedom."[6] Another conclusion Stepan draws to strengthen his argument that secularism is not required for democracy is that actually it also does not necessitate democracy. Looking at several data sets, he shows that as there are democratic "non-secular" countries, there are also authoritarian secular countries.[7]

[4] N. Hashemi, *Islam, Secularism and Liberal Democracy: Toward a Democratic Theory for Muslim Societies* (Oxford: Oxford University Press, 2009).

[5] M. Ayoob, *Many Faces of Political Islam: Religion and Politics in the Muslim World* (Ann Arbor: The University of Michigan Press, 2008).

[6] A. Stepan, "The Multiple Secularisms of Modern Democratic and Non-democratic Regimes," in *Rethinking Secularism*, Craig Calhoun, Mark Juergensmeyer, and Jonathan VanAntwerpen (eds) (Oxford: Oxford University Press, 2011), p. 114.

[7] Hashemi sees that Stepan's theory is completely supported by Jonathan Fox's well-known research, based on Religion and State Database (years 1999 and 2002). The Database has indices of separation of religion and state (SRAS) and government involvement in religion (GIR). One of Fox conclusions is that SRAS is the exception and GIR is the norm for most of the world; "the major difference between democracis and non-democracies is not the presence of SRAS but rather an upper limit of GIR." (Hashemi 2009, pp. 126–127). Cf. Kuru, "Passive and Assertive Secularism: Historical Conditions, Ideological Struggles, and State Policies toward Religion," *World Politics*, 59 (July 2007): 568–594.

In his seminal article, he has more detailed explanation. Twin toleration is defined as "the minimal boundaries of freedom of action that
must somehow be crafted for political institutions vis-à-vis religious
authorities, and for religious individuals and groups vis-à-vis political
institutions."[8] His main question, then, is about the minimal institutional
and political requirements for democracy. Besides the institutional guarantees for an electoral democracy, Stepan adds protection of basic liberties and minority rights and constitutionalism. "Religious institutions
should not have constitutionally privileged prerogatives which allow
them authoritatively to mandate public policy to democratically elected
governments." Yet they have autonomy to worship privately and even be
involved in public sphere to advance their religious interests, with two
conditions that apply to any other individuals or groups: that they do so
nonviolently and without violating the liberties of others. Constraints on
religious groups may be placed only if the two conditions are violated,
and they should be decided by courts—again, just like any other groups.
These are minimal requirements, beyond which there may be many different patterns of state-religion relation—the multiple secularisms.

Examples of the multiple secularisms, different models of secularisms (or religion-state relation), of democratic countries can be cited.
Stepan mentions three examples in Western countries: (1) the separatist
model (US, France); (2) the "established religion" model (Sweden,
Denmark, and Norway); (3) "positive accommodation" model in the
Netherlands, Belgium, Switzerland, and Germany.[9] The fourth pattern
exists in India, Indonesia, and Senegal, following the model of "respect
all, positive cooperation, principled distance." These countries have
large Muslim populations, and as such may also be useful to draw conclusions about the relation between Islam and secularism.

"Respect all" means that the countries embrace an inclusive interreligious positive accommodation (compared, for example, with model
three European countries which embrace a more restricted intra-Christian
positive accommodation). Despite its overwhelming Muslim majority,
Islam is not singled out as *the* offical religion; other than Islam, five
other religions were recognized and granted financial and bureaucratic

---

[8] A. Stepan, *Arguing Comparative Politics* (New York: Oxford University
Press, 2001), p. 213.

[9] A. Stepan, "The Multiple Secularisms of Modern Democratic and Non-
democratic Regimes," in *Rethinking Secularism*, Craig Calhoun, Mark
Juergensmeyer, and Jonathan VanAntwerpen (eds) (Oxford: Oxford University
Press, 2011).

supports (Hinduism, Buddhism, Protestantism, Catholicism, and Confucianism). Further, the three countries have "positive cooperation" approach, in which the state works with the religious communities to advance certain policies (such as the family planning in Indonesia; building religious arguments against female genital mutilation in Senegal). In Stepan's discussion, the fourth model meets the minimum requirements of democracy, obeys the twin toleration principle—in some areas even better than the other three models—and as such the countries are undoubtedly democratic.

Indigenization of Secularism

The twin toleration, just as secularism, may normatively serve as a kind of guideline in the management of religious diversity in a democracy. As mentioned by Hashemi, when he discusses Stepan, the critical issue is to ascertain the boundaries of twin toleration, i.e., "necessary boundaries of freedom for elected governments from religious groups, and for religious individuals and groups from government."[10] Hashemi considers many conceptualizations of secularism and democracy in recent history, and comes to a strong approval of Stepan's twin toleration, which he sees to have many theoretical as well as tactical merits.

In his book he advances three main arguments. First, liberal democracy requires some distance between state and religion ("secularism properly understood" or "multiple secularisms"). Second, in places where religion is a key identity marker, democracy had to go through a politics in which religion constitutes a reference point in political argumentation and mobilization. This is true in today's Muslim-majority countries as well as in the history of Western democracy. Third, typically religious reinterpretation or reformation (on issues such as the moral basis of political authority and individual rights) precedes political development such as democratization or secularization. He argues that succeful democratic consolidation in countries such as Turkey and Indonesia was preceded by some kind of religious reformation or the development of an "indigenous theory of Islamic secularism."

Looking at Indonesia, that is precisely what he found. In his discussion of Indonesia, Hashemi focuses to show how twin toleration principles

---

[10] N. Hashemi, *Islam, Secularism and Liberal Democracy: Toward a Democratic Theory for Muslim Societies* (Oxford: Oxford University Press, 2009), p. 129.

are fought for and given Islamic religious foundation by Muslim intellectuals and organizations. No doubt, the process was not straightforward at all. What happened in the process that started even before the
Indonesian Independence in 1945 was intense and sometimes hostile
debates among Muslim intellectuals and groups took place. (It needs to
be said that similar process also took place in different religious communities). Hashemi concludes that, "Like their counterparts in Turkey,
[Muslim intellectuals, political parties, and religion-based civil society
groups] have developed a de facto theory of Muslim secularism while
maintaining a commitment to the principles and rituals of their religion."
He calls this as "indigenization of secularism," which is a key factor in
explaining Muslim groups' contributions to democracy in their country.
Another conclusion he reaches is his claim that this example from
Indonesia shows the importance of getting the sequence right—religious
reformation prior to the spread of secularization.[11]

However, if democracy requires such a religious reformation,
wouldn't it put too much burden on religion, especially the kind that
lives in a conservative society? Does that not mean that only a certain
kind of religion may be compatible with democracy?

CONSERVATIVE RELIGION AND LIBERAL DEMOCRACY

Beyond theoretical debates, the idea that opens up the possibility of
democracy for religion is attractive for a society with high religiosity
such as Indonesia. However, the requirement of "religious reformation"
may beat the purpose—at least for a large group of conservative people.
While it may be true that Indonesian Muslim intellectuals of the past
have created an "indigenized theory of secularism," today's Indonesia
may be different, and as such two questions remain. *First*, the indigenized theory of secularism that Hashemi talks about was developed
during the pre-1998 authoritarian government, which preferred moderate religion and repressed religious groups or individuals who were
considered "extreme" or harbored the idea of Islamic state. The freedom
opened up by the democratization that started in 1998 has given space
for the religious groups that were repressed, including those which are
explicitly anti-democracy. *Second*, national and international surveys on
Indonesian religiosity have undoubtedly shown Indonesia to be a society

[11] Hashemi, 2011, pp. 165, 170.

with strong religiosity, even compared to other Muslim countries. While the support for democracy is quite high, the support for *shari'a* is also very high.[12] Interestingly, while in general elections Islamic parties got less than 20 percent of votes, there are indications that Indonesian society is experiencing a "conservative turn"—either there has been a rise of the conservatives, or they are gaining stronger ground and managed to influence public discourse of Islam, and to some extent it has been successful to marginalize the more liberal discourse.[13] The rise of the politics of *shari'a* in Indonesia recently is yet another indication of the need to consider whether certain religious aspiration could find a place in a democracy.[14]

To return to my earlier question, the requirement of religious reformation for democracy may make Hashemi's ideas (and his support for Stepan's) less interesting in a conservative society. Religious reformation indicates a liberal orientation, which stands in contrast to conservatism. Without dwelling too much in the semantics, we may characterize liberal religiosity in its tendency to be more open, while the conservative tends to be insular. While the liberal puts an emphasis on autonomy and individuality, including in interpretation of religious texts, the conservatives' main character is in the maintenance of boundaries of the group's identity—to the extent of regulating dress codes or marriage, for example. For the liberal individual autonomy may be the most important, even if it means criticizing what is regarded as normative by the group, but what is more important for the conservative is the idea of the good, even if it is derived from submission to an authority. If a liberal theology tends to be pluralist, eroding the boundaries, conservatism strengthens them by showing their differences from the religious others.

Taking the examples of thinkers of classical liberalism such as John Locke and John Stuart Mill, Jeff Spinner-Halev sees that they did not try to be neutral in speaking about religion, but tried to convince believers to change their religious outlooks and show their theological preference

---

[12] John L. Esposito and Dalia Mogahed, *Who Speaks For Islam?: What a Billion Muslims Really Think* (New York: Gallup Press, 2008).

[13] Martin Van Bruinessen, *Contemporary Developments in Indonesian Islam: Explaining the Conservative Turn* (Singapore: Institute of Southeast Asian Studies, 2013).

[14] Robert Hefner, "Introduction: Sharia Politics—Law and Society in the Modern Muslim World," in Robert Hefner (ed.), *Shari'a Politics: Islamic Law and Society in the Modern World* (Bloomington: Indiana University Press, 2011) pp. 1–54.

178 ZAINAL ABIDIN BAGIR

for a liberal religion. That is, a more open religion, which bases itself on
reason rather than revelation, and make it as a force to bind rather than
divide different people.[15] A pluralist society is expected to acknowledge
religious diversity as much as possible and not excluding the religious
others too soon.

Preference for a more liberal religion is surely understandable and
we may muster many arguments to say that such a religion would
be more conducive for a plural, liberal democracy. Nevertheless, at the
same time it also shows the limitation of political liberalism. If the above
contrasts are accepted, it is difficult to deny the possibility of a tension
between conservative religion and liberal democracy; to ask the conservatives to liberalize their religion may put too much burden on them.
If this criticism is right, then instead of giving generous space for differences, the liberal restricts the space by giving it burdensome qualifica-
tions. So the question is whether the conservatives get sufficient space
in a pluralist democracy.

This question is not meant to privilege the conservatives, but to make
sure that democracy does not put undue burden on religion, because the
spirit of pluralist democracy is to acknowledge diversity, not reduce it.
Methodologically speaking, religious conservatism constitutes a test for
conceptions of management of diversity: assuming that such a conception
is better if it is more inclusive, the question is how inclusive can it be?

Spinner-Halev lists several points of tension between conservatism
and liberal democracy.[16] That is, between individual autonomy versus
group authenticity; the inclusive versus exclusive citizenship or social
behavior; and equality versus difference (in the position of men and
women, for example). What I am interested to see in the case of
Indonesia is not only an evaluation of individual conservatives' views or
behavior, but also attempt to make them public or even to ask the state
to protect the conservative form of life.

What we see here is not only the strong, conservative religiosity as
shown by the surveys[17], which are in general parallel with Spinner-Halev's
description, but also the rise of several conservative organizations. Other
than the new (conservative, hardline, radical, or even militant) groups that
came into existence after 1998 and a few old Islamic groups that have

[15] Jeff Spinner-Halev, *Surviving Diversity—Religion and Democratic Citizenship*
(Baltimore, Maryland: The Johns Hopkins University Press, 2000), p. 11.
[16] Ibid.
[17] Z. A. Bagir and S. Cholil, *The State of Pluralism in Indonesia: A Literature
Review*, Pluralism Mapping Study 1/2008, Hivos and Kosmopolis Institute, 2008.

become more assertive after 1998, a very striking phenomenon can be seen in the Indonesian Council of *Ulama* (Islamic religious leaders; Majelis Ulama Indonesia, or MUI). I will use their attempt to redefine and strengthen the boundaries of Islam through *fatwa* (religious, non-binding edicts) as illustrations and see how they may fit in a democracy.

Conservatism and Pluralism in a Democracy

MUI was established in 1975 at the initiative of the government of the time. They are partially funded by the government, just as it funded other (Christian, Catholic, Hindu, and Buddhist) religions, through the Ministry of Religious Affairs. The establishment of the Council of Ulama has been described either as an accommodation or incorporation of Islam (Muslim authorities or orthodoxy) by the state.[18] It was *khadimul hukumah* (servant of the government). After 1998, they are still funded by the government, but they have tried to become more independent of the government, sometimes even against it, defining itself now as *khadimul ummah* (servant of the Muslim society), claiming authority on issues considered of importance to Muslims—from birth control, *halal* food and cosmetics, TV broadcast, Facebook, to "correct theology" and "deviant" Muslim groups. On these issues, in general they can be termed as conservative. *Fatwa* is non-binding—it doesn't bind the government to enforce it nor the Muslims to adhere to it. However, increasingly the MUI itself has become more assertive, trying to impose its views on public policy, and the government, especially on certain symbolic issues, has increasingly listened to the MUI. So constitutionally and legally it does not have a place in the government, but they have become more effective as a kind of pressure group—and they are still partially funded by the government.

For Stepan, government funding for religion does not necessarily constitute a breach of twin toleration. The question, however, is whether "the boundaries of freedom for elected governments from religious groups" is still maintained. It can be argued that on several issues, such as the ones related to the issues of defamation of religion (or blasphemy), the government does seek their views and enforce their views; this may be argued not as a breach of the twin toleration, since the elected government does have freedom not to enforce their views. To be

---

[18] D. Porter, *Managing Politics and Islam in Indonesia* (London and New York: Routledge Curzon, 2002), 77ff.

fair, it should also be mentioned that on certain issues, such as the certification of *halal* products (which entails a big business of certification),
the government has been in opposition to the Council over which institution is to certify (which is the reason why the bill on *halal* products
cannot be signed into law after years of discussions in the parliament).
However, usually for the sake of political (and eventually electoral)
expediency they choose to listen to the Council and be influenced by
their views which are made enforceable through public policies. In this
situation, twin toleration in general is maintained, but the government's
freedom is compromised.

Among the main criticisms directed toward the MUI was a series of
fatwa they produced in 2005. These *fatwa* attempt to draw boundaries of
normative Islam in their declaration of the deviancy of the Ahmadiyah
sect (which was a reinforcement and strengthening of similar but weaker
fatwa issued in 1986) and the unlawfulness of secularism, pluralism, and
liberalism (of course, in the particular definitions of the terms by the
MUI). This was strengthened by a *fatwa* which defines the criteria of
teachings, interpretations, or practices of Muslims deemed deviant or
heretical. These cases will be looked upon more closely here.

One of the demands of those who oppose the (Qadiani) Ahmadiyah
is to disband the organization in the name of eradicating deviancy from
the true Islam. Indeed the MUI also says that violence should not be
done to them, but MUI leaders repeatedly made public statements that
demand the government to ban them and are much weaker in denoucing
the violence. These statements have been claimed to fuel hostility
toward the Ahmadis, or at least has been used to justify attacks on them.

Statements highly critical of the MUI that come from liberal Muslims
leaders criticized MUI of inciting hate and violence toward groups
deemed deviant, including the Liberal Islam Network. Luthfi
Assyaukanie, a young liberal Muslim leader, even makes a direct link of
the *fatwa* to a series of physical violence toward those groups.[19] While
the causal relation of the *fatwa* to the violence may be questioned, a
question which arises here is whether such a conservative group such as
MUI can express their conservative religious views in a democracy.
Wouldn't demanding all Muslims who regard Ahmadiyah as deviant
(from the true Islam as they see it) to say that it is not deviant be too high
a demand? This is a question about theological pluralism: should everyone

---

[19] Asy-Syaukani, Luthfi, "Fatwa and Violence in Indonesia," *Journal of
Religion and Society*, 1, 2009. Available for download at http://moses.creighton.
edu/jrs/2009/2009-3.pdf (Last accessed: December 22, 2013).

be a theological pluralist for democracy to work? Should a plural democracy force one to change their (theological) views? Couldn't one have such a view and accept the Ahmadis as equal citizens?

The same issue applies to relations between religions, which is an issue of theological pluralism as a subject treated in another *fatwa* issued by MUI in the same year, 2005. In its *fatwa*, MUI defines pluralism as a view teaching that all religions are the same, religious truths are relative, and as such no religious believers should claim that their religion is the only true one and others mistaken. It distinguishes pluralism from plurality, which is a fact that in a place there may be different religious communities living together. The verdict is that pluralism is opposed to the teachings of Islam and such it is *haram* (forbidden) for Muslims to follow it. While in social relations Muslims should be inclusive, meaning that they have good relations with non-Muslims, in matters of theology and religious practices they should be exclusive.[20] Such a view is impossible to be enforced by the state through a public policy. However, besides increasing heavy criticisms toward the liberals following the *fatwa*, there was at least one incident in which the office of the Liberal Islam Network was threatened. Further, just as in the case of Ahmadiyah, there is a possibility, which has not been actualized, that liberal views may be branded as heretical or deviant and as such categorized into "defamation of religion," for which there is a law. In practice, what classifies as "defamation" is subject to government's consultation with the authority of *ulama* regarded as representing the normative Islam, and MUI is one such body.[21]

Many criticisms were directed against the *fatwa*, for example, the very definition of pluralism, or the inappropriateness of using the legal Islamic term, *haram*, to philosophical or theological views. Another thread of criticisms sees that pluralism is in the interest of all religious communities and charges MUI's *fatwa* as, to say the least, not helping in creating harmony between religions, or even creates a possibility of conflict and disintegration.[22] To return to our main question, however,

---

[20] The other part of the *fatwa* on liberalism is in direct confrontation with a kind of religious reformation that Hashemi regards as a requirement of democracy. Liberalism is understood as "interpreting religious texts (Qur'an and the Prophet's tradition) by using free thinking, and only accepts religious doctrines which are considered to be compatible with rational thinking"—and this is *haram* too.

[21] Bagir, Zainal Abidin, "Defamation of Religion in Post-Reformasi Indonesia: Is Revision Possible?", *Australian Journal of Asian Law*, 13 (2), 2013.

[22] This is a statement from a liberal Muslim intellectual, Dawam Rahardjo, as quoted in: http://www.kompas.co.id/kompas-cetak/0602/04/Politikhukum/2409601.htm.

should we exclude such an exclusive view in the name of pluralist democracy? For this, we may question the link drawn between theological pluralism and civic pluralism.

Civic and Theological Pluralism: American Debate

This issue is well illustrated in an American discourse on the US as a democratic country which is grounded in a strong religious ethos. Diana Eck sees the American paradox in its new religious diversity: there is a positive civic pluralism, but one which is in direct conflict with conservative Christian's negative view on pluralism.[23] Theological pluralism is related with an individual theological attitude, while civic pluralism is about the individuals' position as a citizen with equal rights, regardless of their beliefs. On one hand, Eck seems to see that civic pluralism and theological pluralism are different and separate, but on the other hand, she seems to demand that civic pluralism should be supported, or even required, by a non-exclusive theological view of diversity.

She gives several examples of what she calls as the confusion of civic and theological arena.[24] One of the example is a case which involves a parliament member in Minnesota who opposed Dalai Lama's visit because he regards Buddhism as contradicting Christian principles. Another example of an American-Hindu community who was upset when a Baptist church asked its members to pray for the Hindus, who were celebrating Diwali, because they were regarded as being lost and in the darkness of Hindu teachings which do not acknowledge god. Should the Hindus bring the case to the Supreme Court? Isn't it making a theological issue to become a public issue?

The confusion of arena takes place when, on the basis of his or her religious beliefs, one refuses the presence of others, or asks for a different treatment. This view seems to negate the effectiveness of (theological) diversity in the public sphere and, if continued, this would end up drawing strict boundaries between religion which is privatized and the public space in which there is a demand of consensus. If that is the case,

---

[23] Diana Eck, *New Religious America—How a Christian Country has Become the World's Most Religiously Diverse* (HarperSanFransisco, 2002), p. 80.

[24] Diana Eck, "Prospects for Pluralism: Voice and Vision in the Study of Religion," *Journal of the American Academy of Religion*, 75 (4) (December 2007): 10.

then does it not negate the very core of diversity, because the problem we have is with religion in the public, not private, sphere?

For Anatanand Rambachan, while protection of religious freedom by the Constitution guarantees religious pluralism in the US, civic pluralism will be better protected if supported by theological pluralism. A theology of religions would guard the exclusivists from the temptation to make the state as an instrument to force a religious doctrine and restrict the state from making use of religion to defend its policies.[25] Similarly, Rita Gross sees that when pluralism is accepted, the space for public involvement of religions is open. What she means by pluralism here is acceptance of the necessity of religious diversity, which in the philosophical and theological perspective means that believers of all religions have to drop exclusive truth claims concerning their religions and accept that there will never be only one religion that is accepted universally.[26] This is a theology about religious pluralism which does not see other religions as mistaken. When such exclusive claims gone, the public sphere becomes even more fertile and safe for everyone to express their religious views without much resistance from others. Dropping exclusive truth claims would thus make it more possible for believers to color the public sphere with their beliefs.[27] That is understandable. However, in the end the requirement of dropping exclusive truth claims would reduce not maintain, diversity, because there would also be a loss of one view, which is the exclusivist. Gross's position seems to be stronger than Eck's. From the latter's point of view, it may be seen as confusing the theological and the civic. This is similar to the example discussed above about the Hindu-American objection to the exclusivism of the Baptist church.

What I want to problematize here is the relation between theology and social behavior in the public sphere, which sometimes is taken for granted. It would not be too difficult to accept that theological pluralism would be a stronger ground for an ethos of coexistence; it is also true

[25] A. Rambachan, "The Hindu Tree on America's Sacred Ground," in Barbara A. McGraw, Jo Renée Formicola (eds), *Taking Religious Pluralism Seriously: Spiritual Politics on America's Sacred Ground* (Waco, Texas: Baylor University Press, 2005), pp. 177–178.

[26] Rita Gross, "Buddhist contributions to the civic and conscientious public forums," in Barbara A. McGraw, Jo Renée Formicola, eds. *Taking Religious Pluralism Seriously: Spiritual Politics on America's Sacred Ground* (Waco, Texas: Baylor University Press, 2005), p. 216.

[27] Ibid., p. 220.

that rejection of the presence of others could be more easily justified by exclusivist theology. But is it the case that the civic pluralism of a religious society could only be built on the basis of theological pluralism, or, more generally, liberal religion? Further, if what we want is to build an inclusive social ethos that accepts as much of diversity as possible, it is important to not too quickly stop the conversation by drawing a strict relation between conservatism and rejection of the social ethos.

The above examples show the tension between conservatives's exclusivism and the liberal idea of a plural and democratic society. Robert Wuthnow calls this a tension between two discourses: the language of civic pluralism and that of religious commitment.[28] The former has a more legal character, emphasizing on rights and tolerance—that all individuals, regardless of their religion or ethnicity deserve the rights to live, to elect leaders, to education, and others. But this is a way of thinking and speaking which is totally different from the language of religious commitment. Usually this language is more exclusive, emphasizing on the certainty of the good, not the rights to find what one regards as the good—whatever that is. Because of its emphasis on the good, believers also tend to judge other religions outside their own groups.[29]

Wuthnow does not resolve the tension between civic and theological discourses. He disagrees with those who look for a solution which conflates the two. "Many of us are unwilling to go to the trouble of maintaining this tension. We want an easy least-common-denominator civic culture that prevents us from having to struggle with basic tensions in our values."[30] The tension is healthy but implies willingness to respect their differences.

CONCLUDING REMARKS

If there is any solution that I will propose to our problem here, it is not a substantial model of pluralism, but more on how to face the tension in concrete situations. *First*, exclusivism or conservatism should be accepted and given space, as long as it is not imposed on others or manifested in a way that denies space for the others. In general, the

---

[28] R. Wuthnow, *America and the Challenges of Religious Diversity* (Princeton University Press, 2007).

[29] Ibid., pp. 310–311.

[30] Ibid., p. 311.

reason to restrict freedom which is acknowledged in human rights discourse is also applicable here. As long as ideas are concerned, there is almost no limit on what can be expressed in the public space, so that even an idea which is regarded as the most conservative in a society and at a particular time could be put forward. What is more important is that, for the sake of raising the quality of deliberation in the public, there is a willingness to dialogue such views. The kind of intercultural dialogue proposed by Bhikhu Parekh, in the context of minorities in the multicultural Britain, seems to be applicable to Indonesia in the context of the debate on *shari'a* laws, Ahmadiyah, or other contentious issues.[31]

In the case of Ahmadiyah in Indonesia (or other minorities in a religion for that matter), even if a religious commitment of a group demands a space to judge it as heretic, at the same time there should be a civic commitment to make sure that their rights as citizens should not be reduced. This should not be regarded as contradictory, but an expression of multiple identities—in this case, identities as an adherent of a religion and as a citizen. They are contradictory when there is what Parekh calls "pathology of identity," that is, when an identity overwhelms other identities (an example is conflation of a man's identities as a father and a professional military officer).[32] From the side of the state, what needs to be done is to make sure that the public space is safe—that even though there is a tension, it is not manifested in acts that would violate the rights of others.

In a plural democratic society, theological exclusivism should be given space, as part of freedom of expression, just as the Ahmadi has its space. What is not democratic is when the organization is banned, using the deviancy reasoning, their civil rights are restricted or even violence done on them. It is true that for those who do not see the Ahmadiyah as deviant, seeing it as simply one of the plurality of interpretations would be easier to accept the Ahmadis, and vice versa. However, while good relations between groups should be maintained, it should not demand burying the differences. And this means allowing exclusivism. (It is probably worth noting also that to some extent the Ahmadiyah is also exclusivist.) Exclusion should be possible—though not always nice— but not civic discrimination.

Second, there is another space, which is not as public, in which religious communities may be persuaded to change, for example, to be

---

[31] B. Parekh, *Rethinking Multiculturalism—Cultural Diversity and Political Theory* (Macmillan Press Ltd, London, 2000), pp. 264–294.

[32] B. Parekh, *A New Politics of Identity* (Palgrave Macmillan, 2008), 130ff.

more inclusive—but this has to be done authentically, using its own religious tradition. The above constraints are intended to keep the public space safe and open as a condition for acknowledgment of diversity and public deliberation. That kind of society, although it keeps tensions within itself, could already be called as civic pluralist. The next step, after that minimal condition is fulfilled and in to raise the quality of deliberation, is exchange of views among citizens to achieve the common good. One of the agenda that can be attempted here, to produce quality deliberation, is to empower the religious communities themselves and to develop internal debates within a religious community to change or reform its views, including to create more inclusive views.

"Religious reformation" that Hashemi talks about finds its place at this stage, mostly as part of an internal debate. This is also a space that An-Na'im discusses, where reformation of *shari'a* may take place. Within the internal debates, the language may be exclusive—it does not have to be the kind of Rawlsian public reason or an-Na'im's civic reason. As a matter of fact, this can be seen as a kind of internal (within particular religious communities) preparation to develop civic reason. Hashemi's point that I disagree with is his notion that democracy requires an "indigenized theory of secularism"—and he insists that the sequence must be right. While in the long term such a theory of secularism—understood as religious justification for the differentiation between authorities of the state and of the religious authority—will be a solid ground of democracy, it does not have to start by excluding the conservatives.

Abdullahi an-Na'im observes that when fundamentalism and conservatism are on the rise and try to dominate public discourse (or even the state), the most common liberal response is to insist that religion must be relegated to the private.[33] Such a response is actually a denial of diversity in the public. Indeed, the denial is not without its reason, because conservatism often becomes a problem due to its resistance to compromise, yet such a group should still be guaranteed space to express their views.

Furthermore, excluding or marginalizing them will probably force them to find expressions in self-validating enterprises which make them even more insular and, probably eventually, corrosive of civic pluralist

---

[33] A. An-Naim, "The Politics of Religion and the Morality of Globalization," in Mark Juergensmeyer (ed.), *Religion in Global Civil* Society (Oxford: Oxford University Press, 2005), p. 37.

democracy. Contrary to that, inclusion of as much diversity as possible, as evidenced in many countries, actually helps the process of moderation of the conservatives. In the context of American diversity, Spinner-Halev sees that inclusive democratic state that gives space or even accommodate the conservatives' interests eventually will act as a moderating force.[34] This is also a fact we see in Indonesia with regard to new Islamic political parties that could not be established before the 1998 democratization movement. Despite criticisms that the Indonesian state has been involved too much in the religious affairs of its citizens, we also see that it has moderated the religious groups.

In today's Indonesia, much of the difficulty in imagining the idea that democratic inclusion of conservative religion should, to say the least, not be harmful probably does not stem from a principled reasoning or some norm about the place of conservative groups in a democracy. Rather, it seems to originate from the fact of (today's) government's weak response to the domination of the public space by the conservative groups, in which case the government was seen as being indifferent of their acts that may violate or have violated others' rights. Had the government done its job well and consistently in maintaining a safe public space for all, the existence of conservative, theologically non-pluralist groups does not have to be seen as a threat to democracy.

---

[34] Jeff Spinner-Halev, *Surviving Diversity – Religion and Democratic Citizenship* (Baltimore, Maryland: The Johns Hopkins University Press, 2000), p. 206.

14

An Intellectual Catastrophe
of the First Order

Mushirul Hasan

Islam is in its origins an Arab religion. Everyone not an Arab who is a Muslim is a convert. Islam is not simply a matter of conscience or private belief. It makes imperial demands. A convert's world view alters. His holy places are in Arab lands; his sacred language is Arabic. His idea of history alters. He rejects his own; he becomes, whether he likes it or not, a part of the Arab story. The convert has to turn away from everything that is his. The disturbance for societies is immense, and even after a thousand years can remain unresolved; the turning away has to be done again and again. People develop fantasies about who and what they are; and in the Islam of converted countries there is an element of neurosis and nihilism. These countries can be easily set on the boil.[1]

One of the many overseas-based writers who routinely fulminate against Islam and the Muslims is none other than Sir Vidiadhar Naipaul. His ancestors left India in the early 1880s as indentured laborers for the sugar estates of Guyana and Trinidad. He returned to India to publish *An Area of Darkness*, advertised as "tender, lyrical, (and) explosive." Thereafter, he chronicled the histories of a wounded civilization and a million mutinies in India. In between, he fired his shots at the world of Islam not once but twice, in labored projects. Samuel Huntington, a controversial American political scientist, earned his reputation by arguing that the New World Order is based on patterns of conflict and cooperation founded on cultural distinctions and identifications, the clash of civilizations theory. He, therefore, talks of "the indigestibility of Muslims" and their propensity toward violent conflict, which makes them threatening. Naipaul is no different: he, too, alerts readers to Islamic "parasitism" and the menace of Islam and, thereby, sustains the

[1] V. S. Naipaul, *Beyond Belief: Islamic Excursions among the Converted People* (New Delhi, 1998), p. 1.

Orientalist belief that Islam as a coherent, transnational monolithic force has been engaged in a unilinear confrontational relationship with the West. His essentialist reading of history allows him to sustain the myth of an inherent hostility between two antagonistic sides.

C. Snouck Hurgronje (1857–1936), the scholar at Leiden, wrote convincingly about Islam as a living and changing reality: what Muslims mean by it is constantly changing because of the particular circumstances of times and places. He insisted that if non-Muslims wish to understand Islam, they must study it in its historical reality, without judgment of value about what it ought to be.[2] The sense of Islam as something more than words in texts, as something living in individual Muslims, are not known to Naipaul.

His analysis is of a person ignorant of the nuances of Islam and unacquainted with the languages of the people he speaks to. He records and assesses only what he sees and hears from his interpreters.[3] In the most literal sense, he found the cultures indecipherable, for he could not transliterate the Arabic alphabet.[4] He had known Muslims all his life in Trinidad, but knew little of Islam. Its doctrine did not interest him; "it didn't seem worth inquiring into; and over the years, in spite of travel, I had added little to the knowledge gathered in my Trinidad childhood."[5] Yet he was taught to be mistrustful of Muslims: a particular greybeard Muslim, described in *An Area of Darkness*, came to embody "every sort of threat." Much like Nirad Chaudhuri, Naipaul's encounters with Muslims "are suffused with a sense of youthful bigotries."[6] There is, then, a diametrical difference between his empathy for Brahmanical Hindus and the experience of Muslims as opaque.[7] The nature of his upbringing may, therefore, explain the uneasy relationship with Aziz, Naipaul's personal servant for the six months of his sojourn in India, and Sadeq, his first interpreter in Iran. It may also explain Naipaul's ignorance of Islamic theology and his lack of grounding in history and sociological and political theory.[8]

---

[2] Hourani, *Islam in European Thought*, pp. 42–43.

[3] Suman Gupta, *V.S. Naipaul* (Plymouth, 1999), p. 76.

[4] Rob Nixon, *London Calling: V.S. Naipaul, Postcolonial Mandarin* (Oxford, 1992), p. 145.

[5] Naipaul, *Among the Believers*, pp. 15–16.

[6] Nixon, *London Calling*, p. 146.

[7] Sudha Rai, *V.S. Naipaul: A Study in Expatriate Sensibility* (New Delhi, 1982), p. 16.

[8] Naipaul, *Among the Believers* p. 76.

The whole of *Among the Believers: The Islamic Journey* is permeated
with the sentiment that Islam is hostile and aggressive towards the
advanced and "civilized" Western civilization, and that Muslim societies
are, by comparison, rigid, authoritarian, and uncreative.[9] He, therefore,
insists that Islam sanctifies rage—rage about the faith, political rage: one
could be like the other.[10] In Jakarta, Indonesia, he runs into Imamuddin
who confirms his stereotype. In Tehran, Behzad leaves him convinced
that, "now in Islamic countries there would be the Behzad's who, in an
inversion of Islamic passions, would have a vision of society cleansed
and purified, a society of believers."[11] Both Iran and Pakistan, "a frag-
mented country, economically stagnant, despotically ruled, with its
gifted people close to hysteria,"[12] remind him of the power of religion
and the hollowness of secular cults.

In much of the descriptions, otherwise woven nicely into a coherent
story, there is hardly any reference to the debilitating legacy of colonial
rule either in Iran or Indonesia. The civilized, innovative, and techno-
logically advanced West stands out as a vibrant symbol of progress and
modernity, whereas the four Muslim societies, despite their varying
experiences and trajectories, are destructive, inert, and resentful of the
West. With Naipaul relegating colonialism and imperial subjugation of
Muslim societies to the background, the West appears to be an open,
generous, and universal civilization. In fact, it is the West that is consistently portrayed as exploited by lesser societies resentful of its benign, or
at worst, natural, creativity: "indeed, Naipaul is so decided in his distribution of moral and cultural worth between the cultures of anarchic rage
and the 'universal civilization' that he ends up demonizing Islam as
routinely as the most battle-minded of his Islamic interlocutors demonize
the West."[13]

Beyond Belief: Islamic Excursions among the Converted People
(1998), chooses Islamic bad faith as the high theme of the book, portray-
ing "the same primitive, rudimentary, unsatisfactory and reductive thesis" that the Muslims, having been converted from Hinduism, must
experience the ignominy of all converted people.[14] In *India: A Million*

[9] *Outlook*, June 8, 1998.
[10] Ibid., p. 354.
[11] V.S. Naipaul, *Among the Believers: The Islamic Journey* (New Delhi, 1981), p. 399.
[12] Ibid., p. 82.
[13] Nixon, *London Calling*, p. 149.
[14] Edward Said, in *Outlook*, October 30, 2001.

Mutinies (1990), the 1857 revolt is regarded as the last flare-up of Muslim energy until the agitation for a separate Muslim homeland. So far, so good. But, then, Naipaul finds the Lucknow bazaars expressing the faith of the book and the mosque; for example, Aminabad, a crowded marketplace, served the faith.[15] Such notions, as might be expected, exhibit the cocksureness of the autodidact.

Two years after *A Million Mutinies*, Naipaul defends the destruction of the Babri Masjid by calling it "an act of historical balance."[16] "Ayodhya," he rationalizes, "was a sort of passion…Any passion has to be encouraged. I always support actions coming out of passion as these reflect creativity." Whose passion? Of those Muslims who, despite the bitterness since December 1992, still weave the garlands used in the temple and produce everything necessary for dressing the icons preparatory to worship.[17]

It is noteworthy that Naipaul's fraternity of poets and writers strongly contest not only his reading of the calamitous effects of Islam,[18] but also his virtual justification of vandalism in the name of religion. The best examples are of Sardar Jafri and Kaifi Azmi, two senior Urdu poets, who used a secular rather than a religious vocabulary

[15] Naipaul, *India: A Million Mutinies Now*, p. 356.
[16]   I would call it an act of historical balancing. The mosque built by Babur in Ayodhya was meant as an act of contempt. Babur was no lover of India. I think it is universally accepted that Babur despised India, the Indian people and their faith.
[17] Ashis Nandy, Shikha Trivedy, Shail Mayaram, Achyut Yagnik, *The Ramjanmabhumi Movement and Fear of the Self* (New Delhi, 1995), p. 2.
[18] *Outlook*, February 27, 2004.

> Fractured past is too polite a way to describe India's calamitous millennium. The millennium began with the Muslim invasions and the grinding down of the Hindu-Buddhist culture of the north. This is such a big and bad event that people still have to find polite, destiny-defying ways of speaking about it. In art books and history books, people write of the Muslims "arriving" in India, as though the Muslims came on a tourist bus and went away again.

Again, the Muslim invasion had "a calamitous effect on converted peoples. To be converted you have to destroy your past, destroy your history. You have to stamp on it, you have to say 'my ancestral culture does not exist, it doesn't matter.'" He claimed what he called "this abolition of the self demanded by Muslims" being "worse than the similar colonial abolition of identity."

to delineate the tragic impact of the demolition of the Babri Masjid and
its aftermath:

Manaya jaayega jashn-e masarrat soone khandaroan mein
Andheri raat mein roshan charagh-e-chashme-e-tar honge.

Jo yeh tabeer hogi Hind ke dereena khawabon ki
To phir Hindustan hoga na uske deedawar honge.

[Orgies of joy among desolate ruins
Glimmer of tear-rimmed eyes in the black night

If these be the meaning of our ancient dreams
Then the land and its seers will be gone].

There is no place for such sentiments in Naipaul's jaundiced views.
To him, Hindu militancy is a necessary corrective to the past,[19] a creative
force. He, therefore, rejects the possibility of Islam, a religion of fixed
laws, working out reconciliation with other religions on the subcontinent.[20] This is, in just a few crisp sentences, the clash of civilization
theory. In sharp contrast, Mujeeb had written:

> Unless we have decided in our own minds that medieval Indian
> history is not the history of the Indian people, we must coura-
> geously examine our present criteria of judgement and develop a
> perspective on persons, policies and events of the past that will
> enable us to understand and forgive and to obtain a clear vision of
> the past and the future.[21]

Given a choice, Naipaul would give voice to the "defeated people,"
not the poor or the downtrodden, but the *Hindus* living in *Hindu India*.
Among the many choices available in India with its bewildering variety,
he talks of reviving memories of temples being destroyed, of Hindus
being forcibly converted to Islam, and of Sikh gurus being mercilessly
executed by the Mughal. He rubbishes what goes in the name of assimilation, and suggests that the name of Mahatma Gandhi (1869–1948) be

---

[19] Interview with Tarun Tejpal, in *Outlook*, March 23, 1998.

[20] Ibid.

[21] Mujeeb, "Approach to the Study of Medieval Indian History," in Special
Issue on Professor Mohammad Mujeeb, *Islam and the Modern Age*, 34 (3–4)
(August–October, 2003).

dropped from the history syllabus. Even though Indians use the very idea of Mahatma to turn dirt and backwardness into much-loved deities, the Mahatma has no worthwhile message for this generation. The *Hind Swaraj*, which Gandhi himself translated from Gujarati into English, is so nonsensical that it would curl the hair of even the most devoted admirer; the title especially moves him to scorn.[22] The fact is, as a social scientist points out,

> Hind Swaraj is the seed from which the tree of Gandhian thought has grown to its full stature. For those interested in Gandhi's thought in a general way, it is the right place to start, for it is here that he presents his basic ideas in their proper relationship to one another.[23]

Naipaul's exposition is clumsy, naïve, and, if taken seriously, potentially dangerous. He is as much ill informed about India as Huntington is about the world outside the Western Hemisphere. He talks of a fractured past solely in terms of Muslim invasions and conveniently forgets the grinding down of the Buddhist-Jain culture during the period of Brahmanical revival. He fumes and frets even though a fringe element alone celebrates the vandalism of the early Islamists who were driven more by establishing the might of evangelical Islam than having defacement of Hindus as a primary motive. With anger, remorse, and bitterness

---

[22]   Gandhi shouldn't be considered as laying down a prescription for anything. He was uneducated and never a thinker. He is an historical figure. He came at a particular moment; he turned all his drawbacks into religion; and he used religion to awaken the country in a way that none of the educated leaders could have done. He has absolutely no message today. People talk too much about Gandhi and study him too little. His first book, *Hind Swaraj*, written at white heat in two weeks in 1909, is so nonsensical it would curl the hair of even the most devoted admirer. I don't know Indians who actually read Gandhi. They take him some vague idea of a great redeeming holiness and they are free to ignore the practical side—Gandhi the hater of dirt, the hater of public defecation. That last is still very much an Indian sport. In fact, the Gandhian idea of piety and a very holy poverty is used now to excuse the dirt of the cities, the shoddiness of the architecture. By some inversion, Indians have used the very idea of Gandhi to turn dirt and backwardness into much-loved deities.

[23] M. K. Gandhi, *Hind Swaraj and other Writings*, edited by Anthony J. Parel (New Delhi, 2004 reprint), p. xiii.

becoming a substitute for serious study and analysis, Naipaul's plan for
India's salvation collapses like a pack of cards. Hence, the devastating
denunciation of his *Beyond Belief* by Edward Said (1935–2003):

> Somewhere along the way Naipaul, in my opinion, himself suf-
> fered a serious intellectual accident. His obsession with Islam
> caused him somehow to stop thinking, to become instead a kind of
> mental suicide compelled to repeat the same formula over and
> over. This is what I would call an intellectual catastrophe of the
> first order.
>   The pity of it is that so much is now lost on Naipaul. His writing
> has become repetitive and uninteresting. His gifts have been
> squandered. He can no longer make sense. He lives on his great
> reputation which has gulled his reviewers into thinking that they
> are still dealing with a great writer, whereas he has become a
> ghost. The greater pity is that Naipaul's latest book on Islam will
> be considered a major interpretation of a great religion, and more
> Muslims will suffer and be insulted. And the gap between them
> and the West will increase and deepen. No one will benefit except
> the publishers who will probably sell a lot of books, and Naipaul,
> who will make a lot of money.[24]

[24] *Outlook*, October 30, 2001. See also the analysis in Gupta, *Naipaul*,
Chapter 8.

15

Conflict and Violence in the Name of Religion

Steven I. Wilkinson

It may now seem strange, but at the time of Independence in 1947, it was unclear to many observers whether India or Pakistan was likely to be more successful at moderating religious conflict. Pakistan, although it was to be a home for Muslims, was a state in which Jinnah nonetheless promised that members of all religions would be treated equally by the state. Jinnah, therefore, preserved the separate religious electorates that he saw as necessary to guarantee continuing minority influence in politics. And Jinnah himself appointed several minorities to high office, most influentially Zafarullah Khan, an Ahmadiyya, as Foreign Minister and as Pakistan's representative to the UN, charged with leading the country's efforts on the Kashmir issue.

In India, Congress' bitter struggles with the Muslim League throughout the previous decade, the departure of most of the League's senior leaders, and the violence of partition had greatly strengthened Hindu Nationalist sentiments at Independence. The Hindu Mahasabha and right-wing Congressmen forced at least some prominent Muslims—Rafi Kidwai, the Home Minister of Uttar Pradesh, most prominent among them—out of what were felt to be "sensitive" positions dealing with security. The Congress majority in many provinces then passed, from 1947 to the mid-1950s, a whole series of legislative measures, from bans on cow slaughter, the demotion of Urdu, to bans on separate electorates in local governments that were at the time strongly opposed by Muslims.[1]

Despite the uncertainty in the late 1940s and early 1950s over which state would do better, it now seems clear, 60 years later, that India has dealt with the challenge of moderating religious conflict

---

[1] See Wilkinson, *Votes and Violence: Electoral Competition and Communal Riots in India* (New Delhi: Cambridge University Press, 2005), Chapter 3.

much better than Pakistan. Pakistan's Constitutions have progressively deepened the state's mono-religious character (1962, 1973) and degree of discrimination against its Hindu, Christian, and Ahmadiyya minorities. In consequence Pakistan, which at the time of Independence had around the same percentage of minorities as India, now, has—after the flight of most of its Hindus, many of its Christians, and the secession of Bangladesh in 1971—only around a 2 percent minority population. Perhaps the best indicator of religious inclusion is by looking at who fills the most influential leadership positions in each country. In India, at the time of writing in mid-2013, India's Prime Minister, Deputy Head of the Planning Commission (the de facto Head), and Chief of Army Staff are all members of the 2 percent Sikh minority; the Defense Minister and Chief of the Air Staff are members of the 2 percent Christian minority; and the Minister of External Affairs is from the 13 percent Muslim minority. In Pakistan, by contrast, not one influential government position is currently held by a non-Muslim.

The limited public opinion surveys that have been done comparing India and Pakistan bear out these perceptions. A survey of "Democratic South Asia" done in 2006 found much higher levels of minority satisfaction with democracy in India than in Pakistan. In Pakistan, 43 percent of Christians said they were "very" or "somewhat" satisfied with democracy, and only 30 percent of Hindus. In India, on the other hand, 55 percent of Muslims polled were "very" or "somewhat" satisfied with democracy, with 50 percent Sikhs and 50 percent Christians "very" or "somewhat" satisfied. These rates were not very different at all from those of the majority Hindu community, where 48 percent of Dalits, 60 percent of Hindu upper castes, and 56 percent Other Backward Classes (OBCs) were "very" or "somewhat" satisfied with democracy. In India, 62 percent of those polled agreed with the statement that everyone had equal rights compared with only 23 percent in Pakistan. And perhaps the most revealing statistic from the 2006 survey was on the ratio of those who expressed religious majoritarian sentiments—the majority religious views and practices should dominate—compared to those who strongly spoke up for minority rights. In Pakistan, there were far fewer strong secularists than strong majoritarians (only 60 percent as many) while in India there were almost four times as many citizens who held strong secularist views as there were majoritarians.[2]

---

[2] *State of Democracy in South Asia* (New Delhi: CSDS/OUP 2008).

Why has there been such a divergence between India and Pakistan since Independence, despite their common institutional inheritances and the fact that each state had its challenges in the years immediately after Independence? One easy answer is that India is simply much more diverse than Pakistan. India's great diversity of castes, regions, and religions, so this argument goes, means that unlike in many countries no single religious group can dominate. Even at the constituency level, it is very difficult for any single group to win without reaching across caste and community lines and seeking the support of others. But this argument is too easy. It treats the *outcome* of India's good policy choices since the 1950s—strong intra-Hindu competition in politics along many cross-cutting cleavages—as the cause. India and Pakistan were, in fact, similarly diverse at the time of Independence, in terms of religious diversity, language, and caste. It is the combination of bad inheritances and bad policy choices since 1947 in Pakistan that has led to the gradual emergence of solid religious majorities in politics and underemphasized the many cross-cutting cleavages that might otherwise have moderated religious tensions, and which have played such an important role in India.

BAD INHERITANCES

One partial explanation for the relative success of India compared to Pakistan is that Pakistan had a much worse inheritance at Independence. First, and most obviously, Pakistan was split into two units, a thousand miles apart. Pakistan also had to deal with bigger and more significant outflows and inflows of refugees. Pakistan had lost economically critical Hindus and Sikhs, who had run much of the government and administration in Punjab, Sind, and North-West Frontier Province (NWFP), while the effect of losing a roughly equivalent number of Muslims on India's much larger economy was much less.[3] And the proportion of refugees in Pakistan, at 10 percent, was much more of a challenge in terms of integration than the 1 percent of refugees in India. Second, Pakistan inherited a highly imbalanced state in terms of ethnic representation. Punjab, with 25 percent of the country's population, had a 75 percent share of the army, with NWFP having most of the remainder. Bengal, with 54

[3] C. N. Vakil (ed.), *The Economic Consequences of Divided India* (Bombay: Vora, 1950).

percent of the population, had only 155 troops in the army, less than 1 percent. Moreover, much of the Punjabi and Pashtun leadership of the army regarded Bengalis in a patronizing way, as non-martial and "unsuitable" for leadership positions in politics and army. In India, by comparison, though the state Congress inherited in 1947 was certainly imbalanced (with Punjabis and other so-called "martial races" overrep-resented in the army, for instance), the extent of this imbalance was nowhere near as high as that in Pakistan. Third, Pakistan retained for many years the separate religious electorates system that had been in place before 1947. This system—abolished in India in 1946–1950 at all levels of government—provided no incentive for politicians from the religious majority to appeal to minority voters, and instead provided an incentive for what Donald Horowitz terms "ethnic outbidding," in which majority politicians outdo themselves in order to demonstrate that they are the true guardians of the faith, because they have every incentive to solidify the majority vote, and none to reach across religious lines.[4]

The problems posed by these inheritances for Pakistan were real. But we should not overstate their importance and imagine that they explain all the variation in India and Pakistan since Independence. India and Pakistan had many more similarities in 1947 than we would imagine from their divergent outcomes, outcomes that were at least as much the outcome of bad choices as bad inheritances. The strength of the Pakistani state, for instance, was not as weak as it is sometimes portrayed, and Pakistan in fact inherited many civil servants and other government workers from India. Tens of thousands continued to stream into the country in the 1940s and 1950s because of what they felt were diminish-ing prospects for Muslims at home. In Pakistan, as in India, then, the overall high degree of diversity in terms of language, religion, and caste might, had better institutions been crafted, have provided the basis for strong cross-cutting cleavages that would have helped to soften the political intensity of religion.

The most important reason that India has done better at moderating religious conflict and discrimination since Independence was that the country took a number of political decisions, in its first decade, that have both helped India to cross-cut the importance of the religious divide with many other identities, and that have given members of the majority com-munity a continuing incentive since to reach out to members of the

[4] See Donald L. Horowitz, *Ethnic Groups in Conflict* (Berkeley: University of California Press, 1985).

minority in politics. Some of these decisions were not, it has to be admitted, made with the deliberate intention of reducing religious conflicts. But by happy accident they have had that effect.

The first of these decisions was deliberate. Congress decided, in the 1950 Constitution, to end separate religious reservations in jobs and in politics, and to make religious discrimination unconstitutional. This decision was a clear effort to minimize the kind of "divide and rule" politics that, under the Raj, had maximized Hindu-Muslim tensions and disagreements. The new Constitution abolished the separate religious electorates that had played such a negative role before Independence. These separate electorates were now replaced, for all voters (even those in the SC and ST constituencies), with joint electorates in which all voters voted together. These measures were important. But they were not sufficient on their own, I would argue, to diminish the power of religion in politics, especially given the damaging conflicts of the previous three decades. For that to happen, India also needed policies that maximized the importance of other cross-cutting identities that could compete with religion as organizing identities in politics.

These two other important policies came in the early 1950s, when senior Congress leaders, as a result of pressure from the south, rethought their opposition to (a) reservations and (b) linguistic states. The rethink over caste reservations came in 1950, when mass protests broke out in Madras, where caste reservations had been in effect since the 1920s, over a Madras High Court judgment which (correctly) said that reservations for Backward Classes (BCs) in the state were no longer legal under the 1950 Indian Constitution. Given the strength of feeling over this issue in the south (which involved large-scale riots in 1950), and with the first national elections in the offing, Congress, therefore, passed an amendment to the Indian Constitution in 1951 which specified that measures put in place to help "OBCs" did not contravene the anti-discrimination and equal protection clauses of the Constitution. As is well known, this clause has since 1951 encouraged numerous groups since 1951 to mobilize around regional caste identities rather than religion (religious reservations are still unconstitutional) or some other larger national-level identity. One does not have to like all aspects of reservations to acknowledge that, from the perspective of *religious conflict* moderation, caste reservations have played a very important role since 1951, in breaking up solid Hindu majorities as different castes in different regions have competed with each other for jobs, educational places, and other benefits.

   The second important policy choice, in 1952–1953, was a rethink of
Congress' previous opposition to the carving up of large multilingual
states into more homogenous linguistic states. Nehru had originally
opposed this on the grounds that creating new states might intensify
regional and linguistic nationalisms and perhaps lead to another break-
up of India. But the strength of feeling on the issue in Telugu-speaking
areas, which led to large-scale violence, led him to reverse the party's
opposition in 1952, and then appoint a commission to reexamine the
whole issue in 1953. This commission recommended the creation of a
large number of new linguistic states, and laid down the broad principles
for creating more. As a result, and since the passage of the States
Reorganization Act in 1956, India has gone from nine very large states
at Independence to 28 states today, with more states likely to be created
over the next decade.
   Although again this measure was not taken with the intention of
reducing religious conflicts, the creation of more linguistic states has
had the effect of moderating tensions over religion. A larger number of
states have increased the strength of regional and linguistic identities,
and these identities both increase political competition within the Hindu
majority and helped to increase the number of parties and interests
appealing for Muslim and other minority votes.[5] Imagine, as a thought
experiment, if India today did not have 28 states, but had just four, as in
Pakistan, where there has been no states reorganization and one large
state (Punjab) dominates national politics. Imagine if India had one
Hindi-speaking state with close to half the population, one eastern state
(West Bengal, Orissa, and the North-East), one state in the South with
all the Dravidian languages, and one northern state (J&K, Himachal, and
Punjab). We can certainly imagine that, if this happened, the divisions
between these broad areas would be increased, and also that the relative
weight of religious minorities such as the Sikhs, Christians, and Muslims
would diminish as they would form a smaller proportion of the population in these new large states. The creation of 28 states, by contrast, has
created much better opportunities for religious minorities by creating a
host of small states (e.g., Goa, Meghalaya, Kerala, West Bengal) in
which minorities are both part of the local linguistic majority and highly
sought after by politicians from the local and national political parties,
many of which are based around the caste and linguistic identities

   [5] See Horowitz, *Ethnic Groups in Conflict*, for why these two conditions help to reduce ethnic and religious conflicts.

institutionalized by the Indian state in the 1950s. As I have explored elsewhere, wherever there are multiple caste-based, regional, and national parties competing for Muslim and other minority votes, the level of anti-minority riots is sharply reduced.[6]

Because the 1951–1953 decisions over caste and linguistic states make many tangible benefits available on the basis of these identities, the overwhelming majority of the Indian electorate does not vote on the basis of religion, but votes on the basis of caste or some other local identity, or on broader development issues. This fact, together with the fact that all constituencies are mixed and that in most constituencies no single caste is a majority, has been enormously helpful from the perspective of religious conflict moderation. Leaders from one caste or community have to reach out, at the local and higher levels, to members of other castes and communities if they want to get elected. It is this perennial competition for the votes of all castes and communities, more than just the constitutional rules established in 1950, that has been highly effective, since Independence, in keeping India a secular democracy.

In Pakistan, by contrast, cross-cutting cleavages have not been institutionalized in the same way as they have been in India. There has been no major states reorganization, breaking up the major linguistic states and especially Punjab, which exercises disproportionate weight within the state. There was no reform of the separate electorate system in Pakistan for several decades, which gave Muslims no incentive to appeal to members of the country's religious minority communities. And there has also been no attempt to institutionalize caste reservations, which might have—as in India—encouraged intra-Muslim competition along caste and class lines that might have undercut attempts to make majoritarian religious appeals in politics.

WHY THE DIVERGENCE?

The point about the importance of cross-cutting cleavages and intense political competition raises the obvious question: just why did India do better at institutionalizing cross-cutting cleavages within its polity? There are several reasons.

[6] Wilkinson, *Votes and Violence* (New Delhi: Cambridge, 2004), Introduction and Chapter 5.

First, Nehru and the Congress leadership took the decisions they did on caste reservations and linguistic states in the early 1950s because they were members of a broad-based, internally democratic, and federal political party, which was responsive to strong protests from the south over these issues. Nehru certainly had immense prestige within the party, especially after the death of Gandhi in 1948 and Sardar Patel in 1950. But, as his collected letters to chief ministers make clear, he also had to persuade and compromise with many other strong leaders within the party, and he did not always get his way.

The Muslim League, in contrast, was a much more centralized and "brittle" party than Congress, with Jinnah and a couple of other leaders before 1947 taking all the important decisions and quashing local initiatives and autonomy in the interests of having a "sole spokesman" who could negotiate with the British and Congress over Muslim interests at the national level.[7] As late as the summer of 1944, the party leaders in Punjab were reporting that "most district Leagues had existence only upon paper…" and that "the most urgent task was to set up the preliminary scaffolding of the organization in the district(s)."[8] This organizational problem was accentuated by the fact that most of the League's senior leaders and pre-Independence supporters came from Bombay, Uttar Pradesh, Bihar, and Central Provinces, areas that, after partition, became part of India.[9] These leaders, therefore, lacked the strong local political ties to moderate factional conflicts after Independence.

[7] The best book on this is Ayesha Jalal's *The Sole Spokesman: Jinnah, the Muslim League and the Demand for Pakistan* (Cambridge: Cambridge University Press, 1985).

[8] Punjab Provincial Muslim League, Report of work for June and July 1944 submitted to the All India Committee of Action, Lahore, July 28, 1944, reprinted in Amarjit Singh (ed.), *Jinnah and Punjab: Shamsul Hasan Collection and Other Documents 1944–47* (New Delhi: Kanishka, 2007), pp. 56–57.

[9] In the 1936–1937 elections, the Muslim League won only 109/482 Muslim seats (Judith Brown, *Modern India: The Origins of an Asian Democracy* [Oxford, 1985] p. 303) and it performed best in Bombay (51 percent Muslim seats) and UP (43 percent Muslim seats). In the areas that later were to become Pakistan, the League did very badly, winning became winning only 1 percent of the Muslim seats in Punjab 1 percent, 31 percent in Bengal, and none at all in Sind and NWFP. Ayesha Jalal (1985), pp. 32, 42.

The Muslim League after 1947, therefore, did not have the deep link-ages with local politicians in Punjab, Sind, NWFP, and Bengal that might have allowed it to easily manage regional and religious conflicts within the party structure, as the Congress did within India. In the absence of a strong broad-based and internally democratic party organi-zation, people from regions or groups that felt marginalized, or from leaders who lost out in faction fights, could not, be sure of winning within the system. So their incentives were to take to the streets, or to make appeals to the wider population, as a way of outflanking leaders who were protected by their control of the state and a brittle party struc-ture. The first evidence of this, tragically, was in the 1953 anti-Ahmadiyya riots in Punjab, an anti-minority movement that was at root related to intra-league political fights in which Punjab Premier Daultana and oth-ers allowed anti-minority appeals to continue in order to outflank their opponents and appeal to majoritarian sentiments.[10]

The fact that Pakistan's Muslim League had a very centralized party structure magnified the importance of leadership. And here again, India was lucky in that Nehru, whatever his faults, was profoundly committed to the democratic process and believed in consultation and compromise with senior party leaders. Unfortunately for Pakistan, it turned out that the skills that had worked so well for Jinnah and other senior League leaders in forging Pakistan—obstinacy, an unwillingness to tolerate dis-sent, and an unwillingness to share power with other provincial lead-ers—were not so well suited to managing regional and religious conflicts. Jinnah was as unwilling to compromise with opponents within the state as he had been prior to Independence. In March 1948, when Bengalis—who formed the majority language within the country—appealed against the new policy of making Urdu the sole official lan-guage for the whole country, Jinnah traveled to East Pakistan to emphasize that the policy would not change. To the Bengali students and political leaders who, very respectfully, appealed for compromise, he argued that:

> Let me tell you in the clearest language that there is no truth that your normal life is going to be touched or disturbed so far as your

---

[10] *Report of the Court of Enquiry into the Punjab Disturbances of 1953* (Lahore, 1954) [The Justice Munir Enquiry] available online at: http://www.thepersecution.org/dl/report_1953.pdf, last accessed in December 2013.

Bengali language is concerned. But ultimately it is for you, the people of this Province, to decide what shall be the language of your Province. But let me make it very clear to you that the State Language of Pakistan is going to be Urdu and no other language. Anyone who tries to mislead you is really the enemy of Pakistan. Without one State language, no nation can remain tied up solidly together and function...[11]

This reluctance to compromise would, even if Jinnah had lived beyond 1948, have probably led to worse outcomes in India. As a thought experiment, consider what would have happened if Jinnah had been confronted with the same strong movements for caste reservations or linguistic states as Nehru. On the evidence it seems very likely that he would have acted very differently from Nehru—who acted against his own views and backed down on both issues—and that Jinnah would have tried to prevent both policies from being enacted. But, as we saw, Nehru's willingness to allow caste reservations and linguistic states in the early 1950s, despite his worries that they might threaten national unity, have ultimately helped to cross-cut the religious cleavages that might otherwise have proved so damaging to the country.

[11] Speech by M. A. Jinnah at a public meeting at Dacca on March 22, 1948, in Z. H. Zaidi (ed.), *Quaid-i-Azam Mohammad Ali Jinnah Papers—Pakistan: Struggling for Survival 1 January–30 September 1948* (Islamabad: Quaid-i-Azam Papers Project, Government of Pakistan, 2002), pp. 227–235.

16

Interfaith Relations in Sociocultural Context of Kerala

Annakutty V. Kurian-Findeis

INTRODUCTION

Globalization and technology have brought nations, people, and cultures closer than ever before. This makes us constructively and critically aware of the necessity and possibility of cooperative interaction in all possible fields, not only in the field of technology, trade, and commerce, but more so in the field of mutually enlightening ideas—let us say—in the overall development of human spirit.

Human mind is becoming more and more aware of the reality of religious and cultural pluralism in global as well as in national contexts. The religious pluralism and the relationship of religions seem to be the most challenging of all of them, especially for nations which were in the past used to one homogeneous culture, one religion, and one language forming more of a homogeneous identity. Actually pluralism as such means, the acceptance of the other with all its uniqueness. "World religions are beginning to experience that their future does not consist in any kind of isolation or domination over the other, but their readiness to accept and respect each other."[1]

This means religious pluralism should deeply affect the self-understanding and man's mission and vision in the world. Closely related to the reality of religious pluralism is the other challenge—the challenge of "secularization and secular thinking," a challenge that has both positive and negative aspects. Negative because several religions and ethical values, which were considered sacrosanct and eternal, are becoming more and more neglected and abandoned in our times—more so in Europe where we observe the attempt to de-religionize the society (Entreligionisierung)!

[1] Joseph Pathrapankal, *Enlarging the Horizons* (Tiruvalla, 2007), p. 16.

On the other hand, world religions at large seem to be still "the principal and primary sources" of inspiration and guidance for humanity at large.[2] Religious sentiments and search for individual spirituality return to the space of secularized societies as it is noticed by surprise. People try to experience religion (also by adapting to Asian spiritualities) after a period of living in a desacralized man-made world (the "City without God") ruled by the rationality of technological progress, market dynamism, materialism, consumerism, post-metaphysic destruction, and projection.

Our discourse on "World Religions, Diversity, Not Dissension," is, if I understand correctly, placed in this complex global context.

In my chapter, I start with the submission that in difference to the divisive and only difference stressing mode of thought (mostly in the contemporary western way of thinking) in India (may be also in many Asian and African countries), there is an inclusive approach (empathic reception of the other) with the intention not to deny the differences and yet to be in union (unity despite differences)—a kind of openness. After explaining this stand briefly with empirical instances from the pluricultural existential situations, I shall show— in the major section—the possibility of modes of cooperative coexistence of various world religions and ideologies with special reference to Kerala.

APPROACHES TO PLURALITY

In our attempt to deal with the phenomenon of plurality of religions, ideologies, and cultures we can observe different attitudes emerging in world religions. These approaches have been often identified as: exclusivism, inclusivism, pluralism, relativism, ecumenism, and universalism. In the context of my deliberations I would like to begin with inclusivism in the Indian approach to plurality and difference.

Inclusive Approach to Diversity—Theoretical Foundation and Argument

Historically speaking India remained and remains still open for religions and ideologies coming from elsewhere or the differences originating from within. The Indian subcontinent is a habitat of various migrant

[2] Anindita Balslev, Concept note of conference, p. 9.

folks including the Aryans. Hence the discourse on "foreign religions," deals with very sensitive issues. I would rather stress the openness, the inclusive mentality of Indian mind. Paul Hacker, a German Indologist of the twentieth century, called the phenomenon of including others into one's own religious cosmos "inclusivism," that is, according to his studies, very much prevalent in the so-called Neo-Hinduism.[3] Thus for example, Hinduism has no problem in its understanding of divinity to include Buddha or even Christ as avatars. But Hacker points out one further aspect of this inclusive action, namely the included element is often subordinated to the own deity, i.e., some kind of hierarchy is perceived. The Indologist cites many historical examples. But I cannot go into details here.

Sarvepalli Radhakrishnan's encounter with other religions such as Christianity and other world religions is remarkable.[4] At the heart of his program of harmonizing lies, according to the German Indologist Wilhelm Halbfass, the concept of experience.[5] Experience is the soul of religion.[6] "The manner in which Radhakrishnan contrasts Hinduism with Christianity and other religions is more conciliatory than that of Vivekananda," opines Halbfass.[7]

Empirical Observations of Inclusive Attitude

I have observed this inclusive mentality even while worshipping one's ishta devata: The shiva temples have in its *Garbha Graha* (sanctum sanctorum) Shiva Linga. But on the outer entrance there can be a statue of Vishnu. The devotee goes first to the sanctum sanctorum for worship. After performing that, on the way back he would pay homage also to Vishnu.

---

[3] Paul Hacker, Aspects of Neo-Hinduism As Contrasted with Surviving Traditional Hinduism, in: Paul Hacker, Kleine Schriften, ed. Lambert Schmitthausen. Wiesbaden, 1978.

[4] Eastern Religions and Western Thought, 1939; Recovery of Faith, 1956.

[5] Wilhelm Halbfass, India and Europe (Albany/NY, 1988), p. 253; see ibid. 378 (ch. III. p. 21).

[6] S. Radhakrishnan, Religion and Culture (Delhi, 1968).

[7] W. Halbfass, p. 253. On Vivekananda see also: FRONTLINE, The Legacy of Vivekananda. A Critical Reappraisal on His 150th Birth Anniversary, 30 (2) (January 26–February 8, 2013): 5–44.

In the simple day-to-day life we instill in our children this inclusive and open approach in encountering the other. This openness and extension of familial relationship is to be observed. While children being introduced to strangers we say: see that uncle, that aunty, that your brother and that cousin sister..., etc. (A German friend of mine, the daughter of—an intercultural marriage—father Indian and mother German, could not cope with this universally extended joint family relating to the other in her "European" intercultural perception of the other!)

Inclusivism and Respecting Differences

The diversity of religions even within each religion is to be respected and accepted. Very often we forget the diversity within Hinduism, Buddhism, Christianity, Islam, Jainism, etc., itself and use the term uncritically as if we refer to one homogeneous, monolithic religion. D. S. Khan rightly remarks in her interesting study on interactions of various religions in Kerala,[8] "When pondering interactions between different religious communities, most people tend to think in terms of three uniform blocks—Hindu, Muslim and Christian. They believe that coexistence as well as conflict, results from the encounter between monolithic systems of beliefs and practices..." We fail to see "the extreme diversity that exists within the broad denominations 'Hinduism,' Islam (and I would add Christianity, Buddhism, etc., too) as well as the phenomena which result from this diversity."[9]

RELIGIONS OF KERALA

Kerala depicts itself as "God's own country!" This does not mean that Malayalees have only one religion! Since centuries three major religious traditions Hinduism, Christianity, and Islam contribute to the multireligious, multicultural making of the society in Kerala. Kerala has a unique record in India, it is said, for the harmonious coexistence of diverse religions.

[8] D. S. Khan, *Sacred Kerala: A Spiritual Pilgrimage* (New Delhi, 2009), pp. 17, 18.

[9] Ibid., p. 18.

In the past Jainism and Buddhism too (besides Judaism) existed in Kerala. Due to different historical roots and sociocultural backgrounds Kochi Jews developed significant characteristics of their community (caste-like structure of white, brown, black Jews).[10] Christianity in Kerala is as old as Christianity itself and dates back to the 1st century AD. It is mainly this pre-colonial, inculturated form of Christianity in Kerala (known also as Indian Christianity!),[11] and its coexistence with other religions I would like to underline in my chapter.

Muslims constitute a major community in Kerala. The first followers of Islam entered the coastal region of Kerala as traders, and intermingled with the population, intermarried, established the Islamic community and became economically and politically influential.[12] They too feel their Indian inculturated identity and contribute to the composite culture of Kerala. Besides the larger communities of the main religions there are also members of other religions in smaller numbers including Sikhism, Jainism, Buddhism, and Judaism. Adivasis practise their own religious rituals and customs.

The community of the influential religious and social reformer Narayana Guru needs special mention. Sree Narayana Guru attracted particularly the Ezhavas and Dalits. His teaching of equality and social reform movement contributed to the eradication of the caste-based dis-crimination. That was an important factor to construct the socially pro-gressive state of Kerala. People became aware of human dignity and rights. His proclamation of "One caste, one religion, one God for man" could effect positive results for those excluded from temple and for the inner ecumenical dialogue within Hinduism. Guru opened horizons beyond existing structures and traditional forms of religion. No idols, no *murthi* puja, no temples was his stand. His personality and message attracted both: atheists as well as religious people. His ardent disciple Sahodaran Ayyappan (Brother Ayyappan), who was a staunch Marxist,

---

[10] Nathan Katz (ed.), Studies of Indian Jewish Identity (New Delhi, 1995); Who are the Jews of India? (Berkeley, 2000).

[11] J. Valiamangalam, Indian Christian Spirituality, in Hindu Spirituality II (World Spirituality 7), K. R. Sundarajan, Bithika Mukerji (eds) (New York, 1997), pp. 507–529.

[12] J. B. P. More, Origin and Early History of the Muslims in Kerala. 700 AD–1600 AD (Calicut, 2011); Roland, Mapilla Muslims of Kerala, 1976 (Delhi, 1992).

is a fascinating example for this fact. E. M. S. Namboodiripad[13] (the former Marxist leader and first Chief Minister of Kerala) considered Sahodaran Ayyapan as his teacher. Sahodaran Ayyappan (revered by some as a divine incarnation) tried many social reforms shocking both upper and low caste people! He redefined his master's dictum: "One caste, one religion, one God for man" to: "No caste, No religion, No god for man."[14] In Narayana Guru's thinking and action we see an inclusive attitude. Christian and other elements got absorbed in his thought. He was very much influenced by the Neo-Vedanta of Swami Vivekananda, Mahatma Gandhi, and other reformers. Sree Narayana Guru is for Kerala Ambedkar and Gandhi in one person. For Narayana Guru pluralism culminates in Universalism.

In today's scenario of religious pluralism there are other groups and movements coming up like that founded in 1979–1981 by Mata Amritanandamayi (Amma).[15] Besides offering spiritual teaching, *darshan*, and "Embracing the world," Amma as a guru together with her disciples from India and abroad initiated very strong social, educational, health care, and other organizations registered as "Public Charitable Trusts" and effectively functioning as NGO with international recognition and support.

TRADITIONAL CHRISTIANITY AS INTEGRAL PART OF MULTIRELIGIOUS SOCIETY

The origin and history of Christians in Kerala[16] is very different from elsewhere in India due to the continuity of the St. Thomas tradition. St. Thomas Christians believe that St. Thomas, the apostle of Jesus

---

[13] Namboodiripad, E.M.S., The Communist Party in Kerala (New Delhi, National Book Centre, 1994).

[14] D. S. Khan, p. 170.

[15] Maya Warrier, Hindu Selves in a Modern World (London, 2005).

[16] Kurian Mathothu, Sebastian Nadackal: Marthomma Christianikalude Sabha Noottandukaliloode, Pala. English translation of it under the title: The Church of St. Thomas Christians Down The Centuries (Pala, 2010). For further information: C. V. Cheria, A History of Christianity in Kerala (Kottayam, 1973); P. Placidus Podipara, The Individuality of the Malabar Church (Palai, 1972), H. C. Perumalil, E. R. Hambye (eds), Christianity in India (Alleppey, 1972).

Christ, preached the gospel[17] first among Jews[18] in the region of Cranganore/Kodungallur in about 52 AD. The close relation of the first Indian Christians to the Jews is still present in the name Nazrani used for Christians (following the path of Jesus of Nazareth). The tradition says that St. Thomas converted few Brahmin families from whom the Syrian Christians depict their genealogy and social status. It is believed that Apostle Thomas founded seven or eight churches (i.e., Christian communities) in then Kerala.[19] Ancient Greek, Roman, and Syrian Christian writers speak for it, that there have been Indian Christians from second century onwards.[20] This Christian community existed before Shankara (eighth or seventh Century AD[21]), even before the Sanskritization (Srinivasan) of Dravidian society. Historical evidences of the famous copper plates and various traditions prove the integrated and respected status of the Christians living in middle age kingdoms of Kerala: St. Thomas Christianity is not a product or legacy of European Colonialism.

The arrival of the Portuguese changed the pre-colonial situation because the Christians of the West tried to get the administrative and theological control (Padruado) over the socially and culturally integrated, privileged autonomous Thomas Christian communities having their own ecclesiastical authorities and liturgical traditions. The Church administration of Goa divided the resisting Thomas Christian Church in sixteenth century. Since the eighteenth century the ancient Thomas Christian tradition is partitioned in three main sections with various churches of oriental Roman Catholic, Orthodox, Anglican-Evangelical profiles within the Thomas Christian identity.[22] They consider themselves

[17] James Puliurumpil, History of the Syro Malabar Church (Vadavathoor, Kottayam, 2013); also James Puliurumpil, St. Thomas in India (Patristic Evidences, Kottayam, 2012), pp. 55–62.

[18] Th. Puthiakunnel, Jewish Colonies Paved the Way for St. Thomas, in: J. Vellian (ed.), The Malabar Church (Rome 1970), pp. 187–191.

[19] James Kurukilamkattu MST: Ezhara Pallikal (MST Publication, 2013). Arara Palli means not half, but that it was built by the king (Arachan)!

[20] M. K. Kuriakose, History of Christianity in India: Source Materials (Madras 1982), nr. 12; Joseph Kulathramnnil, Cultural Heritage of Knanaya Syrian Christians (Sharjah, 2001).

[21] S. Radhakrishnan, *Indian Philosophy*. Volume 2 (New Delhi 1990), pp. 447–450.

[22] C. George, "The Seven Churches of St. Thomas," *St. Thomas Christian Encyclopedia of India*. Ed. by G. Menacherry, Volume 2 (Trichur 1973), pp. 179–181.

as inner-Indian Churches with strong roots in the Indian Thomas tradition. At the same time, they are able to mediate between the Indian Christian identity and the identity of the old Churches in Asia, Europe, and Africa. St. Thomas Churches sustain the Indian Diaspora communities and their Indian heritage in different cultural and religious contexts.

It is worth noting that two Indian Cardinals of the Thomas Christian Church tradition, the Heads of Syro Malabar Church and of Syro Malankara Church participated in the conclave at Rome for the election of the new pope in March 2013. This is also a symbolic act of unity in diversity in religion for the Indians, for the Catholic Christians, and for global relations within and among religions.

THEOLOGICAL UNDERSTANDING OF THE SYRIAN (THOMAS) CHRISTIANS

It is necessary here to make some reference to the theology of the Thomas Christians in India. Christianity as they understood is more a way of life praxis than dogmatic. Christianity is pluralistic in the formation of its theology: "Three worlds, three cultures, three visions went to the making of the Christian church; the Jewish (Semitic), the Hellenistic and the Latin... There is the Syriac Orient, the Greek East and the Latin West."[23] They did not function in isolation. They have "common roots in the gospel message" and they interacted, and also they can even today enlighten each other. The oriental Syriac Christian churches have, according to the Syro Malabar bishop Kallarangatt "a unique role since they are representatives of and direct heirs to the Semitic world"..."Syriac Christianity is Asian Christianity... Before the arrival of the Portuguese, Christianity was represented here (in India) only by Syriac Orient... which took very easily root in India..."[24] Kallarangatt points to the fact that the St. Thomas tradition of Christianity represents the Syriac heritage of theology which developed outside the Roman Empire. Some peculiarities of this theology: This Theology "comes from prayer, meditation, contemplation, fasting, abstinence and ascetical life."[25] This

[23] Dr Joseph Kallarangatt, *Reflections on Theology and Church* (Manganam, 2001), p. 10.

[24] Joseph Kallarangatt, *Reflections on Theology and Church*.

[25] H. J. D. Drijvers, East of Antioch: Forces and Structures in the Development of Early Syriac Theology in the East of Antioch (London, 1984), p. 18 as quoted by Kallarangatt on p. 11 of the above work.

eastern theology is deeply spiritual, based on faith in the scripture and not so argumentatively rational and dogmatic. It uses more images and the language is poetic and symbolic and suggestive. It is theology inspired by its heavenly liturgy. The theology of the Church fathers was fruits or revelations of their monastic life. It is a theology of Incarnation, the descent of the divine into the human—into the whole creation. The Trinitarian mystery is also central to its theological understanding. The Presence of the Divine which is finally an ineffable mystery—in and from the awareness of it one has to live. Mysticism is at the root of it. It is no wonder that this Oriental theology which is spiritual, mystical, pastoral, ecclesiastical (in the sense of communion of saints), liturgical, and monastic could strike roots in India. Its understanding of church too is different from the Greco-Roman: "The church was a body of people praying and doing penance... The St. Thomas Christian ecclesial herit-age is a living spirituality."[26] Cardinal Tisserant documents the faith and spirituality of the Thomas Christians: "...the ancient Christianity of Malabar is a living witness to the early messengers of faith."[27] Considering the research on Early Church Fathers and the living oriental Church theology, the Vatican Council II promoted "a very strong eastern sense of theology"[28] and accepted the plurality and differences of the-ologies. Regarding variety of theology the council considers this as variety of expressions. "East and west have used different methods and approaches in understanding and proclaiming divine things"...These various theological formulations are to be "considered as complemen-tary rather than conflicting"... All these traditions with their spirituality "belong to the full catholic and apostolic character of the church (UR17)."[29] For the theology and spirituality of the Thomas Christians it became important that they lived in interaction with the various eastern churches such as the Alexandrian, Antiochean, Armenian, Chaldean, and Constantinopolitan.

The Thomas Christians called their living theology "Thommayude Margam" (Law of Thomas) which includes the whole lifestyle of these Christians.[30] The historian Podipara summarizes Thommayude Margam thus: "Hindu in culture, Christian in religion, oriental in worship."[31] This

[26] Kallarangatt, p. 189.

[27] Cardinal Tisserant, Preface, Clergy Monthly 16, 1952, p. 161 as quoted by Kallarangatt p. 190.

[28] Kallarangatt, p. 12.

[29] Ibid.

[30] Kallarangatt, pp. 210–211.

[31] Placid Podipara, Malabar Christians, p. 27.

model of Indian-incarnated Christianity was and is thus the way of life within the Indian world of religions.

INTERACTIONS AND INCULTURATION PROCESS

Examples of Interaction between Christian and Hindu Families

Christians developed certain devices of living interactively and in cooperation with one another.

Born into an ancient Syrian Christian or St. Thomas Christian (Syro Malabar Catholic) family having lived in a multireligious context in Kerala let me begin with my own personal experience as a child: The first day of every month is considered auspicious by our Hindu neighbor. Of course, many Christians too think so. The auspiciousness depends on the fact that whom you see first in the morning (Kanikanuka). Our Hindu neighbor was somehow convinced that if I or my elder brother entered their courtyard very early in the morning and if they saw one of us (Kanikanuka) first, that would be auspicious. My mother who practised loving and friendly relations with our Hindu neighbors, would accordingly wake up one of us to perform this act of friendship. A rationalist may say that the act one was supportive of a superstition! But I am convinced that it taught me to be benevolent to the neighbor and wish the very best for him.

The St. Thomas Christians hold the Jewish Old Testament (Tanakh) practice of Pasha (Peseha perunnal), i.e., the Pass Over Feast in their families on Maundy Thursday in the Easter Week. Thus it relates itself to the Jewish religion by enacting the Peseha—the ritual narration of the Paschal event. The observance of Peseha at home is an unbroken tradition only practised by the Indian Saint Thomas Christians. How they observe this feast in the multicultural context of Kerala is even more interesting from the intercultural or interreligious point of view: One piece of unleavened bread is prepared on a banana leaf under steam. A cross made out of palm leaves is placed on this one bread while baking and many other pieces of unleavened bread on banana leaves are prepared along with it. The bread with the cross (Kurishappam) is broken by the head of the family and shared strictly among the family (joint family, relations, etc.) and eaten (along with a drink [Pal = milk] made of coconut and jaggery), it is accompanied by readings from the Bible. However, the other pieces of bread (Indriyappam) without the cross are shared with the non-Christian neighbors and friends, who may belong to any other religion or no religion. The fellowship and sharing keeps, thus, the communal bond with the other brethren too.

The ritual services of the Thomas Christians are still called Qurbana which is derived from the Aramaic and Hebrew term *korban* which means sacrifice. The Qurbana was till 1970 held in Syriac language. The songs and tunes were of Syrian. Since Vatican Council II and the subsequent liturgical reforms, the Qurbana texts have been translated into beautiful Malayalam texts (also into Tamil, Kannada, Hindi, English, and others) and the Syrian tunes are preserved for the songs, even in Malayalam translation. These are interesting examples of creatively and positively dealing with diversity through dialogical, inculturating incarnational liturgy.

Rituals in Multireligious Context[32]

Some of the religious ceremonies the Saint Thomas Christians shared with the Hindus. Much of the religious ceremonies of the Thomas Christians pertaining to birth, puberty, and marriage —were nearly identical to the ceremonies of Hindus in Kerala. The terminology which they used to refer to these rituals was the same as used by the Brahmins or Nairs. Thus, for example, *Samskaras* (sacraments), *Annaprasnam* (the child's first taste of rice), *Vidyarambham* (initiation into learning): it is done at the age of five. The teacher (guru) keeps the child on the lap and helps it to draw a cross and scribble one or two letters with the child's tender fingers in rice spread out in a brass plate or on the floor. Interesting it is to note that the teachers were often Hindus, they taught the Christian children the Christian prayers written on Palmyra leaf; *Vivaham* (tying of Thali) or *Minnu* (tying of a small gold ornament on the neck of the bride by the bridegroom). The only difference is that the Thali of the Syrian Christians has a small cross on it as the identity marker! *Jatakakarma* (birth ritual) shows inculturation. Immediately after the birth of the child, one would shout in the child's ear "Maron Yesu Mishiha" (Jesus Christ is Lord). The child would be then also fed with three drops of honey in which a little gold has been mixed.

Interactive and friendly relations existed and still exist between Temples and Churches. For example, the tradition of exchanging

---

[32] James Puliurumpil, History of the Syro Malabar Church (Kottayam, 2013), pp. 166–171.

"Muthukoda" (ornamental umbrella) and even temple elephants for church festivals.

The architecture of the early Christian churches looked like Hindu temples from outside and from inside like Jewish synagogue. But after the arrival of the Portuguese the churches resembled more Portuguese in style! Present day there are some efforts here and there to integrate Kerala temple architectural elements. Many of the modern churches are too big and ostentatious. However, the churches have still many elements which are common to Hindu temples. Some of such shared symbols are lotus, peacock, arrows, snakes, half moon, etc. As D. S. Khan puts it, "...the popular traditions of Hinduism, Islam and Christianity in Kerala bear a kind of family resemblance."[33] The flag-post (Kodimaram) has its place in front of the churches even today (also the communists have flag-posts in front of their monuments for communist martyrs— only difference: a red flag with hammer and sickle). The stone multitiered (seven levels) lamp in front of the entrance of the church, oil lamps (Nilavilaku)—one finds in the churches and also at Christian homes. It is important to note that despite the sharing of the common symbols, the Christian identity is signaled by installing a cross on top of the mast and the lamp.

The St. Thomas cross also known as Mar Thoma Sliba or Nazrani Menorah points to the sharing of symbols with Jews, Hindus, and Buddhists. Some say that its design was based on the Jewish seven-branched candle Menorah—an ancient symbol of the Hebrews! Some crosses shown standing in a lotus. It is interesting to note that the St. Thomas cross has no figure of Jesus Christ on it. The flowery arms, as some interpretation goes, symbolize the "joyfulness" (*ananda*) of the resurrection—the risen Christ and points to the resurrection theology. The Holy Spirit on top in the form of dove—suggests the role of Holy Spirit in the resurrection. Resurrection is most central to the Theology and spirituality of Eastern Church and, hence, Easter celebration is important. The Lotus symbolizes Buddhism and Hinduism or, let us say, an Indian symbol at large shared by all. Till the arrival of the Portuguese this cross was the only symbol of the Syrian Christians. They did not use any images, no idols in order to prevent idolatry. That shows a common tradition with Jews and also with Islam.

All these definitely speak for the harmonious coexistence of religions in Kerala.

---

[33] D. S. Khan, p. 99.

The Hindu rulers were mostly very benevolent to the Syrian Christians in the past. The rajas used to recognize the useful role of the early Christian group being an integrated segment of the traditional society. They granted them land, concessions, and privileges expressing their favor, protection, and expectation that the Christian will remain within their territory and contribute to the prosperity of the rajas and the general community. The goodwill of the rulers is recorded on copper plates, which highlight even rights and privileges such as dignitaries (e.g., Tharisappalli Copper plate grant is one of the reliable documentary evidences of the privileges and influence that St. Thomas Christians enjoyed in early Malabar). There were some more reasons why the rulers got interested and tried to be in good relations with Christians. The Syrian Christians were trained (like the Nairs) in military and they were known for their loyalty and ability as soldiers.

All this may show that the Syrian Christians being part of the society willingly and wisely adapted an inculturation process, by which they integrated Hindu themes and rituals in their behavior, yet were conscious of their specific identity and kept it. We could agree with the scholars who say: The Nazranis or Syrian Christians were "Hindu in culture, Christian in faith, and Syrian in liturgy." So are they even today.

Syrian Christians never felt and do not feel as "foreign" in their own land and culture, and among their own people. They are indigenous. Hence, one has to be very careful in using such terms indiscreetly to all Christians in India, when we interact and dialogue with religions. Syrian Christians are, if at all, as much a migrant community which got totally integrated as the Aryans who came also as migrants to India. As far as Kerala is concerned, they point to the fact that these Indian Christians with apostolic roots were in this part of west coast of India (Kerala) much before Sree Shankara Acharya who is recognized as son of the soil. To be aware of these historical aspects of the religion and religious social identity is also important in our interaction and dialogue.

SHARED SPACES AND RITUALS

Particularly significant is the *Sabarimala pilgrimage* (Ayyappa cult) where three major world religions cooperatively interact, i.e., Hindu,

Muslim, and Christian.[34] There exists a special community bond and rituals during the pilgrimage season between the Hindu and Muslim communities, including a Vavar Masjid where Ayyappa pilgrims go and offer coconut, and a Sastha temple where Muslims go and make their offerings.

Also, the Christian community is connected with Ayyappa and Sabarimala cult: one character called Veluthacchan, a white father,[35] is identified with St. Sebastian, the Christian martyr (who is in Kerala, the patron saint who protects and cures from small pox). There is another Christian Kochu Thomman who is said to be a Catholic devotee of the nineteenth century. He is supposed to have protected the temple from a fire and reconstructed the temple. One more Christian connection to Ayyappa is related to the church at Arthunkal built with the help of local Hindus and permission of the Thampuran of the Muthadath kingdom (sixteenth century). This church, famous for St. Sebastian the patron of small pox and great healer, is visited by the Ayyappa pilgrims on their way back from Sabarimala pilgrimage. They remove the chain (*rudraksha mala*) here ending the vrata period. The people appreciate the legendary close friendship of Ayyappa and St. Sebastian/Arthunkal Veluthacchan.[36] Despite changing conditions, the Interfaith solidarity seems to work for the common welfare and peace for all in the society.

According to some legends (a kind of narrative folk theology of Interfaith relations) Bhagavati is the elder sister of St. Mary! St. Sebastian is the brother of Bhagavati! This is illustrated by a legend pertaining to the Church dedicated to St. Mary and Bhagavati Temple, both exist close by in the village Kalissery (Chengannur). The legendary narration is contextually applied to the family-like relation among Christians and Hindus who always easily solve quarrels and reconcile. It is also background of ritual exchange.[37] At another church, though dedicated to St. Mary, St. Sebastian is very popular. There is also a Bhagavati temple

---

[34] In the year 2004, I got the chance to be introduced to Sabarimala pilgrimage tradition in Erumeli by their representatives, the then Vavar and Pillai at their houses. I am very thankful to both heirs of an important tradition.

[35] A parish priest called "white Father" was respected as saint and Ayyappa's friend by the people: Fr. Jacomo Fenicio (1558–1632), Catholic Church (Latin Rite), Arthunkal.

[36] According to D. S. Khan, p. 80.

[37] Ibid., pp. 105–106.

nearby. At this place, St. Sebastian is believed to be the brother of Bhagavati. During the church festival the statue of St. Sebastian can have a *darshan* of his sister in the opened sanctum of the temple.

INTERACTION WITH COMMUNISM

In Kerala, it is almost impossible for any religion to exist without a discourse and interaction with communism in its pluriform: Marxists (Russian version), Communism with affiliation to China (Maoists, Naxalites). It is very much a formative force in the society arguing for secular values, equality, and fighting against communalism. It can be also counted as one of the many faiths which has followers from all religions and all castes. Theists and atheists, Christians from all denominations, Hindus belonging to various groups. A good number of Muslims became Communists without abandoning Islam. Some have even the justification interpreting Islam as an: "ancient form of Socialism in world history."[38] Large number of Christians became Communists without renouncing their religion (many of my Marxist friends baptize their children, go to the church!), some priests even vote for the communists! Similarly, many Hindus became ardent communists keeping their religious affiliation. About 40 percent of the communists in Kerala adhere to their religion. The party leaders downplay the religious issue and maintain that religion is strictly a personal matter. The inhabitants of God's own country have transformed communism to a dynamic faith in its dialectical-dialogue with the existing religions of Kerala. The communists think that they have contributed much in spreading secularism in Kerala. Some Muslims are of the opinion that communism brought a tremendous change in the mentality of Kerala Muslims.

In the political history of Kerala there had been confrontations between Communist government and the non communist sections of people (e.g., the protest movement Vimochana Samaram, i.e., liberation movement of Nairs and Christians together). Some of the recent dialectical-dialogue between communists and the Christians/church authorities is worth noting: The communist party try to appropriate Christian images (e.g., used posters with the picture of Mother Theresa to inspire the communist youth and in another instance used a caricature of the painting Last Supper by Michelangelo for critique of contemporary

---

[38] According to D. S. Khan, p. 172.

world politics) for their political purpose.[39] In the communist party
national meeting Christ was appropriated. They mentioned in the speech
that Christ was the first and best Communist. A section of the Christians
and the church responded and condemned such misuse of Christian
idols. But some other section of Christians responded in a more amica-
ble and reconciling manner.

REFLECTIONS ON INCLUSIVE DIALOGICAL APPROACH—FROM A CATHOLIC/CHRISTIAN (POST VATICAN COUNCIL II) AND HINDU PERSPECTIVE

Now we come back to some reflections on the phenomena of Inclusivism
and Universalism mentioned earlier and try to draw our attention to
some of the recent developments in this regard from the perspective of
Catholic Church and Hinduism. This would also put the Syrian
Christians or Thomas Christians with their multireligious experience
and the Indian inculturation in Kerala in the right global perspective.

Vatican Council II (1962–1965) is one event and the other the World
Day of Prayer for Peace Meet at Assisi on October 27, 1986 under Pope
Paul II and in 2011 under Pope Benedict XVI, which brought significant
changes in the perspectives of interreligious understanding and relations
in the recent history of the Catholic Church:

> Vatican Council II marks a great breakthrough in interreligious
> dialogue with its many Documents. Nostra Aetate ("NA")[40] is the
> most important one as far as the relationship to World Religions
> and interreligious dialogue are concerned. Yet "NA is not to be
> taken in isolation, but rather must be read in conjunction with the
> other documents of Vatican II," says Fitzgerald.[41] Initially the
> intention was to re-examine and correct the relation of the Catholic
> Church with Judaism (in order to counter the anti-Semitism). The

[39] Newspapers such as Deepika, Manorama, 2012, carried articles.
[40] Declaration on the Relation of the Church to Non-Christian
Religions, 1965.
[41] Archbishop Michael L. Fitzgerald, "Revisiting Nostra Aetate after
Fifty Years," in: Revisiting Vatican II. 50 Years of Renewal. International
Conference Papers, Dharmaram College (Bangalore, 2013), pp. 163–168
(quotation from p. 164).

bishops from the Arab world insisted on including Islam too, the Bishops from Asia and Africa pleaded for a broader treatment of religions. The Indian Syro-Malabar Catholic theologians played an important role in including Hinduism and Buddhism in its purview. Thus they could broaden the Eurocentric perspective of the Declaration.

"NA" stresses the unity of humanity in Chapter 1. It accepts the plurality of religions and worldviews, admits the duty of the church to foster unity and charity among individuals and even among nations, calls for fellowship with all religions. In Chapter 2, the Council deals with as first in order Hinduism because of its very ancient origin, Buddhism too is mentioned in its various forms. Though the heterogeneity of Hinduism is not mentioned in detail, the council highlights significant dimensions. The inclusive and all embracing attitude of the Church towards world religions and worldviews is expressed thus: "The Catholic Church rejects nothing of what is true and holy in these religions. She has a high regard for the manner of life and conduct, the precepts and doctrines which, although differing in many ways from her own teaching, nevertheless often reflect a ray of that truth which enlightens all men."[42] It admits that different religions are different ways of encountering the mystery of God.

With regard to "NA," Felix Wilfred, a leading Indian theologian, says that the Asian bishops had the boldness and candor during the council to make clear to the Pope and the Roman Curia, that Asia and Asian churches "have something to teach the Church of Rome as well as the universal church," the understanding of Universality of the church receives a new dimension in the form of pluralism. From Asian churches came the three directions for interreligious dialogue, which are most relevant for Asia: "dialogue with the cultures, religions and the poor."[43]

With Vatican II interreligious dialogue became programmatic for the whole Catholic Church wherever Catholic Christians live and Catholic communities are integral part of a pluralistic religious and cultural society. Asian Christians found the return to the pluralism of earliest Christian tradition consonant with Asian cultural ethos. And in the Prayer Meet at Assisi (1986), Pope John Paul II stressed that there is "the dimension of prayer, which in the very real diversity of religions tries to

[42] Quoted by Fitzgerald, p. 165.
[43] Felix Wilfred, pp. 108, 109.

express communication with a Power above all our human forces. Peace depends basically on this power."[44]

All this shows us the inclusive approach of the Catholic Church as per "NA." Perhaps it differs from the understanding of Inclusivism and Universality of Religions in the Hindu context. Some of Mahatma Gandhi's statements might help us to see the nuances of perceiving and relating to other religions in the Hindu multireligious context. These writings came much before the Vatican Council II and we can see how prophetic and insightful his ideas sound. Thus, for example, Gandhi explains his stand from his personal experience of religions. It is interesting to understand the Catholicity of Hinduism as Gandhi expounds it, "My Hinduism is not sectarian. It includes all that I know to be best in Islam, Christianity, Buddhism and Zoroastrianism," or "It is because I am a *sanatani* (orthodox) Hindu that I claim to be a Christian, a Buddhist and a Muslim...I claim that Hinduism is all inclusive...I am proud to belong to that Hinduism which is all inclusive and which stands for tolerance." He has problem in accepting the concepts of conversion and mission. He explains the century-old interaction between religions and cultures in India and the formation of Hinduism using the mode of evolutionary progress: "It [Hinduism] has no doubt absorbed many tribes in its fold, but this absorption has been an evolutionary, imperceptible character. Hinduism tells everyone to worship god according to his own faith or dharma and so it lives at peace with all religions." He sees the common factor in all religions as nonviolence.

Sri Ramakrishna, Guru of Vivekananda with his view of *Dharma-samanvaya* (harmony of religions), gave us the Indian version of religious pluralism. Vivekananda took pluralism one step further and said it must culminate in Universalism.[45] Sri Ramakrishna's harmony of religions was based on some principles: "The first is the principle of direct experience...direct mystical experience...," i.e., one must attain "direct spiritual experience." Everyone should follow "his own religion and attain the highest fulfilment that it promises."[46] For Ramakrishna the ultimate reality is only one, is known by different names in different religions. Realization of the ultimate reality is the goal of human life. All

[44] Vatican: Address of John Paul II, Assisi, October 27, 1986, §3.

[45] Swami Bhajanananda, "Harmony of Religions." From the standpoint of Sri Ramakrishna and Swami Vivekananda (Kolkata, 2007), pp. 26–36.

[46] Swami Bhajanananda, p. 27.

world religions are valid and true. Views on interreligious existence, envisaged in India from life experience much before Vatican II! Vivekananda has, as an Advaitin, his own understanding of universalism. He seems to see all religions as journey of the soul towards God, of course in an upward evolution. Vivekananda seems to go beyond all religions in his understanding of the absolute. But then he also speaks of a universal religion and all religions are manifestations of the universal spiritual consciousness of humanity.

This catholic and inclusive spirit of Hinduism enables it to keep itself alive. Gandhi cannot imagine an India without religion. "If religion dies, then dies India," said Gandhi. The secularism of Europe is trying to do away with God.

To come back to the Christian perspective of inclusivism. Post-Council view highlights: "Dialogue is the Way of Being the church." The church is understood as "the communion of particular (and sui iuris) churches...though they are particular the universal church becomes present in them with all its essential elements."[47]

Church holds that Jesus is a message for the whole world and he is a witness of the love of God for the mankind. Collaboration and loving participation and not competition and territorial expansion which is desired. The Catholic Church understands itself as a pilgrim community on earth together with all religions and worldviews striving forward to the fulfillment of the kingdom of God or liberation of mankind.

CONCLUDING REMARKS

It is clear that all religions are faced with the phenomenon of plurality. The problem is age old. The novelty lies therein as to how each religion copes with it. We live in the World Parliament of religions. We all have to work together for the welfare of humanity. Various religions can learn from each other and mutually enrich. It is important that we study at least the religions that we practise and, also necessarily, the religions of the multireligious context where we live. Correct knowledge of the religions of our living context helps us to shed prejudices and avoid conflicts. Let us hope that the conference may help us to tap the positive energies hidden in the world religions for the welfare of the entire humanity.

[47] Cardinal George Alancherry, inaugural speech at Dharmaram, Bangalore.

17

Swami Vivekananda and Indian Secularism

Makarand R. Paranjape

INTRODUCTION

This chapter examines Swami Vivekananda's contribution to the discourse of secularism in modern India. Indian secularism served, as we know, not only as a state ideology opposed to religious nationalism, both within India and across the border, but also as a sort of civic faith, a substitute religion of sorts. I argue that Vivekananda, by striving to make religions open and plural, implying an acceptance of religious diversity and respect for all faiths, contributed to this uniquely Indian experiment with secularism. It was this insistence on religious pluralism, rather than the strict separation of the state from religion, that influenced and contributed to the creation of modern Indian secularism. Though both secularism and modernity are often thought of as non- if not anti-religious enterprises, in India we see a different trajectory of their development. In his brief life of less than forty, Vivekananda not only galvanized a demoralized and moribund nation-in-the making, but gave Indian public culture a definite direction and destination. Following his guru, Sri Ramakrishna, but also differing significantly from him, Vivekananda provided Indian modernity its special inflection by reinventing, or rejecting the role of religious tolerance in the shaping of public culture. He also ensured that modern science was guaranteed a space in the Indian religious mentality. Indian modernity, in other words, involved the rejection of certain traditions and the revalidation of others. In this process, Vivekananda played crucial role. He not only internationalized Vedanta, but reinvented a new kind of Hinduism which could face the challenges of modernity without losing its essence. One hundred and twenty years ago, in his concluding address at the Parliament of Religions, Vivekananda wanted "Harmony and Peace and not Dissension" between world religions. Of course, we are still far away from that ideal, but Vivekananda's clarion call for the understanding and acceptance of religious diversity, not to mention the clarity with which he articulated it, ensures that we do not totally lose sight of that ideal today, even in our notions of secularism.

In order to show how Vivekananda contributed to the discourses of India's religion-positive secularism, I propose to look at and examine two crucial moments in Vivekananda's life, primarily his addresses at the Parliament of Religions in Chicago in September 1983 when he first burst onto the world stage, and more briefly the series of lectures he gave from Colombo to Calcutta, from Jan 1897 to Feb 1897 on his triumphant return to his motherland. Essentially, I believe that Vivekananda effected a unique rearrangement of traditional Hindu religious practices by substituting the *karma kanda* of Purva Mimamsa with modern science, while leaving the spiritual, Vedantic component which constituted Uttara Mimamsa untouched.[1] This ensured that modern science and technology rather than mantras and magical formulae became the dominant tools of altering our material reality and manipulating nature. On the other hand, the ancient spiritual quest of the Indian people was not abandoned in favor of a life of sense-gratification and material prosperity. In addition, by combining religion with science in a unique way, Vivekananda also helped fashion the discourse of Indian secularism. This 150th anniversary celebration of his birth thus affords us a new opportunity to understand Vivekananda's ministry in our present-day atmosphere of religious antagonism and competitive politics.

INDIAN SECULARISM REVISITED

Secularism is, admittedly, one of the key words in the self-definition of post-independence India, though it was only introduced into the Constitution as late as 1974 by the then Prime Minister, Indira Gandhi, through a special amendment. However, this term is also vague and shifting, subject to many different interpretations and appropriations.

---

[1] For example in his lecture on "The Vedanta" delivered at Lahore on November 12, 1897, he says, "The Hindus have the greatest respect for the Karma Kanda of the Vedas, but, for all practical purposes, we know that for ages by Shruti has been meant the Upanishads, and the Upanishads alone." Available at: http://www.advaitaashrama.org/cw/volume_3/lectures_from_colombo_to_almora/the_vedanta.htm.

Jakob De Roover in his incisive essay "The Vacuity of Secularism" comments on this difficulty:

> Instead of being embedded in a well-structured theory, the idea of secularism consists of a number of isolated normative proposi-tions regarding the relation of politics and religion, which are proclaimed as though they are self-evidently true.[2]

Indeed, De Roover shows how "these tenets of secularism do not make much sense, because they are based on an arbitrary and unstable distinction between the religious and the secular,"[3] a fuzziness that is not peculiar to India, but persists elsewhere too to such an extent that he wonders "why do so many intellectuals remain under the spell of the principle of the separation of politics and religion, while this principle suffers from a basic lack of intelligibility?"[4] De Roover's undermining of the sacred–secular dichotomy is quite in keeping with a post-secular questioning of such binaries. He demonstrates how such an opposition would collapse without a clear differentiation between the two domains; if there is no precision on the properties of each, then how is separation between the two to be effectuated?[5] Secularism itself takes on the hues of a state religion while religion, for some, being co-extensive with all there is doesn't leave space for a distinct space called the secular.

Given such confusions, what is of much more interest to us is how ideas of secularism operate differently in India and the West. When it comes to this question, the basic Indian position is that secularism in India implies not so much a clear separation of religion from the state as equal sympathy or tolerance to all faiths. As Thomas Pantham summing up the whole debate puts it, "the Indian constitutional vision ... enjoins the state to be equally tolerant of all religions and which therefore requires the state to steer clear of both theocracy or fundamentalism and the 'wall of separation' model of secularism."[6] When the Indian Constitution recommends equal tolerance in treating all religions, the

---

[2] Jakob De Roover, "The Vacuity of Secularism: On the Indian Debate and Its Western Origins." *Economic and Political Weekly,* 37(39) (September 28–October 4, 2002): 4047.

[3] Ibid.

[4] Ibid.

[5] Ibid., p. 4048.

[6] Thomas Pantham, "Indian Secularism and Its Critics: Some Reflections." *The Review of Politics,* 59(3) (Summer 1997): 523.

basis, as Pantham suggests, is the idea of "*sarva dharma samabhava*";[7] when, on the other hand, equal detachment or distance from all religions is implied, it occurred to me that the phrase used is *dharmanirapekshata*. Pantham goes on to elaborate his position by arguing that secularism in India, though it does not imply indifference or negativity towards religions, does uphold "a certain differentiation or relative separation of the political and religious spheres."[8] He suggests that in India, following Gandhi, "the relative autonomy (or, in other words, the nonabsolute separation) of religion and politics from each other is used for the reconstruction of both the religious traditions and the modern state."[9] What this entails is that the antonym of secular in India is not religious, but "communal";[10] what is more, "communal" is also the antonym of religious in the sense of being intolerant to other religions. As I myself have argued, two kinds of pluralism, both sacred and secular, are ranged against two kinds of intolerance, in India.[11] My own position is akin to William E. Connolly's, first articulated in *Why I Am Not a Secularist*,[12] but refined in "Some Theses on Secularism," where he exposes not only the "shallowness" of secularism, but also how it sets off the "reactive resonance machine," which sets about "to *minoritize* the world."[13] The counter to the problems of both neo-evangelical liberalism and narrow-minded secularism in the United States is a deep pluralism:

> Such a double-entry pluralism is *deep* because it reaches into the spiritualities and creeds of participants, rather than trying to quarantine them. It is deep *pluralism* because it promotes self-recoil

[7] Thomas Pantham, "Indian Secularism and Its Critics: Some Reflections." *The Review of Politics*, 59(3) (Summer 1997): 524.

[8] Thomas Pantham, "Indian Secularism and Its Critics: Some Reflections." *The Review of Politics*, 59(3) (Summer 1997): 524.

[9] Ibid., p. 540.

[10] Ibid., p. 525.

[11] Makarand R. Paranjape, "Secularism vs. Hindu Nationalism: Interrogating the Terms of the Debate," in *Dharma: The Categorial Imperative*, Ashok Vohra, Arvind Sharma and Mrinal Miri (eds) (New Delhi: D.K. Print World, 2005), pp. 262–275; *Acts of Faith: Journeys to Sacred India* (New Delhi: Hay House, 2012), p. 22.

[12] William E. Connolly, *Why I Am Not a Secularist* (Minneapolis, MN: University of Minnesota Press, 2000)..

[13] William E. Connolly, "Some Theses on Secularism." Available at: http://www.abc.net.au/religion/articles/2011/04/04/3181942.htm, last accessed April 22, 2013.

on the part of participants so that diverse constituencies can negotiate settlements out of mutual respect across multiple lines of
difference.

It contains a *spiritual* element because it solicits gratitude for
existence as such from a variety of faith minorities, as it seeks to
dampen those waves of hubris, existential resentment and cyni-
cism that can so easily plague a culture during a period of minor-
itization.

It is precisely such a deep pluralism that Vivekananda was attempting
to forge at the Parliament more than a hundred years ago and which is
still relevant to us in India today.

THE PARLIAMENT OF RELIGIONS, 1893

Within six months of its successful conclusion, Charles Carroll Bonney,
Chicago judge, author, the President of the Worlds' Congress, went so
far as to say:

With remarkable accord, the leaders of progress in all lands have
recognised the World's Congresses of 1893, crowned by the
Parliament of Religions, as constituting an epoch-making event in
the history of human progress, marking the dawn of a new era of
brotherhood and peace.[14]

Looking back a hundred years later, Richard H. Seager, gathering
together some of the voices from the Parliament for contemporary
readers, called it *The Dawn of Religious Pluralism*. A year after this
edited volume, he published his detailed study, *The World's Parliament
of Religions: The East–West Encounter, Chicago, 1893*, arguing that
this event signified a crucial change in American religious and cultural
history.

Even by today's standards, the Parliament was undoubtedly an
organizational feat. Four months before it opened 3000 copies of the
preliminary address were sent out, informing various possible participants

---

[14] Charles C. Bonney, "The World's Parliament of Religions." *The Monist,*
5(3) (April, 1895): 322.

and interested parties around the world about the event and inviting them to attend it. Ten of the world's great religious traditions— Hinduism, Buddhism, Jainism, Zoroastrianism, Taoism, Confucianism, Shintoism, Judaism, Christianity and Islam—were honored in the inaugural ceremony, inviting their representatives together to worship. Of the 194 papers presented, 152 were by Christians, with twelve Buddhist, eleven Jewish, eight Hindu, two Muslim, Parsi, Shinto and Confucian each, one Taoist, and one Jain speakers also present.[15] However, the European branch of the largest Christian denomination in the world, the Roman Catholic Church, stayed away from it. Indeed, according to Marcus Braybrooke, "Pope Leo XIII officially censured the Roman Catholic speakers at the Parliament and forbade participation in 'future promiscuous conventions'."[16] The Church of England also did not participate. Its head, the Archbishop of Canterbury, wrote a letter of disapproval, saying quite bluntly: "the Christian religion is the one religion. I do not understand how that religion can be regarded as a member of a Parliament of Religions without assuming the equality of the other intended members."[17] The Sultan of Turkey, Abdul Hamid II, also refused to participate,[18] while Native Americans,[19] Mormons, and several other sects were kept out.[20] Nevertheless, the Parliament inaugurated an age of interreligious dialogue and pluralism. A part of the Columbian Exposition celebrating the European colonization of the world and the ascendency of the new nations of the North Atlantic, its original intention may have been to establish the supremacy of Protestant Christianity in matters of religion as the rest of the Exposition clearly

[15] Richard H. Seager. 1995. *The World's Parliament of Religions: The East-West Encounter, Chicago, 1893*. Bloomington: Indiana University Press.

[16] Marcus Braybrooke, "The Early Years of the Interfaith Movement." Available at: http://www.parliamentofreligions.org/news/index.php/2013/04/the-legacy-of-the-1893-parliament-of-the-worlds-religions/ last accessed April 18, 2013.

[17] John H. Barrows (ed.). *The World's Parliament of Religions: An Illustrated and Popular Story of the World's First Parliament of Religions, Held in Chicago in Connection with the Columbian Exposition of 1893*, 2 vols (Chicago: The Parliament Publishing Company, 1893), vol. 1, pp. 20–22.

[18] Richard H. Seager. 1995. *The World's Parliament of Religions: The East-West Encounter, Chicago, 1893*. Bloomington: Indiana University Press.

[19] Though kept out of the Parliament, they were exhibited in the Columbian Exposition in "mock villages."

[20] Richard H. Seager. 1995. *The World's Parliament of Religions: The East-West Encounter, Chicago, 1893*. Bloomington: Indiana University Press.

showed the West's material superiority over the rest of the world. Yet, the Parliament is often seen as marking the beginnings of American pluralism: "it was a harbinger of the rise of the idea of religious pluralism that is alternatively celebrated, studied, decried, and in various ways struggled over in many different quarters today."[21] Certainly, dialogue and concord seemed to have been central to the vision of its organizers. As Charles Carroll Bonney said in his opening address: "When the religious faiths of the world recognize each other as brothers, then will the nations of the earth yield to the spirit of concord and learn war no more."[22]

SWAMI VIVEKANANDA'S INTERVENTION

It was in such a gathering and context that Vivekananda spoke. By most accounts, his presence and contribution were not only notable but extraordinary, though his followers and admirers have tended to exaggerate it.[23] For our purposes, it might be more useful to look at what he was actually trying to say in the Parliament.

In his first address on September 13, 1893, which was a response to the welcome he received, Vivekananda begins by recalling how earlier speakers have referred to the "delegates from the Orient" as bearers "to different lands" of "the idea of tolerance." This, indeed, becomes his recurrent theme in the Parliament. Representing Hinduism at the Parliament, he says,

> I am proud to belong to a religion which has taught the world both tolerance and universal acceptance. We believe not only in universal toleration, but we accept all religions as true.

[21] Richard H. Seager. 1995. *The World's Parliament of Religions: The East-West Encounter, Chicago, 1893*. Bloomington: Indiana University Press, p. xxix.

[22] John H. Barrows (ed.). *The World's Parliament of Religions: An Illustrated and Popular Story of the World's First Parliament of Religions, Held in Chicago in Connection with the Columbian Exposition of 1893*, 2 vols (Chicago: The Parliament Publishing Company, 1893), vol. 1, p. 67.

[23] See for instance, Rajgopal Chattopadhyay, *Swami Vivekananda in India: A Corrective Biography* (Delhi: Motilal Banarsidass, 1999). All references to Vivekananda's speeches at the Parliament are taken from the online edition of the *Complete Works*; see Swami Vivekananda, *The Complete Works*. 9 vols (Kolkata: Advaita Ashrama, 1989). Available at: http://www.advaitaashrama.org/cw/volume_1/addresses_at_the_parliament/v1_c1_response_to_welcome.htm

Vivekananda shows how India offered refuge to Jews and Zoroastrians in earlier times, anticipating similar hospitality to the Dalai Lama and his Tibetan Buddhist followers, fleeing from China half a century later.

Quoting translations from the Shiva Mahima Stotram and the Bhagavad Gita, he emphasizes how different modes of and ideals of worship nevertheless reach the one universal divine: all paths lead to the one true God. Here, he restates his Guru's message of the equality of religions, *yato mat, tato path,* which is a modern reiteration of the ancient Rg Vedic declaration, *Ekam sat vipra bahuda vadanti*—truth is one; the wise call it by various names.

After a softer statement of the validity of all paths, Vivekananda now goes on the offence against what is the opposite of such pluralism:

> Sectarianism, bigotry, and its horrible descendant, fanaticism, have long possessed this beautiful earth. They have filled the earth with violence, drenched it often and often with human blood, destroyed civilisation and sent whole nations to despair. Had it not been for these horrible demons, human society would be far more advanced than it is now.

Here we see a fundamental difference between Vivekananda's and Ramakrishna's contexts. The latter functioned in a largely Hindu environment in which the different paths and traditions were not antagonistic to each other even if they debated one another for centuries. While there was sectarianism within the Hindu faith habitat, it was, by and large, not marked by hostility and aggression towards other paths, nor an overriding urge to destroy or convert others. Even invader faiths such as Islam were not necessarily inimical to Hinduism during the times of Ramakrishna. The competitive religious politics of communalism was to come later. What the Indians did face, however, was the onslaught of missionary propaganda. Vivekananda, on the other hand, was in the maelstrom of aggressive attacks from Christian evangelists, fundamentalists, and bigots of various hues. Not only he, but other delegates from the East, including Anagakarika Dhammapla of Sri Lanka, found themselves preaching against religious intolerance at the Parliament and elsewhere. This was not merely a philosophical position, but a strategic one too; they were creating space for themselves in a world dominated by Christian theology, which took the superiority of its own faith for granted. It was a matter of sheer survival of non-Abrahamic faiths in the modern world.

In one of the finest analyses of the context of the Parliament, Donald H. Bishop identifies three attitudes that emerged when different religions confronted each other at Chicago in 1893: "exclusion, inclusion and pluralism."[24] Further elaborating on the first, he says:

> Exclusion is the attitude that there is only one true religion which is destined to become universal. It was the attitude or view expressed most often at the Congress; supporters of the assertion that "Christianity is to conquer and supplant all the other religions of the world... and this Parliament is one of the steps toward this ultimate triumph."

The quotation that Bishop cites is from the October 1983 issue of the *American Advocate of Peace*. Bishop goes on to identify two types of Christian exclusivists—those who believed that Christianity was the only true religion while the others were false and those who held that the others may contain some good, but Christianity was the best.[25] Vivekananda was confronted with both kinds of exclusivists; his speeches at the Parliament were thus aimed at countering such positions and showing up their inherent limitations. Such views, according to him, were retrograde in modern times, when scientific progress and inter-cultural interactions had rendered them untenable, if not falsified. Vivekananda's stridency against fanaticism as well as

[24] Donald H. Bishop, "Religious Confrontation, a Case Study: The 1893 Parliament of Religions." *Numen,* 16(1) (April, 1969): 63. Bishop's typology has been cited by several subsequent scholars including Alan Race, Swami Tyagananda, Swami Bhajanananda, and Diana Eck. Alan Race, *Christians and Religious Pluralism: Patterns in the Christian Theology of Religions* (London: SCM Press, 1993); Swami Tyagananda, "Harmony of Religions." Available at: http://vedanta.org/2000/monthly-readings/harmony-of-religions/ last accessed April 22, 2013.

The seventh chapter of Eck's *Encountering God: A Spiritual Journey from Bozeman to Banaras* (1993, 2003), for instance, is subtitled "Exclusivism, Inclusivism, and Pluralism." According to Eck, the Christian position has gradually shifted from exclusivism, which held sway for nearly 1900 years, to inclusivism in the twentieth century, and finally to pluralism in recent decades. Eck cites Race, but does not mention Bishop's essay where these terms were used much earlier. Diana Eck, *Encountering God: A Spiritual Journey from Bozeman to Banaras*, 1993 (Boston: Beacon Press, 2003).

[25] Donald H. Bishop, "Religious Confrontation, a Case Study: The 1893 Parliament of Religions." 16(1) (April, 1969): 63–64.

his occasional claims to the superiority of Vedanta precisely because of the latter's pluralism must be seen in the light of such a context, not as Jyotirmaya Sharma and others have seen it, as a precursor for Hindu supremacism.[26]

In his second address, "Why We Differ," to the Parliament on September 15, 1893 Vivekananda offers a parable to account for religious differences. He uses the analogy of the well view versus the sea view to explain why all religions are limited and partial rather than complete and perfect:

> I am a Hindu. I am sitting in my own little well and thinking that the whole world is my little well. The Christian sits in his little well and thinks the whole world is his well. The Mohammedan sits in his little well and thinks that is the whole world.

Here, Vivekananda was following up on a position already enunciated by President Bonney in his opening speech:

> As the finite can never fully comprehend the infinite, nor perfectly express its own view of the divine, it necessarily follows that individual opinions of the divine nature and attributes will differ... Each must see God with the eyes of his own soul; each must behold him through the colored glass of his own nature; each must receive him according to his own capacity of reception.[27]

Similarly, the Brahmo representative from Bombay, B.B. Nagarkar said, "No nation, no people, or no community has any exclusive monopoly on God's truth."[28]

But one of the frogs in Vivekananda's story is from the sea, the dimensions and vastness of which the frogs in the wells are unable to conceive. Vivekananda, while relativizing the existing religious traditions

---

[26] Jyotirmaya Sharma. 2013. *A Restatement of Religion: Swami Vivekananda and the Making of the Hindu Nationalism.* New Haven, CT: Yale University Press.

[27] John H. Barrows (ed.). *The World's Parliament of Religions: An Illustrated and Popular Story of the World's First Parliament of Religions, Held in Chicago in Connection with the Columbian Exposition of 1893*, 2 vols (Chicago: The Parliament Publishing Company, 1893), vol. 1, p. 68.

[28] Donald H. Bishop, "Religious Confrontation, a Case Study: The 1893 Parliament of Religions." *Numen.* 16(1) (Apr. 1969): 71.

does allow for a view that is vaster than theirs, almost suggesting that the Parliament has enabled the emergence of such a view:

> I have to thank you of America for the great attempt you are making to break down the barriers of this little world of ours, and hope that, in the future, the Lord will help you to accomplish your purpose.

But supposing that well-views are limited compared to the sea-view, what about the various sea-views compared to, say, the planetary view? It would seem that a higher, more inclusive, and vaster perspective is always implied beyond the one that is ours at any given time. In his own parable, Vivekananda refrains from telling us who the frog from the sea was. But presumably being from the sea really means never believing that one's own perspective is the final or the best. The sea view is thus characterized by an openness and non-dogmatism that the well-view lacks. Yet, the notion of openness or its absence only makes sense compared to boundedness of some other views. The positions of both exclusivism and pluralism are contingent and relative; absolute intolerance or openness, in the other words, can only be abstractions or ideals. In the real world, one's pluralism or tolerance will only be in relation to the other, less-extensive positions available. Here, it seems to me that Vivekananda anticipates some of the problems implicit in debates on pluralism.[29] According to him, the partiality rather than the flawlessness of each religion makes it possible for its votaries to recognize and respect one another; we are equal because we are all imperfect. A non-hubristic admission of our limitations will enable us to dialogue.

In his third address on September 19, 1893 Vivekananda delivered his paper on Hinduism. In respect of how he constructs his own tradition, starting with the Vedas, Vivekananda does not differ substantially from another speaker, Manilal N. Dvivedi, who also spoke on "The Religious Beliefs of the Hindus."[30] Vivekananda begins with a historical overview, which he follows by an attempt to define what is common to all the different sects of Hinduism. That common characteristic is the idea that we are spirit, not body. Therefore, the aim of all spiritual endeavor is "Mukti—freedom, freedom from the bonds of imperfection, freedom from death and misery."

---

[29] See, for instance, William E Connolly's *Pluralism* (2005).

[30] Walter R. Houghton, Editor-in-Chief. *Neely's History of The Parliament of Religions and Religious Congresses* (Chicago: Neely, 1894), pp. 105–108.

But where Vivekananda differs radically from nearly all his contemporary commentators on Hindiusm is that he emphasizes the scientific temperament that to him marks the Hindu's quest for the higher truth and reality. The Hindu, like the scientist, is not afraid to say *I do not know*:

> Science has proved to me that physical individuality is a delusion, that really my body is one little continuously changing body in an unbroken ocean of matter; and Advaita (unity) is the necessary conclusion with my other counterpart, soul. ... the Hindu is only glad that what he has been cherishing in his bosom for ages is going to be taught in more forcible language, and with further light from the latest conclusions of science.

To Vivekananda, science, like Vedanta, is a search for unity: "Science is nothing but the finding of unity." The establishment for oneness at the heart of all diversity and duality is thus the aim of both religion and science: "This is the goal of all science. All science is bound to come to this conclusion in the long run." Here Vivekananda not only posits that religion and science have the same end, but also that, at least in the case of Vedanta, their methods are similar too. Further, he believes that the truths of Vedanta will be corroborated by modern science sooner or later.

Vivekananda now proceeds to mount a defence of Hinduism, which has been attacked by Christian missionaries. He explains the basis of Hindu practices and beliefs, including idolatry. He counters the charge that Hindus are superstitious with the accusation that Christians can be bigoted: "Superstition is a great enemy of man, but bigotry is worse. ... If the Hindu fanatic burns himself on the pyre, he never lights the fire of Inquisition." After this defence, Vivekananda returns to his favorite theme, the unity of the religious quest: "Every religion is only evolving a God out of the material man, and the same God is the inspirer of all of them." He explains the contradictions between religions as being only "apparent," not real: "says the Hindu. The contradictions come from the same truth adapting itself to the varying circumstances of different natures." Actually, the core of all religions is the same: "It is the same light coming through glasses of different colours. And these little variations are necessary for purposes of adaptation. But in the heart of everything the same truth reigns." Ending with a passionate plea for a universal religion, he says:

> if there is ever to be a universal religion, it must be one which will have no location in place or time; which will be infinite like the

God it will preach, and whose sun will shine upon the followers of
Krishna and of Christ, on saints and sinners alike; which will not
be Brahminic or Buddhistic, Christian or Mohammedan, but the
sum total of all these, and still have infinite space for development; which in its catholicity will embrace in its infinite arms, and
find a place for, every human being....

Such a universal religion would reject intolerance or hatred, devoting
itself to reveal the divinity imminent in every man and woman:

It will be a religion which will have no place for persecution or
intolerance in its polity, which will recognise divinity in every
man and woman, and whose whole scope, whose whole force, will
be created in aiding humanity to realise its own true, divine nature.

For such a universal religion, Hinduism may serve as a model. For it
accommodates such a plurality of views within it:

From the high spiritual flights of the Vedanta philosophy, of which
the latest discoveries of science seem like echoes, to the low ideas
of idolatry with its multifarious mythology, the agnosticism of the
Buddhists, and the atheism of the Jains, each and all have a place
in the Hindu's religion.

Ecumenism, according to Vivekananda, has a history. In the past,
both Ashoka and Akbar, two great emperors in India, tried to offer such
a universal religion. But they were only precursors for "It was reserved
for America to proclaim to all quarters of the globe that the Lord is in
every religion." His last lines, then, are a paean to the glories of the
United States:

Hail, Columbia, motherland of liberty! It has been given to thee,
who never dipped her hand in her neighbour's blood, who never
found out that the shortest way of becoming rich was by robbing
one's neighbours, it has been given to thee to march at the van-
guard of civilisation with the flag of harmony.

In his enthusiasm, Vivekananda ignores the bloody history of conquest and liquidation of the native Americans by the colonizing
Europeans who founded the country.

In his very brief fourth address, "Religion Not the Crying Need of India," on September 20, 1893, Vivekananda again exhorts the Christian missionaries not to denigrate Hinduism. He minces no words when he says:

> You Christians, who are so fond of sending out missionaries to save the soul of the heathen—why do you not try to save their bodies from starvation? In India, during the terrible famines, thousands died from hunger, yet you Christians did nothing. You erect churches all through India, but the crying evil in the East is not religion—they have religion enough—but it is bread that the suffering millions of burning India cry out for with parched throats.

He also spells out the nature of his mission in the West: "I came here to seek aid for my impoverished people, and I fully realised how difficult it was to get help for heathens from Christians in a Christian land." In return for material aid, he will give them religion, thus reversing the colonial flow of money out of and religion into India.

Vivekananda's fifth address: "Buddhism, the Fulfilment of Hinduism," September 26, 1893, is fascinating as a statement of the unity between the two traditions, at least in India. He begins by asserting, "I am not a Buddhist, as you have heard, and yet I am. If China, or Japan, or Ceylon follow the teachings of the Great Master, India worships him as God incarnate on earth." And, in the end, he declares:

> Hinduism cannot live without Buddhism, nor Buddhism without Hinduism. Then realise what the separation has shown to us, that the Buddhists cannot stand without the brain and philosophy of the Brahmins, nor the Brahmin without the heart of the Buddhist. This separation between the Buddhists and the Brahmins is the cause of the downfall of India. That is why India is populated by three hundred millions of beggars, and that is why India has been the slave of conquerors for the last thousand years. Let us then join the wonderful intellect of the Brahmins with the heart, the noble soul, the wonderful humanising power of the Great Master.

Vivekananda's call for unity between Hindus and Buddhists is all the more pertinent in today's India, after B.R. Ambedkar's movement to separate the two, pitting the latter against the former. While some may claim it as an appropriation or even an unjust attempt to collapse the two, Vivekananda did not wish India to forgo its claim to Buddhism, whose birthplace it was.

In his sixth and final address at the concluding session of the Parliament on September 27, 1893, Vivekananda reiterates his call for the unity of religions. But how is his "common ground" to be achieved? Not, says he, by "the triumph of any one of the religions and the destruction of the others. Do I wish that the Christian would become Hindu? God forbid. Do I wish that the Hindu or Buddhist would become Christian? God forbid." Instead, "each must assimilate the spirit of the others and yet preserve his individuality and grow according to his own law of growth." It is this approach that has been termed "integral Vedanta" by Bhajanananda[31] and others. It also anticipates Sri Aurobindo's integral yoga as outlined in *The Synthesis of Yoga.* Vivekananda, thus recommends co-existence not conversation, assimilation, not rejection of other faiths. He also repeats his attack on fanaticism and exclusivism:

> holiness, purity and charity are not the exclusive possessions of any church in the world....In the face of this evidence, if anybody dreams of the exclusive survival of his own religion and the destruction of the others, I pity him from the bottom of my heart....

Instead, he asks for a new religious spirit in keeping with a new age of unprecedented closeness between various continents and cultures. This new spirit will have a motto such as: "Help and not Fight," "Assimilation and not Destruction," "Harmony and Peace and not Dissension." The last of these admonitions forms the subtitle of the very conference in which this paper was first presented.

In brief, Vivekananda's addresses at the Parliament had two key thrusts: to call for an end to religion intolerance and to defend Hinduism against such fanaticism. In the process, he offered a new definition of religion, as a quest for truth, like modern science itself was; he saw that religion and science could be allies. He also offered a new method to discover a universal religion, a graded, cooperative ascent to the Divine among the denizens of the planet.

On his return to India in January 1897, Vivekananda delivered a series of remarkable lectures, during his triumphal progress from Colombo to Calcutta. In these lectures he provided his own vision and plan for the religious, cultural, economic, and political regeneration of India. He advocates nothing short of a total national resurgence,

[31] Swami Bhajanananda, *Harmony of Religions* (Kolkata: RMIC, 2008).

rebuilding India from the bottom up, brick by brick, as it were, by the power of the spirit. Spiritualizing life, to Vivekananda, meant finding out who one is, cultivating one's inner being, discovering the strength of the self (*atman*), and deploying these resources for social welfare, not just personal well-being. This was the essence of the "practical Vedanta" that the Swami preached, all of it is based on simple religious truth that we are not merely our bodies but immortal selves, essentially one with the Absolute Brahman. One important ingredient of practical Vedanta was the upliftment of the downtrodden, especially of women and depressed classes. Science and religion were not at loggerheads, but the former would aid the latter in the integral development of the new human being.

Admittedly, Vivekananda's agenda was much wider, deeper, and more ambitious than merely the fashioning of modern Indian secularism that came to serve somewhat inadequately, as our state religion. But what is important to note is that Vivekananda wanted a tolerant and religiously-sensitive polity, precisely what Indian secularism came to embody at its best.[32] Indian secularism, in other words, is not irreligious, nor does it build an insurmountable wall between the state and religious practices of the land. Instead, it is meant as a safeguard against intolerance and fanaticism. If various political parties in India have misused religion for political ends or if Indian secularism has come to be equated with minoritarianism, then this is clearly a distortion of the ideal. If Vivekananda's practical Vedanta is taken as one of the sources of Indian secularism, it will be obvious how both are a concern for the depressed castes, as well as inclusiveness were a part of the religious ideology of modern India. Hence, neither religious intolerance nor secular fundamentalism can be the answer to the failures of Indian secularism. Likewise, religious intolerance or supremacism, either of the right-wing Hindu variety or of Islamist or Sikh fanaticism are the alternatives to "pseudo-secularism." If a vibrant and sincere Indian secularism may be seen as underwritten by Vivekananda's call for a pluralistic and practical Vedanta, then Indian secularism may be realigned with its well-springs. Indeed, it would be a unique contribution to democratic societies all over the world to show how a country can be secular in a deeply religious way, allowing for a free expression of a diversity of faith traditions, without allowing any to become intolerant or dominant.

[32] Indeed, it is this religious basis and bias of Indian secularism that has led some critics to allege a "Hindu Bias in India's 'Secular' Constitution." Pritam Singh, "Hindu Bias in India's 'Secular' Constitution: Probing Flaws in the Instruments of Governance." *Third World Quarterly,* 26(6) (2005), 909–926.

CONCLUSION

We have seen that Indian secularism does not entail strict separation between state and religion nor irreligiousness, but rather respect all religions both by the state and civic society. India invented a new kind of secularism, a *dharmic* secularism, if you will, one of whose founders was Vivekananda. This *religious* or dharmic secularism was first proposed by Vivekananda at the Parliament of Religions in Chicago in September 1893, but then refined and adapted to the Indian situation during his *digvijaya yatra* or victorious journey from Colombo to Calcutta, January–February 1897, when he returned to India. Vivekananda's neo-Vedanta thus became the basis not only of a new, engaged Hinduism, but also undergird Indian secularism, as it developed later. It is hardly farfetched to consider that Vivekananda's practical Vedanta was the ground of Indian secularism just as many have argued that Western secularism came out of Christianity. No wonder Vivekananda's definition of Hindu as including all the indigenous religions of India such as Buddhist, Jain, and Sikh was accepted by the architect not only of the Indian constitution, but of the Hindu Code Bill, Dr. B.R. Ambedkar. Ambedkar ensured that these latter communities are *constitutionally* and legally Hindu, whatever they may be theologically or politically. Hindu in India thus came to represent not any one religious tradition but a non-exclusive faith continuum. It is this plural and inclusive redefinition of Hinduism that has allowed Indian secularism to be open to all religions rather than intolerant of them. Vivekananda wanted Indians to spiritualize their lives, to realize their own strength based on their self-identification with the *atman* rather than the body; he considered this, rather than political independence, as true empowerment. Practical Vedanta meant service and charity, which is what he enjoined upon sannyasins or renunciates rather than a turning away from the world and its responsibilities. Like other modern Hindu sects such as the Swaminarayans, Vivekananda wanted practical and service oriented, rather than ascetic, spirituality. As Amiya Sen observes in "Swami Vivekananda and the Making of Modern India," faith to him was thus not merely private belief, but a social responsibility.[33] It is this civic faith that is at the root of Indian secularism rather than a denial or turning away from religion; after all, Vivekananda repeatedly declared the key

[33] Amiya Sen, "Swami Vivekananda and the Making of Modern India." *Times of India,* Jan 12, 2013.

element of the Indian psyche was religion. In times when a recrudes-
cence of religious intolerance threatens the world, Vivekananda's practical Vedanta and the religion of civic responsibility, nation regeneration,
and service of the poor, such as Indian secularism aspires to, may provide both an alternative and an anodyne.

Picture 1
*Anindita N. Balslev addressing Karan Singh, the President of India, and
Suresh Goel and the crowd at the inaugural session at Rashtrapati Bhavan*

Picture 2
Pranab Mukherji inaugurating at Rashtrapati Bhavan

Picture 3
Karan Singh at Rashtrapati Bhavan

Picture 4
Anindita N. Balslev at Rashtrapati Bhavan

Picture 5

All contributors to the volume in a meeting at Azad Bhavan

Picture 6

Seated beside Anindita N. Balslev, Karan Singh speaking at Azad Bhavan

Picture 7

Anindita N. Balslev greeting Dalai Lama and Karan Singh the valedictory session at India International Centre

Picture 8

Anindita N. Balslev, Karan Singh, Dalai Lama, Maulana Wahiduddin Khan, and Mpho Tutu at India International Centre

Picture 9

From the front: Jeffery D. Long, Annakutty V. Kurian-Findeis, Karan Singh, Dalai Lama, Dr Anindita N. Balslev, Whitney A. Bauman, and Shernaz Cama. From behind: Steven I. Wilkinson and Makarand Paranjape at India International Centre

PART III

Conversation with Eminent Personalities

Dr Anindita N. Balslev in conversation with His Holiness Dalai Lama, Maulana Wahiduddin Khan, Dr Karan Singh and Reverend Mpho Tutu

The Four Clusters of Questions

Anindita N. Balslev

Namaskar! We are celebrating the 150th Birth Anniversary of Swami Vivekananda by holding this international conference "On World Religions: Diversity, Not Dissension." We are doing this precisely because this is a topic on which his thoughts are particularly relevant to our contemporary multireligious situation worldwide. This conference has been inaugurated by the Hon'ble President of India, Shri Pranab Mukherjee at the Rashtrapati Bhavan itself. During the past two days we have been deliberating on key issues focusing on multiple aspects of this large and complex theme at the Azad Bhavan, which is the seat of ICCR. This morning's session at the India International Centre is the valedictory session of this international conference.

Almost three decades ago, I heard with a sense of profound disbelief about a forecast made by certain futurists. These futurists, it was said, were pretty much convinced that with the spread of secular political ideology and the increasing sharing of scientific technology, the influence and impact of the religions of the world will gradually subside and even that in due course of time these were likely to vanish from the face of this earth. I recalled that prophecy and how it has proven to be utterly wrong with almost a sense of amusement, while providing the concept note for this significant international conference.

Indeed, the religions of the world are still very much with us. A common sharing of advanced technology in a global context, while facilitating travel and communication in an unprecedented manner, has made it all the more clear to us that we are by no means living in a post-religious era.

Swami Vivekananda had observed: "Of all the forces that have worked and are still working to mould the destinies of the human race, none, certainly, is more potent than that, the manifestation of which we call religion."

Perhaps the single most dominant criterion used in the public discourse for distinguishing the largest human aggregates one from the other is by their religious identity associated with one or another of the religions of the world. Indeed, the world religions are still continuing to be the primary sources from which people derive their sense of collective identity, draw their norms and values and seek guidance in times of need. Consequently, the presence of the plurality of religious identities is an inalienable fact of the contemporary global scene. It is a phenomenon that has to be dealt with at multiple levels of exchanges and interactions by all of us.

Today, the central question before us is: Can we move on to a plane of collective existence where the presence of diversity of religious traditions will no longer be perceived as a cause for dissension—as it has so often been so far? Is it at all possible for us to view the religions of the world as our common resource that can enrich and empower us in ways that we cannot even imagine today? If we could or even give it an honest try we could then claim that we are indeed seeking to carry forward a project that was initiated by Swami Vivekananda.

While exploring these issues with the eminent personalities present here, I have chosen this conversational format in order to highlight that the endeavor here is not simply to invite a series of monologues but about how to innovate a setting especially with a view to facilitate the bridge-building task among the religious traditions. This is a humble attempt to carry forward Swami Vivekananda's unfinished project of enhancing "harmony" and avoiding "dissensions" among the religions of the world.

Speaking of religious identity, let us use just a couple of minutes more while trying to understand the genesis, that is the beginning and the constitution of religious identity for us as individuals—as it is generally referred to in ordinary parlance and in our everyday socio-political contexts. Let us begin by asking whether we deliberately choose these identities or are these by and large attributed to us by the accident of birth? The picture seems to me at least to be very much as follows: one is first born into a religious tradition, belongs to it and only later on one can say that a given tradition comes to belong to one. While considering the question of dissensions that often happens in the name of religious identity, it is indeed interesting to note that comparatively only a small number of people among us who actually choose their religious identity, as that would imply exiting from the ones into which they are born. There are such cases of course—as exemplified by a few persons present here—where one has been born into a given tradition but has decided to choose another. We also know that there are many cases where people have been persuaded, forced and even persecuted to exit from traditions into which they are born but even in such instances would we not hesitate to call that these are actually cases of deliberate choice? In other words, wherever there is no real option before us, there is no question of exercising choice.

Thus, to start with we are born into a given religious tradition and this is not a case of choosing. I assume—like most of us present here—that to be the case for all four of them (pointing to Dr Karan Singh, HH Dalai Lama, Reverend Mpho Tutu and Maulana Wahiduddin Khan). Their religious identity is a part of the givenness of their lives—born as a Hindu, born as a Buddhist, born as a Christian and born as a Muslim. May I ask whether this is a correct assumption on my part?

(They nod, but see video to note how Maulana Saab answers. My comment to that response is that he chose to "remain" a Muslim.)

Let me now say that I am truly honored for having this opportunity to share the stage with you all. You have before you my *four clusters of questions* that are the same as those that were sent to you and I request that each one of you respond to the same question or questions but only from the vantage point of your own tradition.

Let this be an opportunity for all of us to start from the scratch. Every time I read out one of these four clusters of questions and share these with the members of the audience, I request each of you to fully utilize 5–6 minutes for each cluster of questions and let us benefit from your knowledge.

Friends, we are now going to listen to the practitioners, who are also all authors and have very ably propagated the core ideas of their respective traditions in their published works.

Q 1. What do you consider to be the principal teaching of your tradition? What is it that has especially inspired you most, impelling you to serve your tradition all throughout your life that we cannot simply attribute to the fact of your being connected with it by the accident of birth but will be willing to grant that it could just as well be the case had it been a matter of deliberate choice?

In other words, is there a central message that is specific to your tradition that you wish to share with the entire humanity because you firmly believe that we will all live in a better world if we pay heed to it?

Replies to Question No. 1

HH Dalai Lama: Respected spiritual brothers and sisters. I also recognize some long time friends in the audience. I am very happy to have this opportunity.

I am a Tibetan. Since seventh century, and particularly eighth century, and ninth century, Buddhism very much flourished in Tibet, particularly the Nalanda tradition. Pali tradition provided the basis for mainly Vinaya practice, monastic discipline. On top of that, Sanskrit tradition provided lots of philosophical ideas and practices including some yoga or Tantric practices.

My parents were uneducated farmers. I think my father knew more about a variety of horses rather than Dharma. In early period, when people chose me as a reincarnation of Dalai Lama, I studied Buddha Dharma with little interest; it was compulsory. Gradually, I have studied it seriously. Buddhism, particularly Nalanda tradition, puts emphasis not on faith but on reasoning and experiment. Buddha himself stated: All my followers should not accept my teachings out of faith but rather through investigation and experiment. In the meantime I also developed interest in learning about technology and science. Since my childhood I have been curious by nature. The more you investigate, the more you engage in thoughts and thinking. As we observe our world and its lots of problems, essentially many of these problems are our own creation. No one wants problems, but we create many problems. Then the big question is why? I think it is due to too much self-centered attitude and lack of holistic view.

One of the main Buddhist concepts is Pratityasamutpada or everything is interdependent. This concept gives us a holistic view. No event is absolute and independent. Good or bad events happen because of this and those factors. Thinking this way always brings us a holistic view. It is quite useful to reduce narrow-mindedness. Additionally, there is altruism, sense of concern for other's well being. Altruism is the direct antidote to reduce self-centered attitude. These are good and useful practices. These are also immense help to understand other traditions. In spite of different philosophical views, all major religious traditions talk about practice of love, compassion, forgiveness, tolerance, individual contentment, and self-discipline. All major religious traditions carry the same message. In order to strengthen these sorts of practice, use of different philosophy is necessary. Why? Because among humanity there are many different mental dispositions. Even among Buddha's own students, there are different mental dispositions. Therefore, Buddha taught different philosophies which may appear contradictory. I often tell people these seemingly contradictory philosophies came from the same teacher. This is not because Buddha is confused in his own mind. One day he taught some different philosophy; next day, next audience, another sort of philosophy. All of this is neither due to his own confusion nor for deliberately creating more confusion among his followers. He taught many different philosophies out of necessity. For different mental dispositions, different ways of approach are necessary. I personally find this reason immensely helpful to understand and appreciate different traditions—both theistic and non-theistic religious traditions. Needless to say, within these traditions we find differences as well. I feel different philosophies are necessary in order to fulfill a variety of people's wish.

Maulana Wahiduddin Khan: I was born in a Muslim family. My education and my upbringing were totally on the traditional lines. But when I reached the age of maturity, I became a seeker; I wanted to discover the truth on my own. I studied many books on different subjects, including religion, that were related to my search. Finally, I discovered the truth that my nature was seeking. This discovery was Islam. I can say that Islam is my discovery. I'm a Muslim not by birth, but I'm Muslim by choice. Then I published a book with the title *Islam Rediscovered.*

My main search was regarding the purpose of life. In the Quran I discovered the Creation Plan of God. This discovery led me to understand the real purpose of life. According to the Quran, after the creation, God Almighty settled man on the planet earth. The planet earth is a selection ground. Here man is constantly under divine watch, and God Almighty will select those men and women, on the basis of merit, who prove to be deserving candidates for Paradise. This selection depends completely on everyone's personal record. In the end, God Almighty will select all those individuals from entire history and settle them in Paradise, which is the perfect world, free from all kinds of limitations and disadvantages.

This discovery helped me understand the purpose of life. Here I found the justification of settling man on this planet. This discovery helped me understand the creation of man as unique. It helped me understand the pre-death period, and also the post-death period of my life. Before this discovery my feeling was that I have strayed into a world that was not made for me, but now everything seems to fall into place.

I was born as an idealist, but according to my experience the present world was less-than-ideal. It seemed that a perfectionist was compelled to live in an imperfect world. My discovery solved this problem, and I realized that the present world is not my final abode, my final abode is Paradise, and Paradise is undoubtedly the ideal place to live in.

I wanted to know the interpretation of human history. But my problem was that I wanted to interpret history in terms of humanity at large, which seemed impossible. Because, man enjoys freedom and he is also free to misuse his freedom. As we cannot abolish this freedom, we cannot establish an ideal system. It is this fact that in this world finding perfect individual is possible, but establishing a perfect society or system is simply not possible.

Then I discovered that according to the Creation Plan of God, it is persons who are required and not the masses. Gibbon has remarked: "History is indeed little more than the register of crimes, follies, and misfortunes of mankind." This remark seems to be right when you see history in totality. But when you see history in terms of individuals, the scene is quite different. Now the world becomes a vast garden of beautiful trees.

Reverend Mpho Tutu: John 3:16 "God so loved the world that he gave his only Son, that whoever believes in him shall not perish but shall have eternal life." This is probably the most often quoted verse of the Christian Bible. It encapsulates the principal teachings of my faith tradition. First that God loves. The fullest expression of God is love. God's love is creative, generative and generous. Second that the world is the object of God's love. The world is not described here as a mistake, a lack, an incompleteness but is described as loved. Because the world is loved the world is, by definition, lovable. This quotation does not make a division between what is spiritual, beautiful, acceptable and lovable and what is fleshly, ugly, wrong and therefore unlovable. What this teaching contains is a statement of God's vastness and God's goodness. God is vast enough and good enough to love the world, not as it will be when it is perfected but as it is. God will love the world into perfection.

I am Christian. I was born into a Christian family and so this was my first exposure. It is the third aspect of the quotation that holds me to my faith. God became human and dwelt among us in the form of the man Jesus Christ. The reason that paying heed to incarnation will make a better world for all of us is the message it conveys. That God took human form tells us that our bodies matter. Our bodies are not an irrelevancy. Our bodies are not a prison for our spirits but, rather, there is something very particular and very holy, about our human form. The scriptures of the Christian faith describe the last judgment thus:

> When the Son of Man comes in all his glory, and all the angels with him, then he will sit on the throne of his glory. All the nations will be gathered before him, and he will separate people one from another as a shepherd separates the sheep from the goats, and he will put the sheep at his right hand and the goats at the left. Then the king will say to those at his right hand. "Come, you that are blessed by my Father, inherit the kingdom prepared for you from the foundation of the world; for I was hungry and you gave me food, I was thirsty and you gave me something to drink, I was a stranger and you welcomed me, I was naked and you gave me clothing, I was sick and you took care of me, I was in prison and you visited me."[1]

As described in this passage of scripture, when in the last days God returns to weigh our deeds in the balance the standard against which we are measured may surprise us. They are not the questions that one would typically be those with which religiosity is concerned. The questions that Christian scripture says we will be asked are not "How many hours did you spend in prayer?" or "What was your liturgical practice?" but, "Did you clothe the naked? Did you feed the hungry? Did you visit the prisoner? Did you care for the sick?" These questions demand that we keep our eyes on the eternal by acting in the present reality. These questions and the teaching that they encapsulate are the teachings that Christianity has to offer humanity.

The three claims of my religion as expressed here: That God is love and God loves the world as it is—and therefore the world is lovable; that God has taken human form—therefore our bodies matter; and that how we treat human beings in the here and now is what will shape our place in eternity, are all teachings that can improve human experience.

---

[1] New Revised Standard Version Bible, copyright 1989. National Council of the Churches of Christ in the United States of America (Matthew 25: 31–36).

Let us consider each proposition in turn: in the first instance, that the world is lovable even with all the faults, terrors and disasters it contains. This truth offers us an approach to changing the world that is based on love rather one based on anger and hatred. Hatred, we know, can never overcome hatred. As only light can overcome darkness, so only love can overcome hate. In the second instance, that God took human form and therefore our bodies are good and acceptable to God. This truth should give us each a particular reverence for human flesh and blood. The reverence with which we meet our fellow human beings should be as the reverence with which we approach a temple or a place of worship. Treating our bodies with reverence will make rape, torture and other forms of human brutality not only wrong and distressing but, actually, blasphemous. In the third instance that what determines our place in eternity is our action in the present reality. We cannot win paradise by ignoring or injuring our fellow human beings. There is no prayer, song or meditation or liturgical practice that will earn us heaven. We are made fit for the promise of everlasting life by the practice of human kindness and concern.

Dr Karan Singh: In my view, the principal teachings of Hinduism are to be found in the Upanishads where the all pervasive divine power—the Bramhan—and the Divinity within each human being—the Atman—have been analyzed in detail. There is also the concept of Yoga as the philosophy and methodology of joining the Atman and the Bramhan. There are four paths in Yoga with hundreds of by-paths. These are Jnana Yoga, the way of Wisdom; Bhakti Yoga, the way of Devotion; Karma Yoga, the way of Dedicated Works and Raja Yoga, the way of Psychospiritual practices.

I have always been attracted to the universal values contained in the Vedanta, and find that they are compatible with the Interfaith movement with which I have been involved for four decades. The Rig Vedic dictum "*Ekam Sadvipraha Bahudha Vadante.*" "The truth is one, the wise call it by many names," is the keystone of the whole Interfaith philosophy. We must accept that there are multiple paths to the divine, and whereas our own path may be the best for us, this does not mean that people following other path can be murdered or tortured or persecuted in any way. This is the central message in Hinduism which needs to be shared with the entire humanity. We will certainly live in the better world if this is accepted.

Anindita N. Balslev

We all know of the dual impact of religious affiliations—benevolent and pernicious—as it is demonstrated in the history, be that of two denominations of the same religious tradition or of two religions, that is, where the religious context is definitively plural in character.

Swami Vivekananda said:

> No other human motive has deluged the world with blood so much as religion; at the same time,…no other human influence has taken such care, not only of humanity, but also of the lowest of animals, as religion has done. Nothing makes us so cruel as religion, nothing makes us so tender as religion.

Indeed, this cruel aspect has been played out in such gruesome manner in the name of religious identity that we really need to understand what makes that possible, what is at the root of it. I have said in the beginning that we draw a sense of collective identity from our religions. Let me now ask what is entailed in the teachings of these diverse traditions—explicitly or implicitly—that influence us to construe the "otherness" of other traditions in specific ways that has impact on those whom we do not perceive to be belonging to "our own" religious community.

So my second cluster of questions to you is:

Q 2. What is the status of the other in the philosophy of religion of your own tradition? What is the explicit or implicit teaching that is bound to influence the attitude of the members of your own community as and when they invariably encounter these "others," that is, those who happen to derive their sense of religious identity from "other" sources than your own? That they are to be gradually vanquished? To be eventually converted for the sake of their own good? That those who are reluctant to do so are to be perceived as doomed or at best to be situated at a lower level in the hierarchy and somehow tolerated?

In other words, the question is whether it is possible to be more inclusive? Can these "others" be at all accepted as followers of a distinctly different path yet recognizably a legitimate path? If yes, on what ground?

Replies to Question No. 2

HH Dalai Lama: I think I already answered it. As I said, there is variety
of people. I may add one thing. Recently, I saw one report that out of
seven billion human beings; about one billion are non-believers. In this
regard, I want to say that even though I am a Buddhist and accordingly
I do my practice daily, but I never try to propagate Buddhism. Of course,
I do understand my responsibility and duty to explain what Buddhism is
to Buddhists and those who ask about it. In the Vinayapitaka it is clearly
mentioned that unless someone asked you for teaching, you should not
teach. This goes well with respecting individual's sort of rights.
Realistically speaking, on this planet, there are so many religious traditions. When Buddha and Mahavira came, there were already other religious traditions in India. Buddha and Mahavira never tried to convert all
Indians into Buddhists and Jains.

The fact of the matter is today there are many religious traditions. In
Arab and eastern as well as many other areas in the world, a large number of Muslims follow Islamic tradition. In the whole western countries
most people are from the Judo-Christian background.

India actually is home to many great religious traditions. That said,
quite often religious followers, including Buddhists, forget their religions when things are going well. They do not follow religious principles at the time of need. Instead, people let destructive emotions act like
god. So many problems are actually our own creation. There is too
much greed, too much anger, and too much suspicion, but not enough
practice of compassion and forgiveness. All major religious traditions,
for the past thousand years, helped humanity. Today also millions of
people get immense inspirations from them and it will be the same in
the future as well. I think for at least a few centuries it will remain like
that. After that nobody knows. So, that is the reality. I always expressed
that religious conversion is not good. For example, there are quite a
number of Tibetan Buddhist centers in the west. I always tell them they
should not convert people into Buddhists. Only if people really come to
learn something about Buddhism, then it is ok to teach them Buddhism.
Actually, a German friend of mine who is a businessman wants to build
a Buddhist meditation center in France, but I told him this is not right.
France is a Judo-Christian country. If he really wants to build a
Buddhist meditation center, then he should construct it either in
Thailand, or Burma or even India. Like that, we must respect individual's wish and his or her tradition.

As for the question about non-believers, I think their number will increase. Non-believers are part of humanity and they also have the every right to be happy and successful members in human community. In this regard, without touching religion, usually I talk about secular ethics. Here I do not talk about God or Buddha, but simply about ethics according to our common experience and common sense. Everybody is born from a mother and that is our common experience. Rajas are also born that way. I, as a peasant child, also have been born that way, and you too. I think I want to tease my long time friend (Dr Karan Singh), that perhaps a peasant child is much closer to his mother than Raja's son. Rani lives there and someone takes care of her prince. In that sense a simple peasant's son has been more fortunate because he has received mother's affection and mother's breast-feeding with full of care and affection. Mother's affection and care for a child are extremely important. That bond and experience remain deep in child's blood till death. All of us who are in this hall, outwardly everybody look very smart, but deep inside those of us who have received maximum affection from their mothers when we were young, I think, are much happier and more firm deep inside as compared to those who did not receive the same affection and care from their mothers at a young age. Individuals may be successful today, but at the young age, did not receive affection from their mothers or their mothers died at delivery or those who are born as an "unwanted child" or abused, then such person may outwardly look very smart, but deep inside they feel a sense of insecurity. All of these are our common experiences.

Importantly, we must respect people, and value human affection and compassion. These are very important values even from health viewpoint. Medical scientists clearly say that constant fear; anger and hatred are actually eating our immune system. Calm and peaceful mind is a very important factor to sustain our immune system. You just mentioned that I look healthy. According to my own experience, I think calm mind is immensely beneficial for good health. In our discussions some scientists talk about healthy body and healthy mind. It is not sufficient just taking care of physical health by taking medicine. Ultimately, source of healthy body is peace of mind. I think we can educate non-believers to be warm-hearted persons without necessarily becoming religious minded. They can be more compassionate persons for their own interest, not for the next life. In our everyday life if we become more compassionate and more caring for others' well being, then we would have no room to harm others, to cheat others, and to bully others. Not at all.

ON WORLD RELIGIONS

Actually, you care for others' well being. Compassion is the very basis of non-violence, India's thousand years old tradition. Ahimsa is not a weakness or indifferent attitude. Not at all. Ahimsa (Nonviolence) means even though you have the ability to harm, but you respect their life, their right and so deliberately restrain from harming others. That is nonviolence. With Ahimsa, religious harmony will automatically come because you respect the followers of other religions. Therefore, I feel sometimes compassion and human affection is Universal Religion. No need of complicated philosophy, creator or Buddha. Karma means action. As you mention karma yoga, everything depends on action. Action depends on motivation. So that is my view. Too long, thank you.

Maulana Wahiduddin Khan: The word conversion is totally alien to Islam. Islam believes in spiritual development rather than religious conversion. According to Islam, religion is completely one's own intellectual choice; it is the result of one's own discovery rather than getting direction from some outside agent. The Creation Plan of God in this regard is mentioned in the Quran in these words: "This is the truth from your Lord. Let him who will, believe in it, and him who will, deny it."[2] As far as salvation is concerned, it will be determined by one's personal record. In Islam there is no race-wise salvation or community-wise salvation. Islam very clearly declares that salvation is individual-wise. It is a matter that is completely between man and God, and not between man and man.

The rationale behind this theory is that salvation is the result of personality development. Only those persons will find entry into Paradise who have developed their personalities in such a way that they deserve settlement in Paradise, which is a highly refined society.

For example, the people of Paradise will be completely free from all kinds of negative thought. So, only those people will be selected to be included in the high society of Paradise who have proved in this world that they are such developed souls that they can live in Paradise as is required.

In the Quran Paradise is described as the "Home of Peace."[3] So, only those people will qualify to find entry into Paradise who have proved themselves to be peace-loving persons in the complete sense of the word.

[2] 18:29.
[3] 10:25.

In the later period of history Muslims jurists legislated the law that one who commits apostasy will be given capital punishment, or one who is involved in blasphemy will be given capital punishment. This kind of legislation is completely un-Islamic, it is an innovation of a later period of history, and has no sanction in the Quran. According to the Quran, everyone is free, no one can impose curbs on anyone's freedom. It is God who will decide whether someone misused his freedom or he used his freedom properly. Laws on apostasy or blasphemy are like entering into the domain of God.

It is not a question of acceptance by Muslims, only God will accept or refuse, even those who claim to be true Muslims. The status of everyone, including those who claim to be Muslims, is one and the same, and that is, their fate will be decided in the Hereafter by God Almighty.

The Prophet of Islam has declared that although I am the Prophet of God, but I don't know what will be decided about me in the Hereafter, and what will be decided about you.

The attitude of Muslims towards others will be based on common brotherhood. Everyone is made by God, so Muslims must see others as God-made persons, they have no right to issue a decree about the fate of other human beings. Islam believes in common ancestry. The Prophet of Islam has said: "All men and women are Children of Adam." According to this all men and women are brothers and sisters to each other.

Reverend Mpho Tutu: Christianity has so much variety within itself and the posture towards other has been contested since the beginning of Christianity. Christianity began as a faith, a tradition, a path, an "other" in the center of a dominant and established faith. The Christian religion was born out of the Jewish faith. The first disciples of Jesus Christ—indeed, Jesus himself—if asked, would have described themselves as Jewish. Christianity was a minority sect within a dominant religion. Christianity stood in the posture of being the other religion to religion that already existed. Christians have adopted various postures with respect to the other throughout the history of the faith.

The Apostle Peter writes this:

Wives, in the same way, accept the authority of your husbands, so that, even if some of them do not obey the word, they may be won over without a word by their wives' conduct, when they see the purity and reverence of your lives. Do not adorn yourselves outwardly by braiding your hair, and by wearing gold ornaments or fine clothing; rather, let your adornment be the inner self with the lasting beauty of a gentle and quiet spirit, which is very precious in God's sight.[4]

He advises that Christians can, by being exemplars of their faith win converts to Christianity.

The history of our faith is replete with examples of zealots who have done far more than offer a shining example of Christian living in order to win converts to the faith. The Spanish Inquisition and the Crusades of the Middle Ages are early examples of violent conquest and conversion. Western Christianity spread with western colonialism. More or less bloody means were used to win converts. From the fifteenth through the seventeenth centuries the Conquistadors spread Spanish and Portuguese rule through much of the world. The Conquistadors were soldiers, explorers and adventurers. They were accompanied on their voyages by Roman Catholic clergy who fulfilled administrative functions and spread the Christian faith. Converts came to Christianity because the religion told a compelling story. People were converted because they saw disciples of the faith who were genuinely people of good will. Many were converted from the margins of their societies, the Christian religion has a place of preference for the poor, the weak, those marginalized because of physical or mental ability. These were attracted to the faith rather than driven into it. In the colonies the attraction of a high quality education brought many converts, Christians of convenience. Many who were brought into the fold by educational opportunity remained because the teachings of the faith were compelling and engaging. Christians of convenience were drawn into the faith by the offer of boons for membership. But some were propelled into the faith by fear. During the Nazi holocaust many Jewish families converted to Christianity in fear for their lives. Rather claim a Christian identity and live than proclaim your Jewish heritage and die. In the modern era Christian fundamentalists have used less brutal means to enforce a type of orthodoxy. Political maneuvering and social ostracism have been used within communities to ensure adherence to the Christian faith. America of the 1950s comes to mind. Membership in social clubs and respect in the local community were a function of Christian identity. As the dominant religion Christianity won many social converts. As we see, down through the

[4] 1 Peter 3: 1–4.

ages the attitude of the Christian faith towards other faith traditions has been contested. It continues to be so.

Jesus, is quoted in the Gospels as saying to his disciples that:

> In my father's house there are many mansions.[5]

and that

> I have other sheep that do not belong to this fold.[6]

Indicating to his disciples, that their particular expression of faith is not the only valid way to serve God.

Perhaps in contrast Jesus is also quoted as saying:

> I am the way and the truth and the life. No one comes to the Father except through me.[7]

This line of scripture has been taken by many Christians through the ages to mean that Christianity is the only true religion and that all people must be converted to Christianity in order to find salvation.

I understand all this to mean that we have really no concept of the vastness of God. We have little understanding of how it is that God speaks into the hearts and into the lives of even the people who sit next to us, the people who are closest to us. There cannot be a one size fits all expression or experience of faith, even as there is no one-size-fits-all expression of Christianity. We are bound by Christian teaching to be exemplars of our own faith. We may win converts to our faith by the manner of our lives but the earliest teachings of the Christian faith do not require that we proselytize. If the words of Jesus Christ in the Gospel of John are to be believed then those of us who profess the faith must stand in profound respect of the way other people experience and express their faith. Who are we to know whether people of faiths other than ours are own "sheep of another flock" or "dwellers" in a different mansion in the household of God.

---

[5] John 14:2.
[6] John 10:16.
[7] John 14:6.

Dr Karan Singh: While from the purely Vedantic point of view there is no*other*, we find that in history India has been subject to a constant series of invasions and iconoclasts have destroyed hundreds of temples and inflicted great pain upon the Hindu community. In response to that, the *other* came to be known as Mleccha or the unclean, and this was further strengthened by the fact that the proselytizing religions often used force to bring about conversions. I must add that in sharp contra-distinction to these invaders were the Sufis who brought with them the message of love and harmony, and whose shrines are still revered throughout India.

Anindita N. Balslev

Now let me move on to the next concern.

Those who are familiar with Swamiji's writings know that in many places he has pointed out how noble ideas get trivialized by people of sectarian mentality. He has joked about how, for example, the idea of "universal brotherhood" has been used by some Muslims and Christians. However, when referring to failures and shortcomings of the Hindu community, he has expressed his disapproval in strong terms, sometimes even very harshly but always in all cases with the intent of reminding the followers of specific traditions that they have to live up to the highest ideals of their own traditions, that their social practices and institutions have to comply with those ideals.

Q 3. So, I will now request you to take on a self-critical posture and tell us openly whether you have noticed any event or a display of an attitude or an institutionalized custom or practice that has been carried out in the past or is still in vogue in the name of your own religious tradition that you abhor because you are convinced that no matter how that has come about is surely against the spirit of your tradition. Please give us one example and then tell us what you think needs to be done in order to eradicate it or prevent it.

Replies to Question No. 3

HH Dalai Lama: Frankly speaking, I think in all major religious tradi-tions, many of the followers are not serious and sincere. I observe in various religious traditions, I think due to lack of knowledge and the real message of your own tradition and practice, many people simply carry rituals and some ceremony. For example, many Christians during their service in the church, at that moment, everybody seems very serious, but outside the church, they simply carry their usual way of life and activities such as cheating and bullying. These people are not very serious about their faith. Among Tibetan Buddhists also there are those who do the same.

Unfortunately, religion is also used as an instrument of exploitation. Among Tibetan Buddhists also, quite seriously, some lamas sit on high thrones and appear as very holy but may exploit other people. I actually criticize these practices. I also publicly criticize Buddhist practitioners who attach much importance to wearing ceremony dress or different hats or instruments. I always tell them, we have never heard in the Nalanda tradition that great masters like Nagarjuna, Aryadeva, Bhavavevika, and Buddhapalita wear different hats and carry some instruments in their hands. Not at all. They mainly did thinking, analysis, writing, and meditation. That is the proper way to follow Buddhism. Sometimes we, the Tibetan Buddhists, put too much emphasis on superficial things. You know, for example, monks wear masks and do some rituals. These rituals are supposed to destroy the enemy of Dharma but they failed. We are too much involved in superficial things. Similarly, many Hindu families simply worship Ganesh, Shiva, and Saraswati in the morning; they offer them flowers, incense and recite some Sanskrit shlokas (stanzas) without knowing the meaning. Much importance is given to rituals, not the real religious message. Sometimes, I jokingly tell my friends that in the morning you worship in front of Ganesh or other deities as if you ask for their blessing to be successful in your practice of corruption and hypocrisy. How can that be? That shouldn't be. Impossible! Historically, India is our Guru and I feel very close to India. All our Buddhist knowledge, we learnt from Indian guru. That is clear.

Similarly, some Muslim friends also seem to pray to Allah for success in doing wrong things. That shouldn't be. How can it be? Sadly, religion is also used for conflicts. For example, followers of the same Allah but from different sects fight with each other. People who use religion for conflicts do not know the real meaning of their teachings and follow them seriously and sincerely. Religion is just a lip service for them. Whether you accept religion or not, I think, is up to individual. Nobody can force you to believe in a religion. For example, during Buddha's time there were nonbelievers like Charvakas. But Buddha never imposed his view on them. In Ancient India, at the intellectual level, followers of different philosophies engaged in argument and debate but with respect. That is ok. For example, Charvaka's philosophy was challenged in debate but the challengers respected Rishis or saints of their tradition. My point is this that it is up to the individual whether to accept or not any religion. Once you accept a religion, you must be sincere and serious about it. That is my general critique of any religious follower. As I publicly criticize others, I also know I have to check myself. Every day from early morning onward, I should practice Buddha's teaching sincerely and seriously. If I tell others one thing, and I myself do another thing or do it differently, that is hypocrisy. Sometimes, I tell people, religion seems to teach us how to act hypocritically. That's telling others to be truthful, honest, compassionate and forgiving but one's self practice none of these.

Investigation and analysis are crucial to understand Buddhism and be realistic. Let me tell you a story about my own disagreement with Vasubandhu's cosmological description of universe with Mt. Meru in its center. Vasubandhu and Asanga are brothers and public proponents of Chitamatrin philosophy (Mind Only Philosophy). Both are great scholars of the Nalanda tradition. Vasubhandu, in his Abhidhamakoshakarika, describes Mount Meru in the center and sun and moon go like that at the same level. I no longer accept that explanation. I am a little bit rebellious but with respect. Sometimes, I jokingly tell people that for Vasubhandu, who had no glasses and telescope, sun and moon almost looked the same size, may be with a slight difference. He described that the difference of sun and moon in terms of their size is just one yojhna (one league?); otherwise, just fifty fifty. Actually, the difference between the two is vast; sun is huge but moon is much smaller. As a Buddhist and follower of Nalanda tradition, we must accept reality. Therefore, it is important that one should apply Buddhist logical approach to investigate things and accept reality as it is found through systematic and scientific investigation and must reject false perception and explanation of reality. All the great Nalanda masters like Nagarjuna, Chandrakriti and Shantideva thoroughly investigated Buddha's words. If certain points mentioned in Buddha's own words go against our experiment and investigation, then we have a right to reject that. Therefore, I also follow that tradition. So, I respectfully disagree with Vasubhandu's description of Mount Meru. I think his description is an old fashioned thinking and not a reality. Excuse me for saying that. That's my usual critiquing method.

Maulana Wahiduddin Khan: According to my study, there is nothing in texts of Islam that I dislike. But, Muslims as a community have developed some traits that are quite against the Islamic teachings. And, here comes my difference with other Muslims. For example, present Muslims have developed a self-made criterion. According to them, one who seems to them not following the interest of the Muslim community, they believe that these kinds of persons or groups are enemies of Islam. But this kind of Muslim-oriented thinking is completely wrong. In Islam there are no such enemies. The Quran says: "Good and evil deeds are not equal. Repel evil with what is better; then you will see that one who was once your enemy has become your dearest friend."[8] According to this Quranic verse, there is no one as enemy of Muslims. Everyone is either your actual friend or potential friend. If you find someone who seemingly goes against the interests of your community, then don't dub him as an enemy. But, try to establish normal relationship with him. Try to turn his potential into actuality by doing good deeds with him.

Muslims have formed numerous non-governmental organizations, and under the banner of these NGOs they have waged jihad against their enemies. But this kind of thinking is completely un-Islamic. Jihad in the sense of war is exclusively the prerogative of an established state solely for defence purpose. Even states are not allowed to wage any war other than defensive war. The term "non-state actors" is totally an innovation, it has no basis in Islam. All those wars are un-Islamic that are called guerrilla war, secret war, undeclared war and also proxy war.

To eradicate this mind-set, it requires long educational efforts, which includes that all Islamic ulema should issue a joint fatwa and declare openly and clearly that these kind of violent activities are totally against the teachings of Islam. It is the ulema's greatest duty, if they fail to perform this duty they will be accountable before God.

In the later period of history, Muslims have coined a host of new terms for describing the Islamic position regarding different issues. One such term is *Dar al-Kufr*. According to this term, the whole world was divided into two parts: Dar al-Islam and Dar al-Kufr. Dar al-Islam was that part of the globe in which the Muslims were living in majority and Dar al-Kufr was that part of the globe in which communities other than Muslims were living.

This kind of terminology was completely un-Islamic. The Prophet of Islam never used the terms Dar al-Islam or Dar al-Kufr. If you read the

---

[8] 41:34.

Quran, which is the most authentic book on Islam, you will find that the Quran again and again uses the term *Ayyuh al-Insaan* (O Man) or *Ayyuh al-Naas* (O Mankind). The word al-Naas and al-Insaan are repeated in the Quran more than three hundred times. According to this, the world is neither Dar al-Islam nor Dar al-Kufr, instead it is Dar al-Insaan (world of mankind).

I strongly differ with the above theorization and I believe that our world is Dar al-Insaan, and nothing else.

Reverend Mpho Tutu: My critique is, perhaps, a very self-interested one. Our tradition, not our religion, but our tradition does not accord women and girls the regard and the respect which they so rightly deserve. There are positions of power in our church communities that are not open to women. There are whole denominations, which will not allow women to exercise roles of liturgical leadership. Within my own denomination the role of women as ordained leaders is still contested. We have recently ordained the first two women as bishops in the Anglican Church in Southern Africa, but you know that has come as a hard fought battle. In the Church in England there still hasn't been an agreement that women can be ordained as Bishops. There is no tenet of our faith that says that women are not fully human and so cannot occupy roles of leadership within the faith community. Our Lord Jesus Christ was quite radical in his regard for women. The Gospel tells the story of two sisters, Martha and Mary as follows:

> Now as they went on their way, Jesus entered a certain village, where a woman named Martha welcomed him into her home. She had a sister named Mary, who sat at the Lord's feet and listened to what he was saying. But Martha was distracted by her many tasks; so she came to him and asked, "Lord, do you not care that my sister has left me to do all the work by myself? Tell her then to help me." But the Lord answered her, "Martha, Martha, you are worried and distracted by many things; there is need of only one thing. Mary has chosen the better part, which will not be taken away from her."[9]

Jesus' words and action are doubly radical. In a society that placed a high premium on the value of hospitality Jesus privileged learning and

[9] Luke 10: 38–42.

discipleship. In a society that had very little regard for the personhood of women, Jesus recognized Mary as a disciple and allowed her to sit at his feet, it was only disciples who had the privilege of sitting at the teacher's feet. And women at that time were never accorded the status of disciple. In the Christian Bible it is women who are the first witnesses to the resurrection,[10] women who were the first to see the risen Christ,[11] and women who became apostles to the apostles, the first messengers to the Christian messengers.[12]

Even so in our religion the roles, rights and responsibilities of women continue to be contested. I would venture that Christianity is not the only religion that must contend with this issue.

Dr Karan Singh: In Hinduism, as I have mentioned, we must accept different paths to the divine provided they do not attempt to force themselves upon the Hindu community. We must eradicate the practice that has dogged Hinduism down through the ages, the discriminative and cruel practice of untouchability. Whatever may have been the origins of this custom, it clearly violates Vedantic principles and has condemned millions of human beings to an inferior position for centuries.

It is interesting that the whole Hindu social reform movement which began in eighteenth century in Bengal with Raja Ram Mohan Roy and included a number of organizations such as the Arya Samaj and the Ramakrishna Mission has targeted this practice. In our Constitution, we have not only abolished untouchability by law but have undertaken affirmative action by reserving 12.5 percent of all government jobs for the Scheduled Castes (former untouchables) and 6.5 for Scheduled Tribes which cover our substantial tribal population particularly in the North-East. Despite this, the prejudice still continues and we have to sustain our thrust for equity and social justice.

Anindita N. Balslev

While Swamiji was alive, already during that time there was keen concern in some circles with regard to the presence of religious diversity and that attempts need to be made to bring diverse religious traditions together. The culmination of such efforts was what led to the setting up

[10] John 20; Matthew 28:1–6; Mark 16:5; Luke 24:1–9.
[11] John 20:11–16; Matthew 28:8; Mark 16:9.
[12] John 20:18; Matthew 28:10; Mark 16:7; Luke 24:10.

of the First Parliament of Religions of the World, held in Chicago in 1893 where the young Swami Vivekananda participated. Candid and fearless as he was, he openly said that "harmony among religions of the world" has still remained merely a goal. He had frankly admitted that if that goal has not been reached so far, it is because of a want of a plan that is practical.

He wrote: *"That plan alone is practical, which does not destroy the individuality of any man in religion and at the same time shows him a point of union with all others."*

I now come to the fourth of the cluster of questions.

Q 4. Please take a few minutes each and indicate a plan of action so that a point of union among diverse religious traditions can be demonstrated as achievable on a collective plane. What is it that we are not doing because of which you think that diversity leads to dissension even in our time when technology has bridged physical distance in an unprece-dented manner? How do we transform ourselves so that in our zeal to emphasize our distinctness, we no longer feel the need to overlook the overlaps that are there and get ready to recognize our shared common values?

Replies to Question No. 4

HH Dalai Lama: I always tell people about the concept of one religion and one truth and the concept of several religions and several truths. These views seem contradictory. Every religion seems to claim one ultimate truth or something like that in its own tradition. I feel, in order to develop or keep single pointed faith towards your tradition, the con-cept of one religion and one truth is relevant. But in terms of a larger community, obviously in this room, one religion and one truth is not relevant. That fact is that several religions and several truths already exist here and in larger community. Therefore, in terms of a larger com-munity, the concept of several religions and several truths is relevant. In contrast, for an individual practitioner, the concept of one truth and one religion is relevant. Looking from different perspectives, you can see there is no contradiction in my earlier proposition.

As for religious harmony, for the last several years, one time I dis-cussed some ideas with Bishop Tutu. Firstly, interreligious pilgrimage can promote religious harmony. I have implemented the idea since 1975. I have been on pilgrimage to different religious holy sites with groups of people from different religious traditions. I had one pilgrimage to Jerusalem, I think twice. I also went to Lourde and Fatima in Portugal and many Hindu temples and Jewish temples to pay my respect. I found such pilgrimage very, very helpful for mutual appreciation and harmony. I also paid my respect to a mosque in Jordan and also a Bahai temple. As I said, I find it very, very beneficial.

Secondly, it is important to meet with different religious practitioners and exchange different experiences with each other. I found it very, very helpful to understand and appreciate the value of other traditions. At the academic level, scholars can discuss commonalities and differences. Naturally, we will find differences but what is very important is to discuss the purpose of differences and different approaches. Different approaches can lead to the same goal—how to be a compassionate, sensible and honest person. Some religions say God created us all. If you truly believe that and implement that belief, there is no basis for conflicts among human beings, among brothers and sisters. Belief in one Creator God is very helpful to reduce differences and conflicts because of single pointed faith towards God, our creator. It helps us to reduce self-centered attitude. In Buddhism there is the Anathma or Selfless theory, which claims that there is no intrinsic difference between self and others or you and me. This view also helps reduce self-centered attitude or the same purpose. In contrast, there is the concept of Atma or Soul that eventually merges with Brahma, which serves the same purpose. I have used Anatma concept to reduce self-centered attitude and develop faith towards Buddha and Boddhisatvas. My point is this that there are different approaches but they serve the same purpose. Once we are clear with that then there is hardly any basis for conflicts, arguments and fights.

To Christian practitioners I want to say that when you think of your father, beloved and merciful, the whole atmosphere will immediately become very warm and very frank. With meetings like this where religious leaders sit together and send the same message of peace and harmony from the same platform, I think it will have significant impact in the eyes of ordinary people, millions and millions people.

Looking at Rev. Mpho Tutu HH Dalai Lama said, "Your father told me that whenever disaster happens, people from different religious faith could come together and serve the needy together." I think that is also a very good idea. All religious traditions teach us to serve people and serve the needy. In this respect, our Christian brothers and sisters,

I think, are more dedicated than Buddhist brothers and sisters. Many of you already practice these things, you know it very well as we discussed it on few occasions.

I very much feel that India is the only country where all major world religions exist harmoniously together, as you mentioned. Two years ago, in Jodhpur I met a Romanian who carries research work on religious harmony in this country. He told me that he visited one Muslim village, with at least a few thousand population there, but only three Hindu families. They live without fear, completely safe and friendly with rest of the Muslim community. That is India. I feel it is worthwhile to share this story here in the gathering of many great scholars. Some of my Muslim friends told me that real Islam practitioners should not create bloodshed to people. If you shed blood, then you are no longer an Islam practitioner. The reason, they said, is this that Islam practitioners must extend love towards the entire creatures of Allah. Here I should also mention about the concept of Jihad. Some said Jihad actually means combating your own negative emotions; it does not mean engaging in violence or fighting with other people. It means combating your own wrong, mistaken, inner destructive emotions. So, my point is this that all religions have the same message and the same purpose.

My main point is this that religious harmony in this country has not politically developed recently, but has existed for thousand years. We must make special efforts to promote it within the country as people take it for granted; this is not sufficient. We must educate people about it within the country. India also should show to the rest of the world that different religious people could live together harmoniously and serve people without creating problems. I think we should have this kind of meeting not just occasionally but quite often. We should invite people from different countries, and show them this living spirit of India as an example. My Indian brothers and sisters—Hindus and Muslims—time has come to make continuous effort to promote this living Indian religious spirit of harmony within this country and abroad. We may prefer leisure but now is not the time. We should be more active now. I say to my friend, your age is already 82, but you should be more active. More active means more exercise. Sometimes, I jokingly tell people, age is also setting on me. I am now nearly 78 and I have some problem with my knees. But I tell them that this problem does not matter much because my main interest and main commitment is talk, not sports. If my main interest is sports, then this really is a problem. But for talk, it is not much of a problem. So, I can be active at least for the next ten to fifteen years. I will be active talking even in a wheelchair. Thank You.

Maulana Wahiduddin Khan: In this regard Islam follows a very natural formula. This formula is given in the Quran in these words: "For you your religion, for me mine."[13] This formula is based on the principle of mutual respect, that is, follow one and respect all.

To illustrate this point I would like to cite one event from the prophetic life.

> The Prophet started his mission in Mecca, but after some years he migrated to Medina. At that time there were three Jewish tribes living in Medina. The Prophet, as head of the Muslim community, issued a declaration that is called in Islamic history the Declaration of Medina. In this declaration it was mentioned: "For Jews their religion and for Muslims their religion." One instance of the Prophet gives a very beautiful illustration of this principle. The history of Islam tells us that one day the Prophet of Islam was at some place in Medina. At that time he saw a funeral procession passing by. The Prophet was seated at that time. On seeing the funeral he stood up in respect. One of his Companions said: "O Prophet, it was the funeral of a Jew, not a Muslim." The Prophet said: "*Alaysat nafsan*" (Was he not a human being?)

This instance shows what the prophetic vision was. He was able to realize a commonality between himself and that non-Muslim. He demonstrated by this event that all the human beings are one and the same. In terms of social behavior, everyone is equal. All men and women are brothers and sisters to each other. This is the true basis of social harmony.

According to my experience, the basic hurdle in this regard is that people want to make other people according to their own thought. This kind of practice is quite unnatural. Because, difference is a part of nature. Everyone is born as Mr Different and Ms Different. In such a situation harmony can be achieved only by mutual respect and not by eliminating the differences. Moreover, this difference is not evil, it is rather a blessing. Difference leads to discussion, and discussion always results in intellectual development. There is a well-known saying that "Where all think alike, no one thinks very much."

In other fields people have adopted this formula on a large scale, which is called coexistence. It is said that mutual coexistence is the only way of living on the earth. The same universal formula is also applicable in the religious field.

[13] 109:6.

Unity is very important, but unity can be achieved only by accepting the difference and not by eliminating the difference, which is impossible. History confirms the veracity of this theory. There is a very relevant reference. The government of Canada had adopted a theory after the WWII which was called uniculturalism. They wanted to establish a society of a single culture, that is, Canadian culture. But, in spite of great endeavors, this campaign failed. Then, there was a reversal, and multiculturalism policy was officially adopted by the Canadian government during the 1970s and 1980s. And today Canada is considered to be a multicultural society rather than a unicultural society. This experience is an empirical proof that in this world of differences, only multiculturalism is possible and not uniculturalism.

In the end I would like to add one more point. I am fond of studying. I have spent almost whole of my life in study, the library was my second home. I can say that without study man is a half man. When you read books, you enable yourself to share in with others' wisdom, both contemporary and ancient.

But, according to my experience no study is sufficient. No study can give you all that you need. The other source of learning is interaction. When you discuss with others, you not only enhance your knowledge, but also increase your capacity. It is my experience that new ideas are bound to emerge during discussion. In other words, discussion increases your creativity. Without discussion you are a reader, but after discussion you become a creative thinker. Study is unilateral learning but interaction is bilateral learning, provided it is done with the true scientific spirit.

There is a necessary condition for making discussion fruitful, and that is, objectivity. You have to listen to others' point of view with an empty mind, try to understand it without any bias. The purpose of interaction is nothing but learning. The learning spirit is very important for a person who wants to know the truth.

Study can give knowledge, but study cannot decondition one's conditioning. It is interaction that helps decondition one's conditioning. It is a fact that deconditioning is very important for a person who is a true seeker, but the process of deconditioning cannot take place in isolation. It requires an intellectual partner. This is the greatest experience of my life.

Reverend Mpho Tutu: Some years ago Karen Armstrong articulated a Charter for Compassion based on the shared values of every religious tradition. She noted that every major religion had as a tenet some form of the Golden Rule "Do unto others as you would have them do unto you" or restated "Do not do unto others what you would not have them do unto you." This statement forms the basis upon which we can engage to create a better world for every person. It is the basis upon which we can create mutual respect and mutual regard. It is also the foundation upon which people of diverse faith experience and expressions can work together on issues of common concern. People of every faith can agree that it is good to halt environmental degradation and work together to that end. People of every faith can agree that people need shelter, food and clothing and can cooperate across the religious spectrum to achieve those goals. We can unite across the religious spectrum to respond to human need at times of strife or natural disaster. We can unite across the religious spectrum to respond to human need when government fails us. South Africa's anti-apartheid movement was spearheaded by people of faith from diverse backgrounds. Hindus, Muslims, Christians and Jews joined arms with people of every faith to bring down that oppressive system of government. With the political leaders in jail or in exile it was left to religious leaders to unite based on their common humanity and the tenets of their faith. Now we are faced with environmental degradation; international and civil strife; famine; and disease. It is time for a new unity for people and our planet.

In the United States the country continues to be tormented by the spectre of 9/11/2001. The attacks drove a wedge between religious communities. One initiative to respond to the division was the 9/11 Unity Walk. Each year since the tragedy people of different religious backgrounds have walked from the largest Synagogue in Washington DC down Embassy Row to the Mahatma Gandhi statue at Dupont Circle. Every place of worship alone the way opens its doors to this diverse band of pilgrims. The walk begins with the Muslim call to prayer echoing through the synagogue. Along the way walkers stop at the National cathedral for prayer. They are welcomed into the Sikh Gurdwara for a meal. At the Islamic Center they may listen as a Christian choir sings Amazing Grace. There is no incongruity. It is because the walkers come to this pilgrimage with an attitude of profound respect and an openness to learning about the traditions of people of different faiths that the walk is such a meaningful witness. Most faiths have a tradition of pilgrimage. Pilgrims travel in humility. They trust that there will be a place where they will be welcomed. They trust that there are lessons for them to learn in each encounter, blessings to give or to receive in every interaction. As people of faith we can meet each other as pilgrims. As pilgrims we offer no insult to our own faith. As pilgrims we experience no threat from any faith.

Dr Karan Singh: The point of union among diverse traditional religions has to be the Interfaith movement. This can be traced back to 1893 when the first Parliament of World Religions was held in Chicago and where, incidentally, Swami Vivekananda made such a dramatic impact. In the twentieth century, a considerable number of Interfaith organizations came into being including the one of which I am Chairman worldwide, the Temple of Understanding. Between us, we have had a large number of meetings around the world in the twentieth century. The second Parliament of World Religions was held in Chicago in 1993 exactly a hundred years after the first, the third in Cape Town, South Africa in 1999, the fourth in Barcelona, Spain in 2005 and the fifth in Melbourne, Australia in 2011. Another one is due in 2017 but the venue has not yet been decided. There was also a memorable millennial event in the United Nations in the year 2000 bringing together religious and spiritual leaders from around the world.

Despite all these efforts, however, I am constrained to say that the Interfaith movement has not yet become central to the concerns of humanity. As a result of this, fanaticism and fundamentalism in many parts of the world continue to haunt our civilization, creating havoc and disaster wherever they strike. It is, therefore, essential that the movement should be strengthened, and particularly that Interfaith values should be introduced at the school level so that young people grow up with an awareness of the importance of multiple traditions instead of getting stuck in stereo-typical images and postures.

To conclude, I reiterate that the Interfaith movement has a crucial role to play in the future of human civilization. Without harmony among great religions of the world, there will never be peace on Planet Earth.

Swami Vivekananda:

We want to lead mankind to the place where there is neither the Vedas, nor the Bible, nor the Koran. Mankind ought to be taught that religions are but the varied expressions of The Religion, which is Oneness, so that each may choose that path that suits him best.

Our watchword, then, will be acceptance, and not exclusion. Not only toleration, for so-called toleration is often blasphemy, and I do not believe in it. I believe in acceptance. Why should I tolerate? Toleration means that you are wrong and I am just allowing you to live. Is it not blasphemy to think that you and I are allowing others to live? I accept all religions that were in the past, and worship with them all; I worship God with every one of them, in whatever form they worship Him.

About the Editor and Contributors

EDITOR

Anindita N. Balslev is a philosopher based in India and Denmark. She obtained her MA (Calcutta) and PhD (Paris) degrees in philosophy. Her educational and professional experience in India, France, the US, and Denmark has inspired her to create a forum for "Cross-cultural Conversation" (CCC). The international CCC conferences that she organizes have led to thought-provoking discussions and publications.

She serves on the boards of several important international organizations/societies and is a founding member of the International Society for Science and Religion.

Apart from contributing many essays in professional journals in the areas of philosophy, religion, and culture, she is the author of *A Study of Time in Indian Philosophy*, *Cultural Otherness: Correspondence with Richard Rorty*, *Indian Conceptual World*, and *The Enigma of I-consciousness*. She is also the editor of the volume entitled *Cross-cultural Conversation*, *On India: Self-Image and Counter-Image* and the coeditor of the volumes entitled *Religion and Time* and of *Compassion in the World's Religions*.

CONTRIBUTORS

Zainal Abidin Bagir is Director of Center for Religious and Cross-cultural Studies Graduate School, Gadjah Mada University Yogyakarta, Indonesia.

Whitney A. Bauman is Assistant Professor, Department of Religious Studies, Florida International University, Miami.

Swami Bhajanananda is the Assistant Secretary of the Ramakrishna Math and Ramakrishna Mission, Belur Math, Kolkata.

Shernaz Cama is Director, Parzor Foundation.

Mushirul Hasan is ex-Vice Chancellor, Jamia Millia Islamia University, New Delhi.

Steve Killelea is the Executive Chairman and Founder, Institute for Economics and Peace.

Annakutty V. Kurian-Findeis is Professor Emeritus of German and Former Head of Department of Foreign Languages, University of Mumbai.

Jeffery D. Long is Professor of Religion and Asian Studies, Elizabethtown College, Pennsylvania.

Rabbi Ezekiel Isaac Malekar is Priest and Honorary Secretary of the Judah Hyam Synagogue, New Delhi.

A. K. Merchant is a National Trustee of Lotus Temple and the Baha'i Community of India; Chairperson, Sarvodaya International Trust, New Delhi.

Makarand R. Paranjape is Professor of English, Centre for English Studies, Jawaharlal Nehru University, New Delhi.

Karan Singh is the President, Indian Council for Cultural Relations (ICCR) and Member of Parliament.

Mohinder Singh is Member of the National Commission for Minority Educational Institutions.

John A. Teske is Professor of Psychology, Elizabethtown College, Pennsylvania.

Steven I. Wilkinson is Nilekani Professor of India and South Asian Studies and Professor of Political Science and International Affairs, Jackson Institute for Global Affairs, Yale University.

Santiago Zabala is ICREA Research Professor of Philosophy at the University of Barcelona.

About Cross Cultural Conversation

CROSS CULTURAL CONVERSATION

The CCC conferences aim at exploring the contending visions and choices that are before us today. Based on the recognition of a call for human solidarity as a powerful rhetoric in national and international contexts, these conferences seek to bring about changes in the present environment, drawing on the perception that respect for cultural diversity demands a more complex understanding of what a pluralistic society really entails. Indeed, there are many voices that express this common human aspiration for achieving solidarity in all its various facets—social, ethical, religious, economic, and political. The modes of persuasions are diverse, as is to be expected. Approaches and preferences may be secular or religious, philosophical strategies can be of various genres (essentialistic, pragmatic, or otherwise) just as suggestions for practical, political implementations may also vary.

The participants of this open conversation attempt to closely examine a range of issues and concerns with the hope that the very richness of the interactions and exchanges will make us all aware of various asymmetries that are there in different contexts. This in turn will gradually help us to envision—through repeated cross-cultural conversation—how to build those bridges that are lacking at present. The endeavor here is to provide a positive ambience where it is possible to diagnose in collaboration those collective prejudices that act as a divisive force, how these are actually perpetuated in and through theoretical discourse affecting negatively practical policymaking. On the other hand, the aim is to unlearn these prejudices while projecting visions for the future in the name of human solidarity.

About Indian Council for Cultural Relations

Indian Council for Cultural Relations
भारतीय सांस्कृतिक सम्बंध परिषद्

Maulana Abul Kalam Azad, the first Education Minister of independent India, founded the Indian Council for Cultural Relations (ICCR) on April 9, 1950.

The objectives of the Council are to participate in the formulation and implementation of policies and programs relating to India's external cultural relations; to foster and strengthen cultural relations and mutual understanding between India and other countries; to promote cultural exchanges with other countries and people; to establish and develop relations with national and international organizations in the field of culture; and to take such measures as may be required to further these objectives.

The ICCR is about a communion of cultures, a creative dialogue with other nations. To facilitate this interaction with world cultures, the Council strives to articulate and demonstrate the diversity and richness of the cultures of India, both in and with other countries of the world.

The Council prides itself on being a preeminent institution engaged in cultural diplomacy and the sponsor of intellectual exchanges between India and partner countries. It is the Council's resolve to continue to symbolize India's great cultural and educational efflorescence in the years to come.